Discerning the Subject

Theory and History of Literature
Edited by Wlad Godzich and Jochen Schulte-Sasse

For other books in the series, see p. 186

Discerning the Subject

Paul Smith

Foreword by John Mowitt

Theory and History of Literature, Volume 55

University of Minnesota Press, Minneapolis

Published by the University of Minnesota Press
2037 University Avenue Southeast, Minneapolis MN 55414.
Published simultaneously by Fitzhenry & Whiteside Limited, Markham.
Printed in the United States of America.

Library of Congress Cataloging-in-Publication Data

Smith, Paul, 1954–
    Discerning the subject/Paul Smith; foreword by John Mowitt.
      p.   cm. – (Theory and history of literature; v. 55)
    Bibliography: p.
    Includes index.
    ISBN 0-8166-1638-8   ISBN 0-8166-1639-6 (pbk.)
    1. Criticism–20th century. 2. Self in literature. I. Title.
II. Series.
PN94.S65 1988
801'.95'0904–dc19   87-35926
                                                             CIP

The Venn diagram on p. 73 is reproduced from
Jacques Lacan, *Four Fundamental Concepts of Psychoanalysis*,
with permission of the publishers: W. W. Norton & Company, New
York, and Tavistock Publications, London.

The University of Minnesota is an equal-opportunity
educator and employer.

Dedicated to Britton Harwood,
with gratitude and by way of recompense.

Contents

Foreword
The Resistance in Theory
John Mowitt

Avoiding the Subject

Few critical issues are as pressing as those animating the pages of this book. Specifically, *Discerning the Subject* broaches the problematic that structures the core of contemporary political reason, namely how one grasps the very agent of radical criticism. Within this context, Paul Smith argues that a distinction between the subject and agency needs to be introduced within the critical theory of society[1] in order to sustain the historical possibility of the political resistance that is currently exemplified within international feminism. The urgency of this argument derives from Smith's comprehensive, though partisan, survey of the humanities and the social sciences—a survey organized around an investigation of the status of the subject as a disciplinary construct. What stands exposed by this survey is the fact that the subject functions within the disciplinary structures of knowledge to provide their adherents with an alibi for the consistent inadequacy of disciplinary self-reflection. Smith is not primarily interested in overcoming this inadequacy, but rather in examining the peculiar duplicity of the alibi—a duplicity that rests upon the counterintuitive fact that whether the subject is explicitly problematized or not, its disciplinary function remains constant. In fact, I will argue that the strategic character of Smith's approach to the inadequacy of disciplinary self-reflection harbors insights into the notion of agency that cannot be fully detailed within it.

Crucial to both the conceptualization and the realization of the distinction between agency and the subject is the project of discernment. In his preface, Smith
explains what is at stake in his choice of the verb "discern." Two meanings of the
etymological root of the word are at play within it: (1) a negative construction
of the verb "to cerne," which means to enclose or encircle (one is reminded here
of Elias's discussion of *homo clausus*[2]), and (2) a negative construction of the verb
"to cern," which means to assume responsibility for an inheritance. These terms
are not merely *applicable* to the concept of the subject, they actually constitute
its disciplinary character. Smith argues essentially that the subject, as it has been
traditionally theorized, is at once enclosed by or set off from its enabling conditions and thereby marked as the bearer of an empowering legacy. To discern the
subject then means to disclose and dismantle it by contesting the subject's traditional theorization. What separates Smith's project from others like it is that he
insists upon connecting the "cerned" subject to the fact of its disciplinary theorization. This permits him to do two things. First, he is able to criticize the subject's
function as a disciplinary alibi without rejecting the activating dynamic which the
subject inadequately designates, namely agency. Second, he authorizes himself
to draw upon the reassociation of agency and theory to insist upon the indispensable relation between political resistance and the negativity disclosed by theoretical
criticism. Thus, while it would be fair to say that the project of discernment has
both theoretical and practical aims, its investment in the delimitation of agency
promises that it will proceed according to means that are, strictly speaking, neither. To understand the significance Smith attaches to feminism in this context
it will be necessary to confront the specific positions taken within his project of
discernment. Therefore, let us turn to a characterization of the strategy that moti-
vates the project.

Smith organizes his project around a return—though I hasten to add that this
return is not merely a repetition, a distinction whose significance I will spell out
shortly. As a strategy, it is perhaps both necessary and necessarily limited. Its
necessity, while ultimately requiring a detailed elaboration, can be made tangible
by considering two previous moments in the reception of poststructuralism,
aspects of which explicitly embody what Smith is seeking to avoid through his
strategic return. What limits this strategy, namely the relation it constructs between the inadequacy of disciplinary self-reflection and the instance or performance of critical reading, can be spelled out more efficiently once this prior issue
is settled. As with all limits, this one hinders and facilitates at once.

Both Foucault's "What is an Author" and Derrida's "Structure, Sign, Play in
the Discourse of the Human Sciences"[3] were initially delivered as papers that included among their auditors and respondents Lucien Goldmann. With an almost
uncanny, though predictable, tenacity Goldmann pressed both men with the same
question: Where is the subject? With equal tenacity both Foucault and Derrida
responded to Goldmann by insisting that contrary to his assertions they had not

rejected the subject, but rather had "situated" it (in Derrida's case) or "analyzed the conditions of its possibility" (in Foucault's case). Goldmann, as we know, was able later to make his peace, at least with Derrida, by proposing the congruence of *écriture* and praxis.[4] But what I would like to emphasize here is that while post-structuralism (if one will grant the representative status of Derrida and Foucault) undertook a decisive and systematic remapping of the category of the subject, it has nevertheless remained unable to develop its problematization of the subject in a manner that satisfactorily rewrites the socio-political functions served by this category within theoretical discourse. This is the unfinished business, as it were, that Smith's book returns to. What prevents it from being a repetition is the fact that, on the one hand, Smith's return recovers a moment that was itself divided by controversy (he is not recovering *the subject*, but its problematization) and, on the other hand, it refers us to specific figures (Althusser and Lacan) whose works were themselves carried out under the heading of "returns" (to Marx and Freud, respectively). In short, Smith's strategy is designed, in the name of a "discernment" of agency, to avoid affirming either the subject *or* its poststructuralist problematization. As we will see, the significance of agency for Smith derives from its utility in the execution of this double avoidance.

There is more to be said for the necessity, if not the urgency, of Smith's strategy. This is made particularly clear when it is contextually situated. Quite early in the book Smith issues the now compulsory call for a theoretical revision of Marxism in light of historical developments. This call underscores the fact that within the tradition of the critical theory of society a troubling delay has opened between the moment of critique and the activity of political resistance. More than a split between theory and practice, this delay traverses the two, obstructing their enabling relations to the historical process. It is important to stress this because the contextual urgency of Smith's work does not derive, as one might think, from the much decried delay between theory and practice as such, but rather from the impact the current organization of this delay has had upon theory — particularly as theoreticians seek to reflect upon theory and define its social obligations.

Marx is an indispensable reference point for Smith here because his critique of the political economy of capitalism contained a necessary reference to the concretization of this critique in the social praxis of the working class. What has, in part, provoked Smith's reflections is that the critical theory of society has, in the name of a deconstructively "principled" rejection of the limits of Marxist theory, tended to abandon the responsibility of effective concretion. Agency as the activating dynamic of political resistance has been, as it were, thrown out of critical theory with the working class. The consequences of this gesture, hence the necessity of Smith's strategy, are made plain in his chapter on deconstruction.

In his reading of this increasingly legitimated critical practice, Smith proceeds to dispel the myth that has often served to protect Derrida from the attacks on deconstruction that are now attaining the level of intellectual sophistication necessary for them to acquire credibility. The myth is inappropriately, though predictably, paternal. Though Derrida's work is often read as a definitive critique of the function and meaning of the father, he himself has ineluctably come to be identified as the father of deconstruction. In the reception of deconstruction, this contradiction is mythically articulated in the following manner: the father's epigones (particularly his American epigones) may be politically problematic, but the father is, if not politically correct, at least politically redeemable. Smith, in decisively distancing himself from this perspective, attacks the father who wasn't supposed to be one.

Crucial to the Derridean critique is the protocol by which one, as I have said, "situates," and thereby surpasses, the subject. At stake here is a rejection of the punctual simplicity of the classical juridico-philosophical subject—a rejection Derrida has been at pains to differentiate from the version of this project articulated by Lacan. As is evident from his title, Smith is committed to this rejection as well and extends his solidarity with Derrida up to this point. But then he executes what can only be called a Marxian move by insisting that critical theory— even metacritical or deconstructive theory—take responsibility for an account of its own relation to agency and the agency of those who presumably are to realize its critical effects. Derrida is thus attacked for foreclosing the question of agency by reducing it to a paradigm of subjectivity that renders Derrida's own critical practice unthinkable. Here Smith effectively exploits the distinction between the subject and agency by reminding us (and Derrida) that even the theoretical negation of the subject comes from somewhere. Nevertheless, while it is true that Derrida's circumspection concerning the subject provokes him to designate, rather flippantly, the "text" as its own agency—thus inviting Smith's criticism—it is worth pointing out that the notion of agency deployed here is a limited one. At least at this juncture Smith appears willing to identify agency with the general preconditions that make the theoretical articulation of the critique of the subject possible. Supplementing this, one might also insist upon agency's pertinence for an inquiry into the mode of "performativity"[5] that operates in the very inscription of deconstructive theory. Such an insistence would enable one to separate agency from the shadow cast by the subject and focus on the sites where this shadow falls upon what, as a consequence of this fact, remains misrecognized in, and as, the object. If the "text" in some sense adequately names that which propels and yet eludes the activity of reading, then perhaps there is something to be said for Derrida's designation of it as its own agency. Only if one is overeager to restitute a causal (and therefore accountable) historical principle does agency have to answer to the demands inappropriately placed upon the subject. Though Smith is concerned that the contemporary critical theory of society has failed to connect its critical character to an agency of political resistance outside the compromised academic public sphere, he does not thereby reduce agency to a mere extratextual collectivity. Nor, however, does he clarify how we are to connect what he calls "active agency," with its accent on activism, to agency as activation in general. There are good political reasons for this and they derive from Smith's assessment of the failure of theory to connect with a mobilized constituency.

This failure is particularly important because the present historical conjuncture is so bleak. For Smith this bleakness has two sides. On the one hand, there is the fact that the revolutionary subject of Marxism (the proletariat) has both atrophied and multiplied. Since the critical power of Marxism was tied to the necessary and sufficient negativity of the proletariat, this power has withered with the emergence of the "other" revolutionary subjects—the ones we inadequately summon through the term "new social movements." The critical theory of society has splintered in its practitioners' efforts to embrace these new "subjects" and, as a consequence, has been politically paralyzed by the loss of its self-legitimating notion of "totality." On the other hand, the political Right has capitalized on this paralysis, recasting political discourse in its terms and appearing to address the need for revolutionary subjectivity by empowering people to unleash the economic forces that actually enslave them. This potentially permanent fixed counterrevolution has made it necessary to contest both the subject and its problematization: the subject, because of the way this concept operates to reduce agency, obscuring the very rhetoricity of this concept; its problematization, because of the way this strategy has tended to both absorb and neutralize agency, undermining the possibility of theoretically sharpened political resistance. Smith articulates this necessity in his account of what I will call the "conflict of interpellations"—an account that joins the notion of agency to the intellectual generator of his entire project: resistance.

As has been indicated, a recovery of the "returns" of Althusser and Lacan is crucial to Smith's project of discernment. Not surprisingly, Althusser's much debated notion of the ideological interpellation of the subject figures prominently in Smith's return, even though the latter's reading of this notion fundamentally displaces it. Interpellation is the name Althusser gave to the process through which the human being is constituted as a subject through its relation to the ideological practices of society. However inadequate Althusser's discussion of this process was (Smith scrupulously details its central limitations), interpellation remains an absolutely crucial contribution to the contemporary practice of ideology-critique. It is perhaps then not accidental that Althusser's theoretical discovery of the ideological significance of the subject occurred at that moment in the history of Marxism when it was being confronted by the insurgency of several other "subjects of history." Theory is thus rather like philosophy for Hegel—always late.

What then is meant by the phrase "the conflict of interpellations?" To begin with let me suggest how interpellation functions in the Althusserian account. In "Ideology and Ideological State Apparatuses,"[6] ideology is presented as an imaginary relation to the real relations of production—a relation that participates in the reproduction of these real relations and is to that extent real. Althusser complains that Marxism has devoted itself to accounting for the economic production of the positions to be filled within these relations, as if the mere existence of positions explained their filling. In essence, the concept of interpellation accounts for the filling of these positions. Specifically, ideological practices, as discursively mediated constructs, contain references to subjects understood necessarily, though not exclusively, as grammatical subjects. These references call or invite human beings to see themselves as the addressees of these discourses. Interpellation is then this "hailing" which incites human beings to identify their self-experience with the image of that experience that comes for them in the discourses emanating from the ideological state apparatuses. This is not a question of intellectual manipulation. The identification with an image of one's self is constitutive of that self, and this constitution is the structural precondition for any manipulation at the level of ideas. The headway made by Althusser's account of how subjects are invited to take up the positions offered to them by the mode of production nevertheless exacts a high analytical price. His commitment to the totalizing function of the mode of production forces Althusser to ignore the qualitative differences and tensions that comprise the relations among the subject positions it supports – differences which are not merely external to the subjects occupying them. Because Althusser still wants to see that which operates through subjects as instances of "determination" (even if only in the last instance), he is obliged to assume that ideological interpellation can and must always homogenize the results of its functioning. In refusing this Althusserian stricture, Smith secures an important conceptual feature of agency – its relation to resistance, both within the subject *and* the object.

Smith exploits the possibility of multiple subject-positions by submitting Althusser to a Lacanian gaze. In doing so, he weaves together two theoretical strands in order to relocate in the concept of interpellation an irrepressible moment of resistance. On the one hand, he rescues the notion of subject-position from Althusser's latent economism by following the interpretive leads of those who have located this phenomenon in the workings of literary and cinematic enunciation. As a result, he is able to insist that all subjects arise at a temporally shifting intersection of *multiple* interpellations. In effect, one is the subject of race, gender, and class discourses as they are disproportionately activated by different cultural media. These subjects are not isomorphic and cannot, therefore, be homogenized, nor, for that matter, determined. On the other hand, Smith insists upon the importance of Lacan's description of the subject's entry into the symbolic order of language, and three moments in Lacan's discussion are particularly important to him. First, because human reality is irreducibly mediated by language and because language is the differential system described by Saussure, the subject that arises in language is structured by the differential logic of the linguistic signifying chain. In short, the subject is divided by that which enables it to articulate its experience as its own. Second, the linguistic constitution of the subject predisposes it toward its others: the unconscious and the social domain of other subjects. Thus, the subject is not only divided, but it is energetically entangled in the social construction of reality. Third, the subject's desire (structured by its linguistically mediated intersubjective constitution) not only destabilizes the subject, but also attaches the impossible structure of the subject to the lived inadequacy of social reality.

In short then, Smith's reading of Lacan enables him to locate an intrasubjective corollary to the mechanisms of interpellation described by Althusser. What does he gain by doing this? If he were merely discovering a way to establish a homology between the two theaters of the subject's infrastructure, he would have gained little and certainly *not* the motor of resistance he was seeking. Interpellation would simply have been causally linked to the inner structure of the post-Freudian subject. Instead, Smith introduces a crucial nuance in the account of interpellation, neutralizing forever its transcendental pretensions. In Smith's Lacanian reading, interpellation becomes a locus of negativity and conflict – not between experience and ideology, but *within* ideological experience. He does not theorize a subjective moment *outside* interpellation that could then serve as the fulcrum of resistance, but rather a conflict *within* the social practices of interpellation that, when understood as the social articulations of the constitutional instability of the subject, can be theorized as society's perpetual production of resistance to itself. Agency emerges as the decisive term here because Smith uses it to name the activating dynamic that exceeds individuals at the point where this dynamic nevertheless empowers them to oppose that which confronts them, as individuals, from without. In short, with agency Smith gains a coherent account of political resistance that neither resorts to a metaphysics of voluntarism, nor appeals to a teleologically designated subject of history. He has, in effect, mapped out a multiply and asymmetrically divided interface at the core of the subject/object dyad, one that marks the inadequacy of this opposition just as surely as it founds the possibility of permanent revolution. But an account is merely that. Smith still wants an immanent link to a concrete agency of resistance, a link he provides in his concluding chapter on feminism.

In his solicitous yet judicious discussion of feminism, Smith illustrates that the movements gathered together by this name exemplify the structure of his account of resistance. He does this by reading the oft-cited difference between French (or Continental) and North American feminism in a novel way. Because this difference has itself been historically transformed, Smith is in a position to argue that the theoretical interrogation of "woman" characteristic of Continental feminism merely reflects the instability of the subject that has, as he has shown theoretically, its necessary political corollary in the empirically motivated activism characteristic of North American feminism. In other words, the "double strategy" of feminism (risking essentialism and difference) captures in a "movement" the agential displacement of the subject. Thus the contentiousness that has marked academic feminism within postmodernity is not only to be read as a sign of strength, but as an embodiment of the very historical possibility of political resistance as such. While this might appear to imply that women or feminists have, in spite of all Smith's precautions, become the new subject of history, it is important to note that, in point of fact, what Smith identifies as the locus of resistance are the conflicts and tensions within *feminism*. Presumably, of course, as these are lived by those interpellated within it—subjects who are, as is obvious from contemporary feminist discourse, multifariously shaped by the dynamics of gender, race, and class.

But one should resist proceeding too hastily here. Smith closes his book by invoking the responsibility of theory, not theorists. Clearly, an important moment in his theorization of agency resides in an affirmation, often decried by feminists, of the discursive mediation of the subject. While this affirmation is not to be confused with a consequent determination of agency, it nevertheless problematizes subjectivity in a way that necessitates a reexamination of the performativity of discourse. I stress this because otherwise one is tempted by Smith's analysis to regard theory itself as the only way to realize the decisive connection between negativity and resistance, agency and active agents.

Dispossessing the Object: Reading and the Political

I offer the strategy embodied in this subheading as a complement to the project of discernment, one that will suggest how one might pursue some of the issues left undeveloped within the latter project. Let us begin by returning to the problem of the relation constructed by Smith between the necessary inadequacy of disciplinary self-reflection and what I called the instance or performance of critical reading. How are we to understand the necessity of this inadequacy?

By focusing his analysis on the disciplinary function of the subject, Smith invites us to conceive of it as a blindness imposed upon the members of a discipline by their shared commitment to categories that obstruct inquiry into the necessary preconditions of these categories. Both the subject and its deconstruction function this way within the discourses of the humanities and the social sciences. This is obvious in the case of the subject where, in accord with its cerned character, it operates to delegitimate any appeal to constitutive preconditions. Deconstruction similarly, though less obviously, obstructs inquiry because it problematizes the subject so deeply that any inquiry aimed at a disclosure of its preconditions is implicitly trivialized. Given this, would not the discernment of agency permit a discipline to engage in adequate self-reflection? No, because precisely what agency reveals about the enabling conditions of a discipline is that they are riddled with negativity and are, as a consequence, resistant to adequate self-reflection. In effect, the very duplicity of the subject as an alibi registers the negativity that otherwise escapes disciplinary reflection on the subject. This is why it attracts Smith's attention. It might also, however, have led him to seek agency beyond the limits acknowledged by the disciplinary field. When agency is paradigmatically situated in relation to its disciplinary cernment, a certain strategy for its disclosure is privileged implicitly. Since the disclosure of agency clearly involves the decisive shift from activation or negativity to activism, theory as the mediating practice must consequently assume tremendous and paradoxically classical importance. But what then is surprising about Smith's book is the fact that at the level of its own performativity it is so theoretically eccentric. It is actually less a theoretical interpretation, than a reading excercise centered on the disciplinary status of the subject— a reading which, as de Man observed, eludes the very theoretical presentation that necessitates it.[7] The all too familiar discrepancy between what a book says and what it does might have pressured Smith to consider more directly how agency figured in his own procedures. If de Man's thesis is correct, then that which eludes theory would necessarily rebound upon the relation between negativity and resistance in a way that would problematize the mediation of this relation decisively. Recognizing this, Smith would have been obliged to remap the entire discussion of agency.

There is, however, another way to approach the inadequacy of disciplinary self-reflection—a way that leads us more directly to the problematic status of reading and ultimately beyond the disciplinary framework altogether. Instead of stressing the reflective limits imposed by the category of the subject, one might also attempt to specify the resistance embodied in the object. In other words, one could also show how the construction or, more precisely, the activation of disciplinary objects eludes disciplinary self-reflection. To avoid misunderstanding I will put this in terms of Lacan's description of the place of the object within the dialectic of desire.[8] For Lacan the object is that which the subject's desire always misses, not because the object is antithetical to desire, nor because the object is radically extrinsic to thought, but because desire is activated by something which escapes and thereby structures the subject's relation to itself. Put this way, one can see why the disciplinary object is not to be confused either with Kant's thing-in-itself, or with what Adorno knowingly referred to as the "naked sense datum."[9] In a word, the object as seen from within the current disciplinary crisis becomes that which eludes possession, that which is never "given." Lest this be confused with a peculiar form of transcendental empiricism, I will insist that the structure of the object's absence for the subject informs both from a standpoint which is neither that of the subject nor of the object—a standpoint which enables us to see the disciplines as particular modalities of onto-epistemological production.

If we substitute the "will to know" for "desire" in the Lacanian model, then it is possible to rewrite the necessary inadequacy of disciplinary self-reflection from the standpoint of a rethinking of the object. Disciplines are structured by their immanent resistance to that which they claim to know. More precisely, since the previous formulation invites a Kantian understanding of the object, disciplines form around a denial of their activating gestures – gestures which subsequently return, disguised as the objectivity or resistance of the object as "thing." Approaching disciplines in this way puts the accent not on the "nature" of the object as such, but on the aspect of agency inscribed within it. What blocks disciplinary self-reflection then is the untheorizability of the activation of its own objects – their *fabrication* as determinations of experience – and this is precisely why, contrary to certain hysterically defensive views, interdisciplinary reseach has always been immanent to the disciplines. Every discipline is obliged to turn to its "others" to resolve its self doubt. This, however, is also why the crisis of disciplinary knowledge is interminable. One might even say that interdisciplinary study is an institutional analogue to deterrence – a defense strategy destined to precipitate the obvious, namely the advent of postdisciplinarity. Dispossessing the object thus involves recognizing within it that which marks both it and the subject, who can no longer make it his or her own, with a necessarily extra-disciplinary alterity. If social experience has indeed become textual, it is not because deconstruction is merely the cultural logic of late capitalism, but rather because texts arise wherever we struggle to make sense of the resistance that eludes us in this very struggle. This is an experience that is particularly intense at the interchanges among disciplines and at the point where disciplinary objects trail off into the unmanagable flux of daily life. What is more, this is an experience that confronts us with the necessity and inevitability of reading.

This does not yet clarify how an object-centered account of the inadequacy of disciplinary self-reflection leads us more immediately to the problem of reading, nor for that matter why this is important. To make headway here we need only recognize that during the period mapped out in Smith's survey, the disciplines of the humanities and social sciences were witnessing the socio-genesis of "the text" as their paradigmatic disciplinary object. Bakhtin, whose idiosyncratic yet clairvoyant perspective is now much celebrated, put it this way: "the text . . . is the primary given of all these disciplines . . . where there is no text there is no object of study."[10] This need not be taken to mean that all such disciplines are literary, but rather that they work with materials that are irreducibly mediated by discourse. This is, of course, the very type of assertion taken to task by Smith in his remarkable chapter on the text. While it *is* important to resist a textualization of experience that eliminates agency altogether, it is just as important not to overlook the fact that the text operates as a configuration of heterogeneous yet reciprocally conditioned fields – a configuration that signals the dispossession of the object and hence the "presence" within it of agency. The relation to agency made available by the object of the text is not worth sacrificing to a literary (and therefore discipline-specific) reduction of "intertextuality."

But aside from the ubiquity of "textual analysis" within the disciplines under consideration, what more concrete evidence is there of the text's status as a dispossessed object? Though it would take more space than I have here to demonstrate it, the fact that the text was continually theorized in relation to what Julia Kristeva called its "productivity" represents just such evidence. It is worth recalling, for example, that productivity is contrasted by Kristeva with both historical or psychical determinism and phenomenological intentionality, and is therefore positioned in the complex interplay between the subject and the object. As such, the text names the process of cultural construction that both compromises and comprises the subject, but from the "place" of the object. What is crucial about the productivity associated with the text is that it registers the notion of agency implicit in determination without thereby sacrificing the possibility of resistance. When, for example, Marx speaks of life determining consciousness, he is suggesting that some force outside of consciousness sets consciousness in motion, activates it, and thereby shapes its inner character. Even if we restrict agency to the notion of the human agent (which is unwarranted), one cannot fail to see how the concept of determination is, for Marx, bound up with what is at stake in the objectal account of agency. Nevertheless, what prevents the Marxian notion of determination from coming to a standstill is the negativity introduced within it by human labor. In other words, Marx, while prepared to countenance the agency of the object, must resort to the subject (specifically the proletariat) in order ultimately to redeem agency through the activist agent.

A recognition of the text's productivity is designed to resist this exclusive appeal to the activist subject by affirming the agential character of what, in opposition to determination, might better be called conditioning. The text does not eliminate agency, it merely situates it beyond the subject/object dyad. That is, it obliges us to locate the possibility of activism, and therefore resistance (even meaningful political resistance), in the process of activation made particularly available, though not graspable, through an analysis of the object. Again, one returns here to the notion of performativity, the untheorizable instance of the enunciation of the object's analysis. Concretely, this implies that the political activism necessary for social change today is produced, is made available (though by no means exclusively) in the analyses of the institutional formation of disciplinary objects. Why? Because these analyses, conducted as instances of "critical reading," engage the conditioning matrix that plunges both the subject and the object into the general social dynamic that activates them—a dynamic that operates below the level of the disciplines themselves. To see ourselves and the order of things as effects of a general conditioning is to open ourselves to the desire for other conditions, perhaps even those in which the subject/object dyad is eclipsed. Contrary to what one might expect, this does not lead to a politics of resignation. In fact, it is precisely in order to avoid the charge of resignation that one must insist upon the importance of conditioning—the agent is not empowered to negate that which in the text conditions negativity. By the same token, the negativity made legible in the text cannot operate without the agent. Taken together these observations imply that agency is discernible beyond the contradictions opened up within the conflict of interpellations, where the only object present is the subject in the eyes of its others.

In opening this discussion of the object's dispossession, I raised an implicit question about Smith's presentation of the relation between the necessary inadequacy of disciplinary self-reflection and the performance of critical reading. I would like to bring these introductory remarks to a close by specifying what is at stake here.

What makes agency such a powerful critical tool is also what haunts it. This can be clarified by returning to a nodal issue in Smith's book. Crucial to his analysis is the contention that agency embodies both the general dynamic of activation and activism. Moreover, he argues that activism as embodied political resistance is implicit or latent in the general dynamic of activation, what he calls negativity. That is, because agency is, as it were, the backdrop of subjectivity resistance will take place. Now only if one assumes that history is all but totally administered can one be so sanguine about such a state of latency, i.e., one has to assume that *anything* would be better than the present order of things to read sheer negativity as affirmable political resistance in itself. Despite his sensitivity to the bleakness of the present conjuncture, Smith does not seem to share such a view. This means, of course, that he must affirm some sort of mediation between negativity and resistance. For Marx, who is an obvious touchstone here, theory provided this mediation. Marx's critique of political economy grounded theoretical truth in a concrete, practical moment of negation—a negation which captured the presence of capital in the immanent production of its future absence. This perspective was authorized by the relations among theory, the social totality, and the subject of history assumed by Marx. The proletariat qualified as the subject of history because its political activity promised to negate that which Marxist theory identified as the social totality, namely the class organized expropriation of surplus value. No other appeal to negativity was thus necessary, for it was guaranteed by the comprehensiveness of theory itself. Though this gesture identified the working class as the subject of history, it did not sacrifice theory to this subject. In other words, theory remained just as necessary to the negation of bourgeois society as the activism of the working class. In fact, and this became all the more apparent as time passed, theory—once institutionally inflected—became the medium through which the historically sanctioned negativity of the proletariat was communicated to it as its consciousness.

Though Smith has no commitment to the totalizing vision that necessitates such a view of theory, he is clearly attracted to this model of the mediation of negativity and resistance. One has only to consider his own book as a case in point. Despite its theoretical peculiarity—it reads more like an ensemble of "variations" than a sytematic tract—its *raison d' être* is clearly to locate the historical production of negativity and to intervene within it so as to draw upon its political energy. Thus, his discourse assumes the classical burden of theory even as it shrugs off the attendant generic responsibilities. As I have already said, there are irreproachable political reasons for pursuing this strategy, but precisely because the stakes are so high one might prefer that Smith be more suspicious of the kinship between theory and the cerned subject of Western political economy.

There is, to my mind, another way to go here. If the political meaning of agency is that it offers us a way to politicize the contradictions that structure daily life, why not seek to discern agency in those experiences within the quotidian field that do not require *traditional* theoretical mediation in order to become political, that is, explicitly connected to activism. The gain here would be that we need no longer bemoan the absence of organic intellectuals nor need we exhaust ourselves in debating the merits of vanguardism. To make the most of these gains, of course, one has to be able to locate instances of the experiences I refer to. At the risk of appearing to retreat to the very position attacked by Smith in the chapter on the text, I will propose reading as just such an instance. It is attractive to me, not just because I do it, but because it is a phenomenon that mixes and, one might even say, stages, the moments of agency that operate in the subject and the object.

Even in the "ordinary" act of reading, say a "trashy" bus depot paperback (but why not consider here the ongoing struggles over the writing surfaces within a city?), the reading subject cannot help but be conditioned—even at the cognitive level—by the specificity of the text. Either one reads *the* book, the one in his or her hands, or one does not. The intertextual matrix that inevitably complicates this picture nevertheless still surrounds the text one reads. Moreover, the transference dynamic that activates the text's narrative effects clearly places the reading subject at the point where pleasure and an aspect of discernment arise. By the same token, under the conditions of reading one is also empowered to read resistantly, that is, to make sense of the conditions activated by the text. Reading subjects are obliged to confront texts with the communities that have informed their competencies and the interests that inflect them. In short, reading performs the mediation between the two poles of agency: activation and activism. Reading situates one within the experience of being empowered to oppose that which conditions one's opposition. This is not to say that theory plays no role here, but only that theory operates here primarily as a reading, and specifically as a reading that fails to delimit its own performativity. Theory, as a way of seeing, cannot mediate between negativity and resistance because it must deny its own status as a reading to do so. It must, in a sense, fail to perform even while inevitably doing so.

I share with Paul Smith the genuine discomfort one feels when offering up an activity such as reading as an instance of political activity. Nevertheless, what is crucial about reading, namely its instancing of agency, leads it well beyond the rather limited (and therefore politically compromising) practice we associate with typographic literacy. In fact, if texts arise under the conditions outlined above, then the postmodern condition may well oblige us to "read" the worlds that are struggling to occupy the same planet, not in order to render them prosaic, but in order to take responsibility for the changes our interpretations are empowered to effect.

Notes

1. Throughout this text I will use the somewhat cumbersome phrase "the critical theory of society" in order to differentiate the critical projects under discussion from "critical theory" — which I associate with the Frankfurt School. Certainly, I include the latter within "the critical theory of society," but I am trying to avoid collapsing all critical discourse into the project of the Frankfurt School, which is what is often suggested when one uses the term "critical theory" loosely.

2. Norbert Elias, *The Civilizing Process*, Vol. I, trans. Edmund Jephcott (New York: 1978) pp. 246-52.

3. Michel Foucault, "What is an Author?" in *Language, Counter-Memory, Practice*, ed. Donald Bouchard, trans. Donald Bouchard and Sherry Simon (New York: 1977) pp.113-38. The debate that followed the reading of this "lecture" is available in *Screen*, Vol. 20, No. 1 (Spring 1979) pp. 29-33. Jacques Derrida, "Structure, Sign and Play in the Discourse of the Human Sciences" in *Writing and Difference*, trans. Alan Bass (Chicago: 1978) pp. 278-93. The debate that followed the reading of this paper is available in *The Structuralist Controversy*, eds. Richard Macksey and Eugenio Donato (Baltimore: 1972) pp. 265-72.

4. Lucien Goldmann, *Lukács and Heidegger*, trans. William Boelhower (London: 1982).

5. Performativity is a concept introduced into the theoretical debates around postmodernism by Jean-François Lyotard. He presents it as the criterion of legitimation that prevails within the cultural and scientific discourses of contemporary captialism. Rhetorically, Lyotard exploits performativity to undermine the Habermasean notion of legitimation crisis, arguing that the latter depends, for both its analytic power and promise, upon the enervated notion of human emancipation through enlightenment. Even so, performativity is exploited ambivalently. On the one hand, Lyotard tends to restrict its critical power to a quasi-cynical rejection of the historical possibility of emancipation through enlightenment. On the other, however, Lyotard seems prepared to exploit performativity's "other" side — the one turned toward what he calls, following Adorno, the "paralogical." The paralogical refers to those practices that exploit the destabilization of the language game of Truth, in order to underscore the agonistics defining our relations to the discourses that situate us. However, as Fredric Jameson has effectively argued, stressing the *para*-logical suggests one is committed to an undebatable affirmation of sheer discursive incommensurability. Against this, I will reinvoke the notion of performativity, but now mediated through the debates around John Austin's notion of performatives, where the question of the agency or power of discourse has come to the fore. Terry Eagleton in "Brecht and Rhetoric" has broached these issues in a particularly suggestive way. In spite of his explicit hostility towards postmodernism, one could feasibly argue that Eagleton's account of a speech act "deactivated," or as he says "hollowed out," (and therefore capable of producing estrangement) by theatricality is precisely what confronts us in postmodern performance art. One must also consider here Paul de Man's provocative insistance upon the relation between rhetoricity and the performative moment of the literary text. Specifically, de Man's notion that reading performs that which *in the text* always escapes us strikes me as especially pertinent here. Taking advantage of these observations, I will have continual recourse here to the notion of performativity in order to evoke the play of resistances comprising the moment of enunciation in what might generally be called "text acts."

6. Louis Althusser, "Ideology and Ideological State Apparatuses (Notes Towards an Investigation)" in *Lenin and Philosophy*, trans. Ben Brewster (New York: 1971) pp.127-86.

7. I am alluding here again to the extremely suggestive, but rather differently focused essay of Paul de Man's "The Resistance to Theory" in *The Resistance to Theory* (Minneapolis: 1986) pp. 3-20.

Though de Man has been attacked (explicitly by Frank Lentricchia) for having a reactionary political agenda, I think that when this essay is considered in the context of a debate like the one staged here, de Man's position is not so handily dismissed. Though de Man never developed an account of agency, his blind insight (once read outside its restrictively tropological context) penetrates more deeply into parts of this problem than does the view of the *zoon politikon* implicitly supported by Lentricchia.

8. Jacques Lacan, "The Deconstruction of the Drive" and "The Partial Drive and its Circuit" from *The Fundamental Concepts of Psychoanalysis*, ed. Jacques-Alain Miller, trans. Alan Sheridan (New York: 1978) pp.161–186.

9. Theodor Adorno, *Negative Dialectics*, trans. E. B. Ashton (New York: 1983) p. 187.

10. Mikhail Bakhtin, *Speech Genres and Other Late Essays*, eds. Caryl Emerson and Michael Holquist, trans. Vern McGee (Austin: 1986) p.103.

Acknowledgments

These acknowledgments and thanks, the last words of this book to be written, can scarcely even start to recognize the full extent of the personal, professional, and even financial debts that I've run up right from the beginning of this project.

The first words found their way to the page in the autumn of 1982 when I held an Andrew W. Mellon Fellowship at the Center for Humanities, Wesleyan University. That year-long experience, my first job in the United States, will act as a measuring stick for all my future positions. There I found a community of committed and humane people — faculty, staff, and students. I need to thank about two score of them for their unabating kindnesses and stimulation. But I'm sure that most of them will understand if I dispense with the usual device of listing all their names and will know my reasons if I choose to name just one of them to act as their communal debt collector: Khachig Tölölyan.

The bulk of the book was written while I worked as an Assistant Professor in the English Department at Miami University, Ohio. I think of all the people struggling to nurture a more tolerant and tolerable intellectual and political environment in Oxford, Ohio, as my friends and allies; but in particular, for providing all kinds of sustenance in the desert, I want to thank Peter Rose and James Sosnoski.

I was saved from some of my more egregious errors and some of my more intemperate tendencies by the careful commentaries, generous advice, and acute responses of several people, all of whom I thank and who I hope will forgive me for not always grasping the import of their suggestions about parts of the manuscript: Rosi Braidotti, Christina Crosby, Jane Gallop, Henry Giroux, Alice Jardine, Peggy Kamuf, David Konstan, and especially Andrew Ross.

Several portions of the text were first aired as talks. Earlier versions of Chapters 7 and 9 were first presented before frighteningly discerning audiences at Wesleyan University. I thank Nat Wing for daring me to assault deconstruction at the 1985 20th Century French Literature Symposium, Ann Arbor; and Elizabeth Traube for persuading me to talk, at the University of Chicago's Anthropology Department, about my vexed relation both to her deceased cat and to her discipline. Some of Chapter 9 has been published in very different form as "A Question of Feminine Identity" in *Notebooks in Cultural Analysis*, vol. 1, 1984; I thank the editors for their permission to reproduce some material. The Venn diagram on p. 73, from Jacques Lacan's *Four Fundamental Concepts of Psychoanalysis*, is reproduced courtesy of the publishers, W. W. Norton & Company and Tavistock Publications.

Not wishing to be slaughtered on the bench of history — the fate of most women who find themselves mentioned in this slot of men's books — the person who has most affected (even effected) both this book and me during the time it took to write it forbids me to mention her by name.

Preface

This book is an attempt to address the notion of the "subject" as it is either explicitly or implicitly installed within a number of different areas or discourses of the human sciences today. Over the last ten or twenty years those discourses have adopted this term, the "subject," to do multifarious theoretical jobs. In some instances the "subject" will appear to be synonymous with the "individual," the "person." In others—for example, in psychoanalytical discourse—it will take on a more specialized meaning and refer to the unconsciously structured illusion of plenitude which we usually call "the self." Or elsewhere, the "subject" might be understood as the specifically subjected *object* of social and historical forces and determinations. Across the human sciences the term enjoys a wide and varied usage which it is one of the tasks of this book to investigate.

Traditionally, and residually in many of our contemporary discourses, speculation about subjectivity is caught up in the set of philosophical terms and problems which are familiar from Descartes, Locke, Hume, Hegel, Heidegger, Sartre, and many others. The "subject" is generally construed epistemologically as the counterpart to the phenomenal object and is commonly described as the sum of sensations, or the "consciousness," by which and against which the external world can be posited. That is to say, the "subject," as the product of traditional western philosophical speculation, is the complex but nonetheless unified locus of the constitution of the phenomenal world. In different versions the "subject" enters a dialectic with that world as either its product or its source, or both. In any case, the "subject" is the bearer of a consciousness that will interact with whatever the world is taken to consist in.

This venerable opposition or dialectic between "subject" and object, between self and other, does not seem readily susceptible to being radically overturned. The dialectic of the internal and the external will not quite go away, and the human species is not prone to think itself except within some version of that opposition: even the radical questioning undertaken recently by deconstruction has regularly to foreground the impossibility of thinking outside or beyond it.[1] And yet contemporary thought has been concerned to mount at least a challenge to that dualism. In recent years the modes and manners of thinking which we know as "poststructuralism" have consistently concentrated on the "subject" in order to question its traditionally privileged epistemological status. In particular, there has been a sustained effort to question the role of the "subject" as the intending and knowing manipulator of the object, or as the conscious and coherent originator of meanings and actions.

Without a doubt, the most influential and rigorous strands of poststructuralist thought have emerged from and been connected with the names of Marx and Freud. The work of both these thinkers has suggested—or, perhaps, been made to suggest—the inadequacy of any epistemology which would establish some kind of sovereignty for the "subject." Marx, in attempting to turn the Hegelian dialectic on its head and reclaiming the ontological primacy of the material world, and Freud, in formulating the invention of the unconscious, have both fundamentally—though to different effects—challenged traditional concepts of the "subject"; both have facilitated revolutionary ways of approaching the dualism of "subject" and object which to a large extent funded the entire idealist philosophical tradition before them.

Hard on the heels of, and indefeasibly linked to this new development has come an increased attention in all areas of intellectual activity to matters of language and representation. There, consideration of the "subject's" complicity in and reliance upon the structures of language has become paramount. The attempt has been to formulate a theory of "the speaking subject" in such a way as to allow an understanding of the "subject's" place within all signifying practices, and to stress the import and effect of representation in the "subject's" construction. This move has its roots in the work of Saussure and post-Saussurean linguists such as Roman Jakobson and Emile Benveniste, and has been developed more recently after the example of Jacques Lacan's psychoanalytical theories which stress the role of language in the formation of the unconscious.[2] At the same time, in many of the discussions of subjectivity conducted in recent years, there has been an urge to join the political impetus of Marx's description and critique of capitalism with the psychoanalytic conception of subjectivity (an urge evident in the early work of Julia Kristeva, for example).[3]

It is within this multifaceted context that the question of the "subject" needs to be taken up once more, in order to survey the issues surrounding its privileged position in contemporary discourses and also to ask what epistemological and political effects might have been produced as a result of this privilege. In conducting such a questioning this book identifies a number of different intellectual "areas" or "fields" – that is, discursive practices – in which the "subject" has become either overtly or implicitly a major concern, and attempts to discuss and critique them. Of course, many of these discursive practices are interrelated – and, it seems to me, inextricably so – in that they participate in many of the same problematics, suggest the same questions, draw upon broadly similar theoretical notions, and – according to this book's argument – exhibit many of the same fundamental deficiencies and suspect tendencies. Because of this, I have tried in my analyses not to isolate completely any of these discourses from the wider intellectual context in which they are implicated. I have tried, rather, to maintain a sense of the multifold articulation of concerns and problems existing in the "areas" and "fields" which I deal with.[4]

One result of this strategy is that the book's argument can not be conventionally anabatic, as it were. That is, it is not quite an argument beating a determinate linear path toward a firm or conclusive point. Rather, the book makes a series of forays or incursions into particular "fields," all the while refusing to acknowledge the autonomy usually granted those fields. Although the argument does alight at particular and definable points in this network of contemporary discourse, I hope to be able to keep in view the ways in which those points are interdependent, or the way in which they all similarly contribute to a more general theoretical economy. Thus I hope that one of the book's primary effects is to point out the overdetermined structure of the economy of contemporary thought in the human sciences.

This is not to say, of course, that such an almost metonymic crossing of a number of important topoi is in any sense arbitrary, nor to say that it does not seek to present a particular point of view. In accordance with the title of the book, *Discerning the Subject*, all the discussions conducted here around the concept of the "subject" are intended to forward a particular claim: that current conceptions of the "subject" have tended to produce a purely *theoretical* "subject," removed almost entirely from the political and ethical realities in which human agents actually live and that a different concept of the "subject" must be discerned or discovered.

In that sense the book might be seen as a series of observations and complaints about the way in which "theory" in the human sciences has proceeded during the few years since it emerged as an at all powerful discursive force in the academy. In constructing my criticisms I have been continually mindful of a remark of Jean Louis Schefer's: referring specifically to current theoretical work on cinema, he claims that

> those analytical/theoretical approaches didn't really concern anyone; that's to say, they didn't concern any living subject, but were dealing rather with what I'd call a fiction of the subject (1982, p. 39).

So I have tried here to identify, from among the discourses which inform and constitute contemporary academic practice in the human sciences, a number of examples of this tendency to abstract the "subject." In doing so I have tried to point out what I take to be the strategy which commonly accompanies the theoretical abstraction of the "subject." That is, I have identified a process of abstraction which I have called "the cerning of the subject." The word "cerning" conflates and plays simultaneously upon two rarely used English verbs — "to cern" and "to cerne." The first means "to accept an inheritance or a patrimony," and I use it to suggest that the contemporary intellectual abstraction of the "subject" from the real conditions of its existence continues — and is perfectly consonant with — a western philosophical heritage in which the "subject" is construed as the unified and coherent bearer of consciousness. Simultaneously, I have used the second verb, which means "to encircle" or "to enclose," to indicate the way in which theoretical discourse limits the definition of the human agent in order to be able to call him/her the "subject." My project in this book is, then, to be described as an attempt to *dis-cern* the "subject," and to argue that the human agent *exceeds* the "subject" as it is constructed in and by much poststructuralist theory as well as by those discourses against which poststructuralist theory claims to pose itself.

My discussions begin with the questions raised within contemporary Marxist and post-Marxist thought about the place of the "subject" in ideology. In the first chapter I have tried to suggest that orthodox Marxist theories about the hold that ideology seems to have over "subjects" by and large neglect to specify the actual locus of that hold; or, in other words, that the point of interaction between ideological pressures and subjective existence is still a relatively mysterious one for Marxist thinking. In an attempt to offer a clearer sense of what happens between the "subject" and ideology, I have examined Louis Althusser's suggestions about the effect of ideological interpellation on the unconscious. Althusser makes some use of recent psychoanalytical theory in his explanations of the effects of ideology but the exact theoretical value of his recourse to Lacanian concepts has often been questioned. Here I have tried both to clarify and to amend Althusser, in order to counter his ultimately abstract view of subjectivity and in the hope of advancing a more useful explanation of the "subject's" interrelation with ideology.

The questions which Althusser's work raises in relation to the "subject" in ideology have been widely discussed, especially by theorists of literature and film. For such theorists cultural texts such as literature constitute a privileged example of how ideological messages take effect upon "subjects." Chapter 2, therefore, looks at a number of theoretical works on film or literature where the ability of texts to position or interpellate the "subject" is taken as a dominant concern. Many of these critical efforts seem often to burden themselves with the notion that ideological interpellation is monolithic, or that it is theoretically unfailing in its ability to construct a compliant "subject." I argue here that ideological discourses are *not* unstintingly effective in identifying their appropriate "subject," but that manners of resistance to ideology can be glimpsed as soon as the "subject" is no longer theorized as an abstract or cerned entity. I end this chapter by distinguishing between, on the one hand, notions of resistance which rely upon deliberate and conscious activity on the part of the human agent, and, on the other hand, a notion of resistance which would be able to recognise it as, in fact, a veritable *product* of ideological interpellation.

The next chapters take up this question of resistance by examining two particular areas of contemporary discourse which seem to offer analyses and theories capable of projecting radically effective contestatory action. In Chapter 3 I discuss some of the implications of deconstruction—or, more particularly, of the work of Jacques Derrida. I argue here that any potential resistance that deconstruction might mount is in fact compromised by its lack of a theory of subjectivity and agency. In Chapter 4, I look at some work in contemporary educational theory—work which is deeply informed (as, I suspect, is Derrida's) by the writings of the so-called Frankfurt School. Arguing that the calls to resistance made by educational theorists such as Henry Giroux are hampered by a view of subjectivity inherited from Fromm, Marcuse, and others, I suggest that an effective theory of subjectivity and agency must take account of what I call the mediating function of the unconscious in social life. Thus, in Chapter 5, I propose a reading of Lacan's theory of the unconscious which could complement the incipient theories of resistance and agency discussed in the previous chapter.

The main point made in these chapters is that theories in the human sciences which privilege the *subjected* state or status of the "subject," or which construe an abstract or cerned notion of subjectivity, tend to foreclose upon the possibility of resistance. A theory of resistance, it is argued, becomes possible only when we take into account the specific history of the "subject" and its implication into systems of knowledge, power, and ideology. Chapter 6 constructs an argument against the modes of knowledge—the epistemologies—and the concomitant views of the "subject" promoted and upheld by humanist thinking in the academy. The focus here is, locally, upon the discourses of anthropology and, more generally, upon what I describe as the metaparanoid nature of knowledge-construction in humanist thought. This chapter argues for the necessity of breaking down these metaparanoid structures by a disruption of both the conceptual and representational modes in which they are cast; this in the interest of opening up possibilities for new relations of knowledge and thus for new representations of the "subject."

In Chapter 7 I discuss one of the privileged modes in which a "subject" and its unique history might be represented, namely, the genre of autobiography. I take as an instance of the attempt to break down the traditional structures of subjective knowledge the work of Roland Barthes. In attempting to scrutinize and radically alter the privilege donated to the "subject" in bourgeois and humanist discourses, Barthes's writings run many risks. These risks are by and large political ones: for example, his writing is often regarded as flirting with a kind of anarchic or romantic individualism. I recognize the justice of these charges against Barthes, and I use them to assess the opposing claim that his writings can be of use insofar as they hint at ways of constructing a contestatory version of the "subject."

Some of the more relentless and rewarding questioning of the status and representation of the "subject" in recent years has been conducted by feminists. Chapters 8 and 9 try to show the effects of such questioning. First, I discuss the work of Julia Kristeva which shares many of its premises and procedures with that of Barthes, but which also notably concerns itself with the nature and construction of the *sexed* "subject"—a consideration almost entirely absent from Barthes's work. This discussion of Kristeva leads into a series of more general questions which have arisen as a result of feminists formulating and approaching questions of feminine identity, femininity, or the female "subject."[5] I try to show here how feminism's inquiries into subjectivity are undertaken within a sophisticated theoretical problematic and are also and simultaneously directed toward an urgent political project. That is, theoretical elaboration of the question of the "subject" for feminism is properly and crucially accompanied by recognition of the need for effective political strategies of resistance. Thus the "subject" which feminism speaks for and about is not an abstract or cerned entity; this, I take it, is feminism's strength.

The need to produce a notion of subjectivity which will satisfy both the demands of theory and the exigencies of practice is what my short final chapter concerns itself with. There is no warrant to suggest that such a notion is already in place, and I cannot claim that this book will make it suddenly available. Rather, I am simply suggesting here that much of the current spate of theoretical work in the human sciences has tended to produce the "subject" in a way which is (a) flawed, in so far as it has become a theoretical abstraction, and (b) incomplete, in that it fails to meet the goal of a contestatory politics. To the extent that the work in this book will be justly understood as being critical of many of the strands and currents in contemporary theory, I should say that the critique is made in the hope merely of provoking a reconsideration of the "subject"—a discerning of the "subject."

Note on Terminology

One of the problems immediately associated with discussions of subjectivity is quite simply a matter of usage. The word "subject" is not without its equivocity. Often, as I noted above, the "subject" is used synonymously with the word "individual" (itself a word with a less than handy acceptation);[1] indeed, it is common for the word to be used to signify exactly the unary and controlling consciousness that subvents traditional philosophical speculation. This usage is particularly common in psychological (as distinct from psychoanalytical) discourse where it is often conflated with another sense of the word: the person or individual under consideration, the object of study. Equally, in political discourse, the "subject" maintains one of its older senses and signifies a person who is sub-jected, exactly, to a particular form of rule or domination. And that use of the word – in a phrase such as "a British subject," for example – has been extended to include one who is subject to ideology, to particular hegemonic formations, or to power in general. And within psychoanalysis the word refers to the complex of psychical formations which are constituted as the human being is positioned in relation to language.

While these different usages can lead to certain confusions about how and as what the "subject" is constituted, each seems to maintain to some degree or other the etymological sense of the "subject" as something that is sub–jected, thrown beneath; in short, the "subject" is by and large a passivity, something at the behest of forces greater than it.[2] Beneath this etymological accident resides the problem of conflating the words "individual" and "subject." The "individual" is that which is undivided and whole, and understood to be the source and agent of conscious action or meaning which is consistent with it. The "subject," on the other hand, is not self-contained, as it were, but is immediately cast into a conflict with forces that dominate it in some way or another — social formations, language, political apparatuses, and so on. The "subject," then, is determined — the object of determinant forces; whereas "the individual" is assumed to be determining. Thus the phrase, "the individual subject," often used in current theoretical discourse, construes a contradiction.

Such a contradiction may not, however, be totally debilitating. The tension between the supposedly determining "individual" and the determined "subject" can be seen as a dialectic, in that the human being, caught within the trammels of subjection or given over to the social formations which he/she inhabits, is never entirely a "subject." This is to say that subjectivity is partial: certainly, the "subject" can always be conceived as being subject *to* something, but that something is always different, always changing. Thus a British subject, for example, is subject to particular forms of state control and hortation, but the "individual" who is a British subject is also subject to other discourses (to an ethnic and/or a gendered division, for example; or to the discourse of a region like Wales or Scotland; to the discourse of his/her family; to particular modes and languages of advertising which will place the "subject" as a consumer; and so on). These multifarious subject-positions must be considered part of the "individual" who exhibits or inhabits them; yet they never cohere to form a complete and non-contradictory "individual" — let alone an "individual" who determines the character or constitution of his/her own subjectivity. In this light it may be useful to stress the lure that is offered in the very word "individual": in its etymology it suggests one that cannot be divided and, by extension, one that is plenipotent. Thus it offers a fiction of cohesion that bears as its symptom a belief in a fully enabled and self-conscious power. It could even be said that the urge to become such an "individual," and the common consciousness of either being one or having the obligation to be one, is itself only a limited and ideological subject-position within a given experience of subjectivity and is itself produced by particular social formations.

Yet, the hope of this book is that, even within the determination of the human agent through and in different subject-positions, there is always room for change. Dominated "subjects" do not maintain the kind of control which the word "individual" might suggest, but neither do they remain consistent or coherent in the passage of time: both they and the discourses they inhabit have histories and memories which alter in constitution over time. Additionally, the interplay of differing subject-positions will make some appear pleasurable and others less so; thus a tension is produced which compels a person to legislate among them. So, in that light, it can be said that a person is not simply determined and dominated by the ideological pressures of any overarching discourse or ideology but is also the agent of a certain *discernment*. A person is not simply the *actor* who follows ideological scripts, but is also an *agent* who reads them in order to insert him/herself into them—or not.

This question of the human agent, its terms borrowed mostly from the social sciences, has only quite recently become of especial importance in discussions of subjectivity in the human sciences. But it is a question which has disturbed the somewhat placid surface of contemporary thinking there, and one of the tasks of this book is to take into account exactly that disturbance.

The human *agent* will be seen here as the place from which resistance to the ideological is produced or played out, and thus as *not* equivalent to either the "subject" or the "individual."

"The individual" will be understood here as simply the illusion of whole and coherent personal organization, or as the misleading description of the imaginary ground on which different subject-positions are colligated.

And thence the commonly used term "subject" will be broken down and will be understood as the term inaccurately used to describe what is actually the series or the conglomeration of *positions*, subject-positions, provisional and not necessarily indefeasible, into which a person is called momentarily by the discourses and the world that he/she inhabits.

The term "agent," by contrast, will be used to mark the idea of a form of subjectivity where, by virtue of the contradictions and disturbances in and among subject-positions, the possibility (indeed, the actuality) of resistance to ideological pressure is allowed for (even though that resistance too must be produced in an ideological context).

The task of this book is, to a large degree, to try to create a new understanding of the theoretical disposition of these three terms. In an attempt to negotiate this vocabulary I have often used the term *subject/individual* to designate the human entity to whom qualities of being a "subject" or an "individual" are commonly assigned. This, I hope, will mark a certain distance in my usage from the common (and, as I noted above, contradictory) expression, "the individual subject." Wherever it seems more appropriate, however, I have used the terms "person" or "human agent." Wherever the use of the terms the "subject" or the "individual" has seemed unavoidable (because of the context in which they are being discussed), I have usually put them in quotation marks. This, too, is to mark a distance between their common usage and my sense (a) that the term "subject" is best understood as the equivalent of what I call colligated *subject-positions* and (b) that the term "individual" is ideologically designed to give the false impression that human beings are free and self-determining, or that they are constituted by undivided and controlling consciousnesses.

When using the terms "subject" and "individual," I have adopted the neuter pronouns (it, its); whereas I use gendered pronouns (he/she, etc.) in the case of "person" and "human agent." I hope that these rhetorical strategies will underscore the meaning of some of the positions I take in this book.

Discerning the Subject

Chapter 1
Ideology

In the contemporary context of literary and cultural theory, Marxist theory has been such an immense influence that it has inevitably come under the closest scrutiny by both its allies and detractors. This working through the possible usefulness and applicability of Marxism in the academy has led to many attempts to rewrite orthodox or classical Marxism from the perspective of current conditions. Over the last twenty years or so, and especially now, Marxist theory has faced a determined and informed interrogation of its basic assumptions by intellectual systems that it has routinely regarded as elements of bourgeois academicism: structuralism, poststructuralism, radical social science, and so on. However, it should be remarked, to begin, that these confrontations have been (and most often still are) with ways of thinking which share Marxism's radical *tendency* and its desire to comprehend and change existing social relations.

One of the results of this new situation is that, however reluctantly, even the most orthodox of Marxist thinkers have now to admit elements of other oppositional and contestatory discourses into their work. The term "post-Marxist" has come into being, indicating the fruits of this confrontation with or challenge to the fundamental paradigms of Marxist theory. Some versions of post-Marxist thought cast their discourses in such determined antagonism to classical Marxism that it quite often would appear that their desire is to dispense with the older paradigms altogether. However, it is worth considering in this respect another possible emphasis made, for instance, by Ernesto Laclau and Chantal Mouffe who point out that "if our project is *post*-Marxist, it is evidently also post-*Marxist*" (1985, p. 4). That description clearly applies to most contemporary radical thinking whose own history is inevitably and inextricably bound up with Marxism; and it is a description which applies to my own project here. One of the principal areas of investigation for the "new" theoretical discourses of the last few decades has been that of subjectivity or the "subject." At the same time, this has been traditionally an area which Marxist theory has found relatively uninteresting — especially more orthodox, economistic Marxism. My "post-Marxist" claim here will be that Marxist theory has perhaps more to gain from an investigation of subjectivity than it currently admits.

Even despite attempts with varying degrees of success and validity by the members of the Frankfurt School and by such as Wilhelm Reich to introduce a theory of subjectivity into Marx's analyses of capitalism and history, orthodox Marxism still by and large holds to that view of the "individual subject" which installs it as an abstraction, fit only to be assigned a class and thence to be superseded by the processes of history.[1] This is the direct legacy of Marx's critique of Hegel, which claimed that Hegel's view of the person as a "unit" consistently ignored the fact that in any social formation "the unit has truth only as many units" (Marx, 1967c, p. 169).

While the essentials of Marx's theories of class and the state are embedded in this correction of Hegel, it is immediately the question of the subject/individual that is pushed aside by Marx:

> My standpoint, from which the evolution of the economic formation of society is viewed as a process of natural history, can less than any other make the individual responsible for relations whose creature he socially remains, however much he may subjectively raise himself above them. (1967a, p. 10)

Even insofar as Marx's criticism of Hegel can undoubtedly be considered correct for its refusal to accept either that "the human species is only a single individual" (1967c, p. 170), or that social organization is to be modeled on the idea of the individual figure, there is still a continual refusal on Marx's part to consider anything but a metaphorical relationship between social formations and the people who inhabit them. Marx insists that "only the people is a concrete fact" (p. 171) and will allow himself to consider "individuals . . . only in so far as they are the personifications of economic categories, embodiments of particular class-relations and class-interests" (1967a, p. 10). So for Marx, in *Capital* "individuals" are only the ground, the resting place for certain properties which are abstract, and they attain the status of the concrete only at the point where they belong to a class or where "the people" can be discovered or invented.

This is a fairly consistent strand of Marx's thought, but one which is available for use today by only the most obstinate economic determinism. The class struggle is, by this account, that which gives to people the right to be considered concrete. Thus, when Marx claims throughout his work that it is men who make history, it is only ever the plural (and, of course, the masculine) form of the noun which counts. Clearly, what is missing from Marx's proposals — and missing because of the need to correct Hegel — is any sense of how the subject/individual, as bearer on him/herself of given class traits, comes to reconcile existence as "individual subject" with existence as "collective subject," or to convert from one to the other. Marx's theory of history and of the social formation in history relies thus upon a certain neglect of, in Reich's words, "what happens 'in people's heads,' or in the psychical structures of the human beings who are subjected to [social] processes" (1972, p. 284). More specifically, and without at all calling for a return to notions of the genius of the individual or to any kind of Carlylean thesis of history, it can be complained that Marx neglects the way in which people exist in the singular. For Marx subjects/individuals are *cerned*. That is to say, and punning on the words "to cern" and "to cerne,"[2] they must: first, accept a given inheritance or patrimony (the legacy of their class provenance and of its economic determinations); and, second, be encircled or surrounded, in a synecdochal figure or by the definition of the whole in and through which they accede to "real" existence.

In the late twentieth century it has become crucial to *dis-cern(e)* the subject/individual — this, quite simply, because of the failure of Marx's prognoses regarding class and history. As many writers in the Marxist tradition have demonstrated convincingly and in a number of different ways,[3] the existing conditions of late capitalism do not submit themselves to the paradigmatic Marxist definitions and categories. The failure of the working class to fulfill its supposed role, and the continuing — indeed, unabating — ability of capitalist society to react resiliently to (or to actually produce) the global conditions necessary to its continuance are both signs of the current and perhaps radical inadequacy of orthodox Marxist positions. With this in mind it becomes necessary to discover or invent ways in which the social formation can be changed without reference to presignifying theories of historical inevitability and the like.

What is at stake here is a sense of how and under what conditions subject/individuals simultaneously exist within and make purposive intervention into social formations. Such intervention can and does take place, actively or passively, through single people or collectives, privately and publicly. It can take the form of a refusal as much as an intervention; it can be in the service of conservativism as much as of disruption. It may well call upon an experience of class; but more generally it calls upon the subject/individual's history: such a history is not exclusively determined by class or class membership, real, borrowed, or imagined. Oppositional or conservative activity on the part of any person is primarily a mark of a certain engagement with meanings as they exist, circulate, and become fixed within the practices of any given social formation. Those meanings have a history which is, in every case, constitutive of the histories of subjects/individuals.

My point here is certainly not to propose some new consolidation of the "individual" as source of meanings or actions; far less is it one which considers the "individual" as a plenitudinous bearer of consciousness, complete and coherent in itself. Rather, what is being suggested is that the subject/individual exists in a dialectical relationship with the social but also lives that relationship *alone* as much as interpersonally or as merely a factor within social formations: alone at the level of the meanings and histories which together constitute a *singular* history.

None of us lives without a reference to an imaginary singularity which we call our "self." Such a singularity or individuality is to be located in the imaginary register—in that set of images, identifications, and narratives which appears to consolidate the cerned nature of the subject/individual. Acting as the broker of that imaginary is the ego, assigned to assuring a dialectical adaptation to the pressures of the social life which has produced it and which it helps to produce. However, the singular is not necessarily to be conceived of as a unity: to think of it as such would be to posit it as purely the effect of the ideological processes in which it lives. In other words, a unified singularity—the "individual"—would never be anything more than a representation of the social formation or of the ideological. To adopt such a model would amount to a return to the Hegelian notions that Marx dispensed with, in which a complementarity or a relationship of specular identity would be said to exist between a singular, human "unit" and its ambient social organization—an identity mediated in some figure like Hegel's monarch.[4]

And yet it is precisely singularity that Marxist thought has chronically not attempted to theorize, since singularity is seen to be synonymous with a metaphysical and individualistic idea of unity; in Marxist thought, unity or totality is treatable only through the dispensability of the unit. This is demonstrated by, for example, Lucien Sève who, directly addressing the question of the singular, distinguishes on the basis of hagiographic readings of Marx's texts between (a) the notion of the concrete individual and (b) that of real men (1978). The former is that which will be allowed to come into existence at the advent of socialism/communism—indeed, it is the goal of Marxism to usher in, by way of radical social change, the freedom of such a concrete individual, and to promote the "development of human energy which is an end in itself, the true realm of freedom" (Marx, 1967b, p. 820). But for the time being, during a period in which what Marx calls the "higher development of individuality" (1968, p. 118) must be deferred, the concept of real men is all that is important to Marxist science. Real men, of course, are to be considered as the actual bearers of the effects produced at particular conjunctions of social relations. Indeed, Sève rather extremely proposes that it is the ensemble of social relations that produces man's real *essence*.

Marx himself is less extreme, I think, but his formulations continually take for granted that there *is* some essential humanity, but that it cannot yet be theorized since "society does not consist of individuals, but expresses the sum of interrelations within which these individuals stand" (Marx, 1973, p. 265). Thus, concrete individuality does not exist in the current conditions of alienation but rather is smothered beneath the weight of those real conditions. In other words, subjectivity can currently have no force and no effect, and can only await its fulfillment, exactly, in the destruction of capitalism and the building of socialism/communism.

One must, I think, argue that this is a utopian maneuver which effectively deprivileges the very real existence experienced by the subject/individual in any given set of social relations. Marx considers the subject/individual only as a currently unrealized form of exactly that lure which has been offered by traditional notions, including the Hegelian one: Marxism looks forward to bringing about an "individual," exactly, whose unalienated activity "will coincide with material life, which corresponds to the development of individuals into *complete* individuals" (1947, p. 68 – my emphasis). This view of the subject/individual is apparent throughout most of Marx's works – epistemological breaks notwithstanding[5] – and represents a serious problem for all radical attempts to understand not only subjectivity but ideology itself. If the goal of a socialist revolution is to be the development of "complete individuals," this surely marks an appeal to either a pre- or a post-ideological condition where the subject/individual is again a plenitude.

Marx proposes this condition of the subject/individual as the result of a more or less predictable social and historical progression which, although determined by particular conditions not yet in place, is nonetheless inevitable. This is emblematic of the always unresolved tension in Marx's text between, on the one hand, an astonishing materialist grasp of the fundamental import of sociohistorical formations, and, on the other, a transhistorical (almost ahistorical) *faith*. Thus what is sketched out in Marx's work is a putative and utopian passage from "dominated subject" to "fulfilled individual" – a passage which, however much it may be offered as a tactical necessity and whatever deal of hope it proposes for the future of the species, constitutes a contradiction at the theoretical level. This is to say that the very same analyses by which Marx attempts to reinstall "real men" and to grasp the materiality of social relations, also prefigure a plenitudinous "individual" as their target and purposively foreclose on the possibility of talking of the experience of real subject/individuals – except in their theoretical cernement by and in historical, causative processes.

This is all to say that the "individual" destined to appear at the endpoint of Marx's historical processes is yet another version of the familiar liberal "subject" – what we might call "the subject of freedom." Freedom, as it is used in Marx's texts and in the writings of many of his followers, implies a release for the "subject" from its alienation in the social and, more generally, from the ravishes and distortions of ideology. It is to be understood that "real men" are "subjects" living in the realm of necessity; but they become concrete and fulfilled "individuals" in the realm of freedom where ideology no longer alienates and subjects them. Some kind of imaginary wholeness of the human being can thus be seen to reside at the end of Marx's theoretical projections.

Marx's view of the subject/individual is disputable to the extent that it has authorized this dichotomy between the utopian idea of concrete and fulfilled "individuals," on the one hand, and "real men," on the other. Yet in Marxist theory this notion of "real men" has become one of the major premises—which are not, according to Marx, "arbitrary" ones—from which all discussions of the social must begin (see 1947, p. 6). Indeed, those premises are now installed in contemporary Marxist discourse as the most primary of concerns; thus they come with their own sanctified conceptual framework and privileged vocabulary. These premises are loudly claimed in our moment—ringing as it is with the cry to historicize, always historicize—and are specified by Marx in his *quare impedit* against the young Hegelians, *The German Ideology*, as

> *real individuals*, their activity and the material conditions under which
> they live, both those which they find already existing and those
> produced by their activity. (p. 7; my emphases)

This well-known passage and its emphasis on Marx's pre-eminent and "empirically verifiable" premise of "real individuals," when taken in conjunction with the point I have been making about that other "real individual" (the one that is yet to appear), makes it necessary perhaps to question the status of the "real" in Marxist thinking and to interrogate what can be called his *real-ization* of the individual. We might nowadays object to Marx's realizing the "individual" as a cerned entity—one which, paradoxically, has been posed in order to counter the idealist (more specifically, Feuerbachian) abstraction of the "subject." Marx's *Theses on Feuerbach* attacks the idealist's tendency to "presuppose an abstract—isolated—human individual" (1967c p. 402), and thus installs the real as a function of nonisolation. This is Marx's strategy for turning idealist thought on its head. However, such an inversion can be conducted only by invoking a classic binary opposition: that between the abstract and the real. So for Marx, "real individuals" are not to be conceived of as isolated, nor to be subsumed under a notion of "a species, as the inner, dumb generality which unites the many individuals *naturally*" (p. 402); rather, "real men" are a kind of tautological construction of the "real"—that is, they are given over entirely to social formations. This opposition, once it has settled in the heart of Marx's text, then clothes itself in the terms of other oppositions: natural/social, gens/socius, and so on.

Immediately, then, it can be seen that the proposal that humans exist, only and really, through a relation to the social formations in which they produce and are produced, is arrived at through the strangest kind of alliance between a utopian abstraction and empirical *realization*. Knowledge about the actuality of social formations is, says Marx, verifiable "in a purely empirical way" (1947, p. 7); presumably a knowledge of the human is to be thence *deduced*.

Clearly, it would not be part of my desire to argue against the fundamental and determining function of the social in the production of the subject/individual; rather, what may be put into question as a result of Marx's formulations is the actual definition of such a subject/individual and what epistemological force authorizes the adumbration of the *matter* of the "individual" and its reality through a mere inversion of the terms of an idealist dualism. If different social formations and differing means of production can be empirically verifiable throughout the course of history, then the "individual's" existence will have been materially altered in such a way that the appeal to a "real" existence will be as questionable as an appeal to an idea of the natural genus of the human. This is because such a "reality" could be posited only as a transhistorical notion, as a structural instance which itself could not be historicized.

What is finally of interest in this determining instance of the real for Marx is that it is to be regarded as *not arbitrary*; thus it becomes clear that beneath the integument of Marxist thought there is posited an intercessional necessity resting upon the empirical viability of descriptions of the social formation into which "real men" in some way fit. The fact that the social is regarded as historically contingent does nothing to rescue the abstract conception of the "real individual" dialectically involved there. It is, then, in opposition to the fundamental intendment of Marx's "real individual" that any further dialectical investigation of the human subject will have to conduct itself. Insofar as it would reject the abstraction involved in Marx's concept of the "subject," such an investigation necessarily poses difficult questions for the various strands of utopian Marxism to be found in contemporary critical practice.

Once the distinction is drawn in a reading of Marx's work between "real men" and the (teleological) "individual," two things become clear. First, "real men" are destined to change according to changes in historical conditions, but such changes will eventually produce an "individual," exactly, something that is a utopian construct not far removed from what has become familiar in certain discourses as the "whole" or "fulfilled" person. This construct is itself not radically theorized in Marx: there is no sense given—except in the most nebulous vocabulary of fullness, completeness and emancipation—of what such an "individual" would consist in. If the inversion of a Hegelian dialectic and subsequent alterations in the modes of production are to eradicate an alienation in the subject/individual, some sense of a "subject" devoid of alienation needs to be proposed. In Marx it is only ever suggested that the revolutionary "subject" will have access to a manner of existence which has been materially ameliorated; the actual qualities of the post-revolutionary "individual" are adumbrated in terms which are disturbingly reminiscent of those older, humanist formulations in which the potentialities of "man" are mystified.

What becomes clear, second, is that Marx's arguments for the definition of "real men" only in terms of a relation to social formations are based upon a teleological, or evolutionary, conception of the human species which begins with a kind of *tabula rasa* notion of the animal: an originary, presocial human animal is posited as an abstraction for which all differences are null and void and which must await its implication into a social category before actually coming into being. Marx's dealings with the subject/individual thus begin with an empty category (the animal) and move toward a utopian and full category (the "individual") by way of the real. It is tempting to suggest that this is a quasi-religious trajectory, but it is in any case certainly imbued with a teleological and even genetic force: it is a description in which the definition of material or real subject/individuals is predicated upon, or succeeds, some previous form of existence which is *infans* or speechless — animal. Real conditions construct "real men" from animals, and those "real men" interact with real conditions in such a way as to cause their alienation finally to disappear and to allow a fully grown and achieved "individual" to come into existence.

Marx's historical materialism, insofar as it addresses the subject/individual, can perhaps then best be viewed as an explanation of why a certain genetic growth has not yet taken place and of why it is nonetheless inevitable. The principal obstacle to fulfillment and maturity is nothing other than the real conditions of men's existence, or those conditions which Marx has already isolated as the constitutive factors in his definition of the species. Within those conditions certain forces are at work to mystify and sully, and to prevent "real men's" accession to "the perfectly intelligible and reasonable relations" that would mark "man's" maturity (1967a, p. 79).

The growth or evolutionary passage from really existing conditions to the conditions which would favor the developed "individual" clearly involves the eradication of mystification for Marx, and it is around the notion of the real that he conducts his arguments for that eradication. Indeed, as is well known, he continually argues that capitalist conditions themselves constitute a mystification. For example, his celebrated discussion of the fetishization of commodities proposes that real relations of existence and production are mystified in the commodity form: "A commodity is . . . a mysterious thing" (p. 72). This is a typical movement in Marx's thinking where what he calls "a social hieroglyphic" is derived from what "appears to be an objective character[istic]" in social life (p. 74). The problem here of course is that the very conditions which Marx takes to be "real," the "real" conditions of existence, are equally proposed to be constituted in fictions and "fantastic forms."

In other words, Marx does two things. First he valorizes the real — the empirically verifiable — conditions of existence, a description of which is fundamental to his analyses of capitalism. This real is the lived real and it includes "real men," really existing subject/individuals. This is the real which is used conceptually to turn the Hegelian idealist dialectic on its head; it thus has claim as a cornerstone in Marxist method. But, second, Marx also proposes another and more "truthful" real—that which lies beneath the forms and appearances of the first real. This second real is hidden in and by the representations which constitute ideological appearances; in other words, it is actually hidden in the first real, in the real conditions of existence of the subject/individual and his/her social relations. The rhetoric which Marx uses tends to obfuscate the difference between these two reals, but it seems that the one (the one shot through with "illusions" and the "appearance of simplicity") is merely the false representation of the other (the one which will become "simple and transparent" and in which the fully developed "individual" will live) (1967a, p. 82 and p. 79).

This problematic of a "double reality" has taken its place at the heart of discussions of ideology in the Marxist tradition.[6] Yet the proposition that "real men" exist somehow on the brink of another reality that is susceptible of revelation by an adequately conceived and formulated Marxist science cannot, of course, be taken seriously for very long. It is remarkable in this context that the following question is seldom asked with any explicitness:

> why some people—those living their relation to their conditions of existence through the categories of a distorted ideology—cannot recognise that it is distorted, while we [Marxists], with our superior wisdom, or armed with properly formed concepts, can. (Hall, 1984, p. 66)

The implication of the notion of "false consciousness" to which Hall refers here is that "alternative forms of consciousness . . . arise as scales fall from people's eyes. This is an account . . . founded on the rather surprising model of St Paul on the Damascus road" (p. 67).

Marx's theory of the fetishization of commodities through distorted forms is of interest here because it makes explicit that, finally and decisively, his view of ideology and the place of "the subject" therein is guided by a similar metaphor of distortion. Despite Althusser's claims that there is an epistemological break between the early and late Marx, I think it can be argued that there is a certain consistency between Marx's rhetorical figures and their concomitant meanings in *Capital*—a supposedly mature Marxist text, by Althusser's lights—and those purveyed in, for example, *The German Ideology*.

The first chapter of *Capital* deals with the commodity insofar as it "appears, at first sight, a very trivial thing, and easily understood. Its analysis shows that it is, in reality, a very queer thing, abounding in metaphysical subtleties and theological niceties" (1967a, p. 71). Already the language of appearance and reality, truth and falsity is emerging here, and it reaches its culmination in Marx's description of the chiasmatic and distorted structure obtaining between producers and commodites:

A commodity therefore is a mysterious thing, simply because in it the social character of men's labour appears to them as an objective character stamped upon the product of that labour; because the relation of the producers to the sum total of their own labour is presented to them as a social relation, existing not between themselves, but between the products of their labour. (p. 72)

The commodity thus exists as an image of the real relations between producers; but it is a distorted and displaced image, a signifier whose real referent is hidden. Marx here, in attacking the commodity *form*, exhibits at least a rhetorical desire for a clear and transparent relationship between signifier and referent. But he holds two positions at once: one states that the conditions which cause the signifier to become a "social hieroglyph" are real and empirically verifiable; the other states that the real hides another real which it is the aim of Marxism to reinstall.

This doubled notion of the real has promoted the utopianism that has been one of the burdens of a good deal of Marxist thinking since Marx: an insistence on a "double reality" thesis has led to a view of ideology—that which hides the more "truthful" reality—as always and necessarily a negative force, and one which is never *enabling* for the human being who inhabits ideologically determined social spaces. If ideology is seen in this way and if the "subject" in history is always to be seen as simply sub-jected to social formations, there can be no room for a genuine theory of resistance or, indeed, for any impulse to social change on the part of the subject/individual. Paradoxical as it may sound to say this, Marxist theory seems to march toward a vision which eradicates such a possibility; for orthodox Marxism change can only be a product of the inevitability of history in certain class formations, economic formations, or whatever. The only transformatory force would be a subject-less, automatic history.

Such a view of history inevitably calls for or foresees the eradication of ideology, and for the unveiling of history's real "truth." The desire to establish a clear and transparent relationship between the socially active signifier and the real relations to which it might refer is thus expressed in a vocabulary which is familiar— the language of truth and falsity in which the real of everyday capitalism is seen as a false representation or a distorted communication of the real relations of everyday productive life: "a definite social relation . . . assumes, in [producers'] eyes, the fantastic form of a relation between things" (p. 73). Or in other words,

ideology represents real relations in a veiled form, under seal. Rather than as a transparent copy obeying the laws of perspective, ideology functions as a simulacrum: it disguises, travesties and blurs real relations. Marx opposes to it the values of clarity, light, transparency, truth and rationality. (Kofman, 1973, p. 28)

There is, obviously, a certain consistency between this view of ideology and the view that Marx offered in earlier texts. The metaphor which describes ideology is always a visual one. For example, Marx compares consciousness under capitalist ideology unfavorably with the "natural" conditions of vision, and the metaphor comes in its most privileged and celebrated mutation in *The German Ideology:*

> If in all ideology men and their circumstances appear upside-down as in a *camera obscura*, this phenomenon arises just as much from their historical life-process as the inversion of objects on the retina does from their physical life-process. (Marx, 1947, p. 14)

The struggle for the reclamation of the teleologized "real" is to be conducted through and by means of that other "real" which includes ideology within itself and wherein ideology distorts or turns things on their head. What is important there is the fact that a fundamental faith in a real object, which is available for representation in ideology, takes pre-eminence over the sense of ideology *as* reality. The "simple and transparent" social organization of which Marx talks in *Capital* will involve the righting of the lines of light in the *camera obscura* so as to produce an undistorted image. It is in the perception of this undistorted image that the full "individual" of which Marx optimistically speaks will participate. However, the very metaphor of the *camera obscura* undercuts the desired project. The *camera obscura* operates in much the same manner as the human eye, as Marx himself points out. Even if the reception of light on the retina produces an inverted image of a perceived object, such an image nonetheless *is* considered a reality, its effective distortion notwithstanding. And the same must be said of the *camera obscura* of ideology: the reality of ideology should be considered pre-eminent to any idealized notion of the real beyond it.

If the place of the subject/individual continues to be seen as a matter of false consciousness, in which the "truth" of the real is both that it is "empirically verifiable" *and* that it is hidden beneath existing conditions, an argument must be made to indicate the conditions of possibility for the raising of the subjective blinds. Traditionally in Marxism this argument has been conducted around either notions of theory and practice (that is to say, there has been a debate as to whether theory should guide practice, or vice versa) or around questions of a possible theoretical distinction between ideology and science.[7] Both these debates basically circulate around the same truth/falsity distinction which has authorized the contention that ideology can be treated as a device of distortion preventing the establishment of true knowledge. To this extent and in this metaphysical bind, orthodox Marxism has no choice but to predicate the possibility of new social relations on the disappearance of ideology.

However, some recent re-examinations of Marxist thinking in this regard have brought into question the notion that ideology will somehow disappear. If it does

not, then of course the implication must be that the "subject" will still exist, dominated in some way, and the "individual" will never appear, fulfilled and liberated.
Perhaps the most influential figures in this tendency have been Louis Althusser
and his followers.[8] One of the more important emphases of their work has been
the effort to eradicate from the Marxist framework any notion that ideology can
disappear. According to their arguments, ideology should no longer be considered as a distorting lens, but rather as a constitutive component of reality. This
obviously has important consequences for a theory of the "subject."

Althusser specifically argues against what he sees as the humanist-Marxist notions of ideology as "false consciousness" and claims instead that ideology is
properly to be construed as a particular social reality, specific to given social
practices. He claims that ideology has a material existence in these social practices and that its work is to construct "subjects" *for* a particular social formation.
This is the function of ideology-in-general, which Althusser calls

> an omni-historical reality, in the sense in which that structure and func-
> tioning are immutable, present in the same form throughout what we
> can call history, in the sense in which the *Communist Manifesto* defines
> history as the history of class struggles, i.e. the history of class socie-
> ties. (1971, p. 161)

Althusser's saying that "ideology has no history" is different from the meaning
proposed by Marx when he uses the same phrase in *The German Ideology*.
Whereas Marx describes particular forms of ideology—"Morality, religion,
metaphysics, all the rest of ideology and their corresponding forms of consciousness" (1947, p. 14)—as having no history (i.e., as having "no development" but
merely the semblance of being "natural"), Althusser claims that it is exactly those
forms of ideology that do have a history: they have a history that is specific to
the history of the societies, institutions, and thus to the struggles of which they
are part. He proposes that these forms of ideology, these ideolog*ies* be distinguished from ideology in general.

Ideology-in-general is the stuctured existence of the material practice of ideology in all social formations. Althusser claims that this general form and presence
of ideology has no especial origin and no predisposed "subject." It is a kind of
geno-ideology which operates in tandem with pheno-ideolog*ies*. Whereas the latter are particular, having specific historical forms, apparatuses, and subjective
effects, ideology in general is a necessary condition for keeping social formations
and social subjects in cohesion; that general function of ideology is overdetermined by any give ideology whose role it shall be to ensure the continuance of
a particular regime or ethos.

Thus Althusser argues for the permanence of ideology as a mechanism, or as
"a 'cement' that holds society together" (Larrain, 1983 p. 92), *and* for the variable
peculiarities of ideologies which can be grasped in particular historical conjunc-

tions. The distinction allows Althusser to remove (to the horror of many Marxist thinkers)[9] the entirely negative connotation that the term ideology tends to carry. Particular ideologies are for him "systems of representations [in which] . . . the practico-social function is more important than the theoretical function" (1977, p. 231), and they will survive even in socialist/communist societies as forms of practical knowledge. Ideology is inescapable since it is the device which guarantees the cohesion of social formations of any sort. And ideologies can signify the character of any social movement or formation. For example, Althusser speaks of the proletarian ideology on which emancipatory movements can build (v. Althusser, 1978). In this way ideologies come to assume in Althusser's work an objective reality present in the practices of everyday life for subject/individuals and constitutive of them: "an ideology always exists in an apparatus and its practice, or practices. This existence is material" (1971, p. 166).

It can be objected to such a suggestion that to install the ideological as an immutable component of reality in this way "so generalizes the concept as to render it meaningless as an analytical tool" (Giroux, 1983, p. 142). Objections of this sort tend to cling to an orthodox Marxist theory of determination suggesting that ideology must be regarded as a purely negative force; the implication is that emancipation can be achieved only through the removal of ideological blinkers. Furthermore, in such a line of thinking, the import of the theoretical space opened up by Althusser's distinction between ideologies and Ideology cannot be accounted for.

To distinguish between Ideology and particular ideologies is tantamount to distinguishing between *mechanism* and *mode*; or, to put it another way between whole and part. Althusser assumes that an understanding of the most general characteristics and qualities of ideology can help in the formulation of contestatory tactics for specific struggles. If the mechanism of the ideology of schooling, for example, is to be contested, it can be contested only on a ground of a scientific comprehension of its possible mechanisms. Althusser is quite clear that the struggle for social change must be undertaken against a plethora of ideologies, each with specific effects but without any necessary cohesion or alliance with others. Nonetheless all ideological apparatuses, of course, function with what Althusser takes to be a unified goal:

> the ideology by which they function is always in fact unified, despite its diversity and contradictions, beneath the ruling ideology, which is the ideology of "the ruling class." (1971, p. 146)

It is because ideologies function within this more massive strategy that they must become the site of struggle against an overarching ruling ideology. Were this not the case, struggle against any particular ideology would constitute a purely local rebellion, directed not against the classes in power but against particular interests. What is important here is the recognition that there are nonetheless specific sites within social formations where resistance can be mounted. If there are such sites, then it would appear that each is constructed according to particular practices—but practices which are contingent upon more generalized conditions of possibility. To understand the mechanism of ideology, then, will be of use in combatting its particular modes.

Far from being confined to this particular procedural import, Althusser's sense that ideology must be distinguished from particular ideologies is crucial in what it has to say about the subject/individual. The distinction allows space for the construction of a theory to explain how and why human agents are implicated in and act in relation to ideological pressures. That is to say, Althusser's Ideology/ideologies distinction, taken here to operate analogously to the *langue/parole* split which has become so powerful a tool in contemporary thought,[10] seems intended to lay the ground for an examination of how ideology is, as it were, *used* by social agents, how ideology becomes implanted in such a way as to be effective in a person's lived existence. Unfortunately, it would not be true to say that Althusser has provided the theory that he has laid the ground for—despite his attempts to do so. Althusser's contribution to a theory of the interaction between the subject/individual and ideological formations is limited and flawed, precisely on the ground of its definitional view of the "subject."

Althusser's theory of ideology places a great deal of emphasis, as it should, on what he calls the "subject." The "subject" is the function and effect of the ideological since individuals are interpellated, in Althusser's word, as "subjects" for an ideological formation or apparatus. That is to say, people are called upon to be "subjects" by means of a process "which can be imagined along the lines of the most commonplace everyday police (or other) hailing: 'Hey, you there!' " (p. 174). In this way people become the bearers or supports of the relations which constitute social formations, just as they were seen to be in Marx (and it is from Marx that Althusser takes the word *Träger* in the following quotation):

> the structure of the relations of production determines the *places* and *functions* occupied and adopted by the agents of production, who are never anything more than the occupants of these places, insofar as they are the 'supports' [*Träger*] of these functions. (1979, p. 180)

In a later essay, the much discussed "Ideology and Ideological State Apparatuses," this thesis is propounded with more force and elaboration as Althusser examines the modes by which the relations of production are reproduced. "Individuals" are interpellated as "subjects" in the discourses of the ideological apparatuses which guarantee the reproduction of social relations; and Althusser claims that ideologies can only function "by constituting concrete subjects as subjects" (1971, p. 173). The effect, then, of Althusser's notion of interpellation is to construct "subjects" that recognize—that are, indeed, predisposed to recognize—the call of ideological discourses.

It has very often been claimed that Althusser's notion of interpellation has a distinct ring of functionalism about it; this, combined with the charge that Althusser's Marxism was only contaminated and vitiated by the predominantly structuralist ethic of his time and place in the sixties, has proved his undoing, especially in America.[11] The charge is usually that "in this grimly mechanistic approach, human subjects simply act as role-bearers, constrained by the mediations of structures like schools and responding primarily to an ideology without the benefit of reflexivity or change" (Giroux, 1983, p. 136). This objection boils down to the observation that Althusser leaves little room for an elaboration of a theory of human agency, or that compared with the human subjects of Talcott Parsons' functionalism "Althusser's agents are structural dopes of even more stunning mediocrity" (Giddens, 1979, p. 52).

The partial merits of such critiques should not, I think, cause Althusser to be abandoned in the way that he has been. The problem, certainly, with Althusser's account is its stringent or, rather, its uncompromising view, inherited from Marx, that the condition of dominated subjectivity is an adequate and full account of the "real" subject/individual. But the thesis that subjectivity is constructed through ideological intervention and that "subjects" are interpellated, called into position by specific social discourses, remains solid and can be built upon.

In his descriptive theory of ideologies Althusser makes use of the term "individual subject" with considerable abandon. As for Marx, the "individual subject" for Althusser remains simply dominated. Althusser is merely adopting a different vocabulary in order to do the same thing as Marx has done, namely, to grant no specificity to the "subject" apart from positing it to be dialectically implicated in the social structures which it inhabits. Althusser's "individual subject" is no more than the bearer or support of ideological practices that are inscribed upon it. Indeed, Althusser's argument seems to maintain that subjectivity actually constitutes a person's unified identity. Thus ideology interpellates only whole human entities, forming them as "subjects" or constructing subjectivity for them. At the same time he claims that a person is always already a "subject," even before being properly and fully interpellated (he talks of the baby which is expected by its parents, the expectation constituting already a subjectivity for the unborn child). So, for Althusser, the "individual" cannot subsist except as conflated with a "subject," and that "subject" is coterminous with the "individual" and vice versa.

Seeing Althusser's conflation of "subject" and "individual," the question must immediately arise whether or not it *is* possible to conceive of subjectivity as in some way contradictory. This is to ask, instead of conceiving of subjectivity as simply resting upon some unspecified biological mass of human cells, and without proposing some innate human characteristic which resists subjectivity, whether or not a subjectivity can be theorized in an entirely materialist manner (i.e., with the help of dialectics and through the recognition of contradiction). To do so would be to speak more fully about the actual existence of human beings in their concrete existence — a concrete existence which can and does include the registration of resistance to the condition of being ideology's "subject."

So the Althusserian notion of the "individual subject" is ultimately, like Marx's conception of "real men," no more than a reversal of the effect of the bourgeois "subject" which controls its destiny, utterance, and consciousness — even if it does remove the humanist connotations of the notion of the "individual" and refuses the utopian "individual" posited in Marx. More seriously, in constructing this "individual subject," Althusser can be accused of positing a "subject" entirely cerned insofar as it seems to exist as a unity which is dependent upon a supposed unity of interpellative effects. It is by no means obvious that the welter of ideological interpellations that might arise from a variety of sources — state apparatuses, texts, history, whatever — do in fact form any kind of unified social ideology — let alone one bound to class or economic categories. Thus there seems to be no reason to suppose that there exists a correspondingly unifiable subjectivity.

The importance of this objection to Althusser's view of subjectivity is underscored by a glance at one of the main sources from which he derives it — a source that in fact provides altogether different notions of the "subject." Rarely read by Althusser's detractors (and seemingly not taken very seriously elsewhere, for that matter) is the essay which follows the "Ideology and Ideological State Apparatuses" in *Lenin and Philosophy:* the essay, "Freud and Lacan" (1971, pp. 189–219).

It should be said about this essay first of all that it is exceedingly defensive: Althusser is concerned that the chronic dismissal and misunderstanding of Freud that has characterized Marxist thinking in this century might entail a disregard of his own attempt to draw from psychoanalytical discourse. Thus his claims for Freud and for Lacan's reworking of Freud are couched in apologetic tones, and he stresses that his dealings with psychoanalysis are more in the way of an overture than anything else. Nonetheless, Althusser here importantly and quite trenchantly lays claim on certain Freudian/Lacanian problematics as being "of particular concern for all investigations into ideology" (p. 219).

Primarily what Althusser claims is that psychoanalysis is necessary to such investigations because it

> gives us a hold, a *conceptual* hold on the unconscious, which is in each human being the absolute place where his particular discourse seeks its own place, seeks, misses, and in missing, finds its own place, its own anchor to its place, in the imposition, imposture, complicity and denegation of its own imaginary fascinations. (pp. 212–13)

From the above quotation it is easy to notice one of the main watersheds of Althusser's own work and to see how he begins to dispose psychoanalytical work around his own. Notably, the emphasis given to the word "conceptual" begins to make a crucial distinction between psychoanalytical theory and the actual practice of psychoanalysis (which latter, one imagines, Althusser would be inclined to designate as an ideological state apparatus). So far as he is concerned, the value of that theory would reside in its having ordered a conceptual revolution by discovering or inventing a new *object*—the unconscious and its formations (see p.202–4, for example). A similar sort of claim is made in *Reading Capital* for Marx and his discovery or invention of a new object by means of a new epistemology (v. 1979, pp.14–69).

This new psychoanalytical object and its philosophical consequence—that is, the lesson that "the human subject is de-centered," no longer to be conceived of as centered in consciousness—takes its place as a theoretical, revolutionary device in Althusser's armory; moreover, it is a device similar or analogous to that provided by Marx when he teaches that "the human subject, the economic, political or philosophical ego is not the 'centre' of history" (1971, p. 218). Althusser's strategy is clearly one of appropriation: indeed, this will be the starting point for my critique of Althusser's notion of the "subject." The appropriating strategy begins to show itself when he talks of the unconscious as an *absolute* locus for an *anchoring* of subjectivity—an idea which, as I will suggest, is quite at odds with psychoanalytical notions of the "subject" and which is used to promote Althusser's conflation of "subject" and "individual" in his later work on ideology.

If the import of Freud's work for Althusser is the discovery of the unconscious and the beginnings of a theory of subjectivity, then the importance for him of Lacan's work is that it furnishes at least the rudiments for a psychoanalytical discussion of the relation between subjectivity and the social order, as well as an explanation of the power of that social order in constructing the "subject." It is worth quoting at length what Althusser takes as "the most original aspect of Lacan's work, his discovery":

> Lacan has shown that this transition from (ultimately purely) biological existence to human existence (the human child) is achieved within the Law of Order, the law I shall call the Law of Culture, and that this Law of Order is confounded in its *formal* essence with the order of language. What are we to understand by this formula, at first sight so enigmatic? Firstly, that the *whole of this transition* can only be grasped in terms of a recurrent language, as designated by the language of the adult or child in a *cure situation*, designated, assigned and localized within the law of language in which is established and presented all human order, i.e., every human role. Secondly, that in this assignment by the language of the cure appears the current, constant presence of the absolute effectiveness of order in the transition itself, of the Law of Culture in humanization. (p. 209)

Althusser seems to be describing here what Lacan calls the symbolic order, or the articulations that Lacan establishes among the construction of subjectivity, language, and the social order. Lacan claims that the "subject" is constructed in the symbolic at the moment of the accession to language; there is, for Lacan, no such thing as a "subject" before the entry into the symbolic order. It is easy to see what is attractive to Althusser in Lacan's formulations insofar as the "subject" can be read there as a *product* of the symbolic order, and the symbolic order seems to be offered as an overarching, even inescapable monolith having everything in common with the discursive formations which work ideologically. Indeed, Althusser seems to have no trouble establishing a synonymy among Lacan's terms and his own — Lacan's symbolic, Althusser's Law of Culture, Law of Order, or Ideology take on the same connotations and functions and then march inexorably toward a view of the subject/individual as entirely *sub-ject*.

Such a view, however, misappropriates Lacan's concept of the symbolic which is, in fact, simply an array of differentiated elements which carry meaning; it does not take on the characteristic of the historical real as Althusser wants it to, and in Lacan it is certainly not this place of an "absolute effectiveness" where the human person can be anchored. Lacan claims that the symbolic catches up (with) the "subject," as it were, and that the "subject" is a production of the symbolic's determinations. But this is not all there is to the symbolic (or to subjectivity). Where Althusser seems to say that ideology is equivalent to the symbolic and therefore that the "subject" of ideology is the same as the "subject" in the symbolic, Lacan might suggest that the symbolic is not ever completely used up in ideology. As Stephen Heath points out, "language is not exhausted by the ideological" even though it "is never met other than as discourse, with a discursive formation productive of subject relations in ideology" (1981, pp. 105–6).

Indeed, Lacan's notion of the symbolic further escapes Althusser's characterization of it, simply by dint of being posed as only one term in a *description* of the "subject," rather than as that which constitutes its unified existence. The symbolic is in fact indefeasibly caught up with two other terms which continually cut across the subject/individual and help to overdetermine its construction; these two terms are "real" and "imaginary." In the essay, "Ideology and Ideological State Apparatuses," Althusser uses both of these terms specifically — but with altogether different senses than those assigned to them by Lacan — in his definition of ideology: "Ideology represents the imaginary relationship of individuals to their real conditions of existence" (1971, p. 162).

First of all, for Lacan, the imaginary is emphatically not, as Althusser implies, the opposite of the real, nor its direct product. The imaginary is that set of representations and identifications which supports an illusory plenitude of the ego, or acts as the ego's broker; and the real is what, in Lacan's pun, ex-sists, stands outside of all symbolization and is unknowable (as distinct from reality, which is the subject's experience). In Lacan's schemas the symbolic order and the imaginary order constitute a *relation* around the "subject," which is merely the place of their operations. This conception of the "subject" — where its imaginary is just one particular subjective mode in the symbolic and where its real is unavailable — is clearly much different from (and more flexible than) Althusser's construction of the "subject" as nothing more than an imaginary/real dyad. This dyad is finally the familiar one which obtains in theories of "false consciousness," where real conditions are taken up in a distorted, imaginary figuration and where ideology is "the mirror [society] looks into for self-recognition, precisely the mirror it must break if it is to know itself" (1977, p. 144).

The "subject" that Althusser depicts as the bearer of the imaginary representations of real conditions is finally incompatible with the "subject" that Lacan defines as a series of instances in a relation of tension between the symbolic and the imaginary. Indeed, it could be said that Althusser's dominated "subject" is mistaken for what psychoanalysis calls the ego.[12] The ego is for Lacan "an object which fills the function that we call the imaginary function" (Lacan, 1977a, p. 60), or a function of identification; for Althusser this is the function of the interpellated "individual subject," which "always already" recognizes itself as the proper object of ideological hailing. In other words, aside from finally rejoining Marx in a crude sense of ideology as distortion and of "subject" as simply *Träger*, Althusser's theories remove most of the flexibility of Lacan's pronouncements.

Nonetheless, certain of Althusser's formulations remain crucial to any discussion of ideology and the subject/individual: the concept of interpellation, that is, is an indispensable tool for describing the way in which the "subject" is brought into place by specific ideological and discursive formations. Equally, his insistence on the materiality and the permanence of ideology as features of human society seems necessary as a way of forestalling or avoiding some of the traps of the "false consciousness" thesis which, ironically, Althusser himself falls into with his conception of the "subject." It should be possible to add to Althusser's theory of ideology a description of subjective mechanisms which might augment its explanatory value.

In Lacan's re-reading of Freud's metapsychological theory, the "subject" appears as a complicated articulation of different moments or instances and is conceived as a kind of process of production in the symbolic order, rather than as that order's direct and fixed effect. In this sense, and without wishing to adumbrate a theory of the production of the "subject" by analogy with some Marxist theory of production, one might talk of Lacan's notion of the symbolic as more materialist, more dialectical than Althusser's. Certainly, Lacan has not much approbation for Marxism's *points de capiton*, historical and dialectical materialism (see Lacan, 1966, p. 869, for example). Yet the emphasis that he continually places on the construction of the "subject" as a process involving a dialectic between it and what he calls "the field of the Other" (i.e., the symbolic) cannot be taken lightly by materialist thought.

What is crucial — at least as a distinction between the tendencies of Marxist thought and those of current psychoanalytical thought—is that there is in Lacan no proposition of a directly and predictably deterministic effect of (or on) subjectivity in the symbolic. Equally, for Lacan the "subject" is not a formation of the imaginary register. Rather, and central to Lacan's thinking, subjectivity is constructed as a process within the division between the two realms, imaginary and symbolic. That process is always engaged in a multiform and contradictory series of instances of the "subject" and is never transcended in order to allow access either to (a) a fundamental and determining set of unconscious meanings, structures, and representations, or to (b) a plenitudinous and self-vindicating structure of consciousness, nor even to (c) a conscious "subject" threatened by the repressed unconscious. Subjectivity is always a product of the symbolic in an instance of discourse; thus, Lacan leaves room for a consideration of subjectivity as contradictory, as structured in divisions and thus as never the solidified effect of discursive or ideological pressures. Far from being such an *in-dividual*, the "subject" is a divided and provisional entity.

It is this last proposition, of course, that must stand at the head of any attempt to specify a way out of the vocabulary of the "individual subject" and of any effort at locating (and thereby, it is to be hoped, enabling) the notions of resistance and agency. This chapter has thus been concerned to cover some fairly familiar ground where the problematic of the subject/individual is implicated with the question of ideology; covering that ground helps adumbrate a notion of agency which might yet arise out of the Marxist and the psychoanalytical traditions— although married to neither and keeping a distance from "the attempt to coordinate a Marxist and a Freudian criticism" (Jameson, 1981, p. 338) or to join them. In my view, the discourses of Marxism are incompatible with those of psychoanalysis so long as the former continue to subsume the human person under abstract categories that arise directly from a consideration of structural effects in society; and so long as the latter continue to promote a view of the "subject" as a kind of "beginning and end of theory and practice, [the] last instance" (Heath, 1979, p. 38). Nonetheless, an imbrication of the terms and ideas underpinning the two sets of discourses can be attempted in order to clarify the human person who is constructed at different moments as the place where agency and structure are fused.

If the tendency in the rest of my discussions is to lean heavily on the psychoanalytical, this is not at all to denegate the Marxist or any other kind of leftist thinking—quite the contrary. Rather, I want merely to propose that psychoanalytical theory is currently a crucially available key to opening up the useful distinction between "subject" and "individual" which Marxism seems unable to recognize; and to propose that psychoanalysis is potentially in a position to elaborate theoretically, and without falling into abstract humanist categories such as "will" or "false consciousness," some notion of how and in what manners resistance to the ideological is conditioned; that it can, by positing a constitutive non-unity in the subject/individual, point toward a category of agency; and that it can, finally, offer a view of the human person in his/her "precise constituted materiality" (Williams, 1978, p. 7) by involving singular histories into an account of social formations which too are historically specific. Yet, equally, it cannot be forgotten here that psychoanalytical theory is scarcely innocent of three quarters of a century of an institutional practice functioning more often conservatively than not; nor that psychoanalysis is prone to constructing universalist theories through an inability to historicize itself; nor that, as a consequence, its discourse is often essentialist and driven by an epistemological will to mastery.

My complaint about most theories of subjectivity either explicitly or implicitly embedded in the various areas of discourse which have recently become influential will indeed be that the subject/individual is more often than not *cerned* in them. That is to say, those discourses try to catch the subject/individual into a mastering theory which encircles and delimits. As Jean Louis Schefer points out,

> those analytical/theoretical approaches didn't really concern anyone;
> that's to say, they didn't concern any living subject, but were dealing
> rather with what I'd call a fiction of the subject. (1982, p. 39)

To an extent it is true that such fictions are unavoidable; however, it should be possible, through a proper concern for lived activity, to disperse them, question their hegemony. The rest of the work in this book will, then, examine different aspects and problematics of contemporary thought in order to consider ways in which the "subject" is cerned and can be discerned.

Chapter 2
Text

In the previous chapter I have been proposing that it is necessary to guard against the epistemological trap inherent in conflating the "subject" with the "individual;" and, equally, that it is necessary to construct some notion of the place of the living person in the processes of the social in such a way as to avoid seeing him/her as *entire* — either in the sense of being entirely submitted to the domination of the ideological, or of being entirely capable of choosing his/her place in the social by dint of possessing full consciousness or some such version of what can be called sovereign subjectivity. In either case the positing of such an entire "subject" constitutes what I mean by a cerning of the subject/individual; in each case the product is an abstract version of the "subject."

After Lacan (indeed, after Freud), I argue that the human realm is marked by exactly a splitting which constitutes the "subject" as an instance amid all forms of material practice and discourses. That splitting is constitutive and, to that extent, real. My argument also takes a certain cue from Marx's observation that the human being is primarily a political entity "that can individuate itself only in the midst of society" (1973, p. 84). My emphasis, however, is different: I would want to stress that individuation not only can, but already *does* take place in human activity and that, consequently, much of the work of human beings takes place in the singular, as it were. Dialectically implicated in the social, but also turned in upon itself, the subject/individual has to be questioned as to its capacity for decisions, choices, interventions, and the like which are not specifically or solely determined by such categories as class or economics — however much they may be at the behest of ideology in general.

The subject/individual must be put at stake in any discussion of social forma-tions. The "must" in that sentence takes account of the undeniable force of ideo-logical determinations, but I do not wish to delimit the concept of ideology to a purely dominating force into which the subject/individual is implicated to the ex-clusion of any possibility of resistance. On the other hand, it would of course be absurd to suggest that resistance, or human agency, has provenance in some puta-tive space of the nonideological since, as has been already claimed, the ideologi-cal and the place of the subject/individual are both intimately tied into the sym-bolic realm. The symbolic realm, the *place* where we are in language and in social formations and which is also the *process* whereby we fit into them, *constructs* the ideological. In that sense, to regard resistance to ideology as anything but a *by-product* of the ideological itself must be to posit some kind of innate human capac-ity that could over-ride or transcend the very conditions of understanding and calculation—indeed of social existence. Resistance does take place, but it takes place only within a social context which has already construed subject-positions for the human agent. The place of that resistance has, then, to be glimpsed some-where in the interstices of the subject-positions which are offered in any social formation. More precisely, resistance must be regarded as the by-product of con-tradictions in and among subject-positions. The subject/individual can be dis-cerned but not by the supposition of some quasi-mystical will-to-resistance. What I propose, then, is that resistance is best understood as a specific twist in the di-alectic between individuation and ideological interpellation.

With this argument in mind it might be informative to look at one particular form of ideological practice which has served as the object of attention for a lot of theoretical work wishing to formulate a valid description of the place of the subject/individual in relation to interpellative mechanisms:

> Literature, one might argue, is the most revealing mode of experiential
> access to ideology that we possess. It is in literature, above all, that we
> observe in a peculiarly complex, coherent, intensive and immediate
> fashion the workings of ideology in the textures of lived experience of
> class-societies. (Eagleton, 1976, p. 101)

One might argue, equally, that film, as "the art form of late capitalism" (cf. Aronowitz 1981, pp. 201ff.), or television, as the most popular cultural text for western society, might offer equally explicit access; and, indeed, it is around these three practices that much debate has been carried on in relation to questions of subjectivity.

The discussions have often taken as their starting point Althusser's insistence on the material nature of ideology and his account of the process by which sub-ject/individuals are interpellated by ideological apparatuses. The French critic Pierre Macherey, for example, has been an important influence as "effectively, the first Althusserian [literary] critic" (Eagleton, 1975, p. 135), with his book *une théorie de la production littéraire* (translated, somewhat inaccurately, as *A Theory of Literary Production* [1978]). The importance, as well as the flaws of Macherey's work are perhaps still not fully considered, even if they have had some influence.[1] What seems crucial, however, in Macherey's work is his effort to free Marxist literary criticism from the sub-Hegelian manners it inherited and had adopted from critics such as Lukács. Equally important, perhaps, is Macherey's positing literature as a locus of the *production* of ideology, without having recourse to the classic Marxist category of reflection. Part of Macherey's emphasis is on the fact that a literary text is the product of labor (the author's work) and that it can no longer be regarded as the mystified "creation" that much traditional literary criticism has perceived it to be. With these emphases, and guided by Althusser's sense of the material existence of ideology, Macherey develops a Marxist attention to the production of an ideology as it is materially inscribed in those practices of signification which we call literary.

Macherey's application of the category of production to the literary text has, of course, not gone unchallenged. Fredric Jameson, for example, seems to claim that the Marxist notion of production as an activity of labor is not suited to a description of literature, and he has condemned Macherey's drawing a homology between work done on the language and "real work on the assembly line and . . . the experience of the resistance of matter in genuine manual labor" (1981, p. 45). This objection is part of a larger one relating to—and, I think, ultimately mistaking—the notion that ideology has a material existence in particular practices. When contemporary literary and cultural critics talk about a "materialist theory of language," they are not, by and large, claiming that language is "matter" to be worked on; rather they are suggesting that literature constitutes one of the social practices in which ideology is materially active. Literature, the production of literary texts and their readings, cannot be privileged above any other social activity, but it does exhibit the material workings of an ideological mechanism. The *ouvriérisme* of Jameson's objection here hints at an old Marxist sentimentality toward the working class and does not recognize that, if a materialist analysis of culture is to be undertaken, "literary production" needs to be understood primarily as an activity of labor whose result can be designated as a commodity. It is in this sense that one can talk of the production of texts which are, after all, produced for exchange—in systems both of economic and of cultural capital—by the labor of one who sits down to write.

But beyond such objections, it might be claimed that the central problem with Macherey's use of the term "production" is that it does not enable him to specify very exactly what are the particular historical conditions and effects of textual production. Macherey's discussions do not, as Terry Eagleton points out, attempt to ask questions about the actual historical conditions of production, or about "the material apparatus, technological infrastructures, and social relations of an artefact" (1975, p. 134). Rather, Macherey is concerned, as Eagleton puts it, with the text as a kind of *"self* production [in] a chain of significations." In other words, Macherey consistently delves into what might be called the text's "internalization," the processes through which it is constructed as literature and as a unique exemplum of the literary, but he rather pointedly (despite talking of texts which are of commonly identifiable genres and historical provenances) refuses to talk of the work's history. This is not exactly a denial of history on Macherey's part, but it takes him very close to a formalism in which the text's social relations are ignored.

As much of a failing as this is Macherey's attempt to install criticism as a "science"—in the Althusserian sense of an objective practice opposed to ideology—based on its putative ability to uncover "the real process of [the text's] constitution" (1978, p. 49) and to "exorcis[e] the fallacies which have bound literary criticism to ideology" (p. 101). Macherey works with two major assumptions drawn from Althusser: (a) that "the language of illusion, the writer's raw material, is the vehicle and source of everyday ideology" (p. 62), and (b) that criticism should be scientifically constituted as a form of knowledge capable of distinguishing itself from the text's offered ideology.

In adopting these two premises, Macherey inevitably replicates some of Althusser's failings with regard to the place of the "subject." For Macherey the text's effect is simply another institutional practice (i.e., criticism) which appears to have no agents. Or to put it with a different emphasis, what is primarily important for him about literature and what it is the task of criticism to reveal is literature's ability to function as a specific ideological apparatus; but this apparatus seems to require no reference to a "subject," the site (even in Althusser's work) where any such ideology might rest. Rather, in Macherey, the institution of literature functions on its own and is not ever disturbed by the complex activities of either writers or readers. By this account literature would seem to be produced more by an ideological institution than by human agents; equally, literature is consumed by essentially passive readers who thus become the receptacles, or the "subjects," of the text's interpellation. In other words, both producer and consumer of the text appear to be nothing but the effects of an overarching literary institution.

In Macherey's later work, however, and in that of some of his followers (especially Kavanagh), the question of the literary effect is dealt with further, under the heading of "aesthetic effect," which is to be distinguished from (but which is not unrelated to) "ideological effect" (Macherey and Balibar, 1982). In this work the text is seen primarily as the vehicle of an interpellation and its privileged mechanism as that of identification (of author with narrator, reader with character) "which provokes readers to take a stand in literary conflicts as they would in real ones" (p. 54). Thus, the ideological and aesthetic effects of the text lead into one another since the text "endlessly transforms (concrete) individuals into subjects and endows them with a quasi-real hallucinatory individuality" (p. 54). Even though Macherey and Balibar assert that this imaginary effect is "an *uneven* effect which does not operate uniformly on individuals"(p. 57), they make it clear that any such uneveness arises primarily from the same even and unified origin. Here they presumably rely upon the same notion of an ultimately cohesive ideo-logical function or goal as does Althusser:

> Regardless of any question of the *individuality* of the "writer," the "reader" or the "critic," it is the same ideological conflicts, resulting in the last instance from the same historical contradictions, or from their transformations, that produce the form of the text and of its commen-taries. (p. 56)

In other words, what is at stake in literary production insofar as Macherey is concerned is the class struggle as a final determinant. "The literary text is the *agent* for the *reproduction* of ideology" and acts in that role by imaginarily an-nealing the contradictions and struggles of class-society. Naturally, given such a view of the text, the concomitant task of a materialist criticism would be to bring about the recognition that what is "disguised and masked" in the text is "also necessarily given away and exhibited in fictive reconstructions" (p. 57). And this task is to be carried out through critical attention to the text's gaps and contradic-tions, its aporias.

Not surprisingly, this view of the text and of criticism's task has proven con-genial to many an orthodox Marxist critic; one thinks especially of Jameson who, even in despite of his desire to reserve the term "production" for "real" work and workers, often adopts what can be described as a Machereyan stance. For exam-ple, he claims, variously and at various moments, that literature has the "function of inventing imaginary or formal 'solutions' to unresolvable social contradictions" (1981, p. 79). Jameson's working critical method is, most generally, to attempt to bring to the surface that which has been repressed in the text's formation—the contradictory social conditions that underpin it, or the text's "political uncon-scious," as he dubs it. The historical conjuncture in which the text is produced would thus seem to be open to an objective (that is, a Marxist-scientific) knowl-edge, and this leads to the claim that "only Marxism can give us an adequate ac-count of the essential *mystery* of the cultural past" (p. 19). It is not difficult to see installed here a familiar Marxist objective—the breaking of the distorting mirror of ideology.

There is ultimately in Jameson's work less of an emphasis on an indefeasible determination of the text by "class realities" than is to be found in Macherey or in other critics of the Althusserian stamp, such as Eagleton. Nonetheless, his criti-cism is perhaps even more radically reluctant than most of that other work to deal at all seriously with the function of the subject/individual in the relay of these sup-posed imaginary-ideological "solutions." For Jameson, "the problematic of the individual subject . . . is only indirectly useful to us" (p. 66) since for "us" the goal of criticism and theory would be to establish exactly the conditions of possibility for some precocious and new collective "individual," rather than engage in discussion of the "myths" of bourgeois subjectivity. Here Jameson replicates, even intensifies, the traditional Marxist reluctance to view the subject/individual as anything but the bearer of the imprint of bourgeois ideology, or the place for the straightforward inscription of social relations.

In some ways a refinement on both Jameson's and Macherey's views of the ideological functioning of literary production is Terry Eagleton's. Whereas both Macherey and Jameson tend to fall into the trap of assuming that at bottom the text is in some sense simply the *expression* of an ideological message, Eagleton specifies that it is "not the 'expression' of ideology, nor is ideology the 'expression' of social class. The text, rather, is a certain *production* of ideology" (1976, p. 64). Indeed, Eagleton is critical of Macherey's attempts (which bear some resemblance to Althusser's) "to rescue and redeem the text from the shame of the sheerly ideological" (p. 85) and to endow the aesthetic realm with a privileged status — even an autonomy — within social formations (cf. Althusser 1971, pp. 221–42, for example). Instead, Eagleton sees the text as "the *product* of ideology, but [also] as a *necessity* of ideology" (1976, p. 77) and claims that it can in fact constitute "the fullest self-rendering of ideology, the only logical form that such a complete rendering could assume." The logical form that the text takes in Eagleton's view is that of the representation "of situations which, because imaginary, would allow for the range, permutation, economy and flexibility denied to a mere reproduction of the routinely lived" (p. 78).

Despite making distinctions between his own work and that of Macherey, Eagleton finally reduces the text in the same way as does the latter; that is to say, both limit their investigations to the text as vehicle of an ideology which works by proffering an "imaginary" to its readers. In neither author, however, is there any sustained discussion of the actual anchoring of the text in the person who reads it. While it is true that an explication like Eagleton's of the workings of the text's mode of production is useful, it seems at best only partial to finish by calling the text ideological without at least attempting to tackle the obvious difficulty — that is, the fact that any ideology must lodge itself in the subject/individual in order to function as ideology.

Evidently, the notion that the text acts as a privileged display of ideological processes ought to allow for a discussion of exactly its consumption and not only its production. There seems no reason to suppose that literary production is any more open to analysis than, say, philosophical production or, for that matter, the production of automobiles, outside a dialectic of production *and* consumption. What does seem important, however, about grasping texts as ideological functions is the possibility opened up thereby of theorizing them as the place where ideology is represented in a relatively unmediated way *for* the subject/individual.

As soon as the place of the text's consumption becomes of concern and the question of the subject/individual's reading of the text is broached, it becomes less crucial to modulate all the suggestions made by Macherey, Jameson, and others about the text's provenance in class-struggle (often reduced to a question of the text's internalization of its contradictions), and more crucial to attempt an account of the processes necessary for the text-as-ideology to function as such, as an arena where a particular ideological message can be taken up or thrown out or simply registered by its audience.

Indeed, it could be said that the insistence upon a final referent in a certain conception of the class-struggle has been a debilitating feature of much Marxist literary criticism. This is, after all, a conception which in itself remains largely ahistorical, despite being rooted almost as a kind of *sine qua non* in Marxist thought. But—importantly—it is a methodological tool which ignores Marx's own insistence that classes are formed *in* struggle. From this notation of Marx it can be proposed, quoting Ernesto Laclau, that

> 1)Class struggle is only that which constitutes classes as such; 2) Consequently, not every contradiction [in ideology] is a class contradiction, but every contradiction is overdetermined by the class struggle (1977, p. 106).

In other words, to reduce every representation in ideology to a pure and simple instance of class antagonism is to limit the notion of contradiction to a reflection of empirically observable social formations at any given moment in history. It is also to propose that contradiction can be transcended through the disappearance of classes: thus it is to return to Marx's vision (tirelessly reproduced by Jameson, for example) of Marx's clear and transparent social relations. Such a view seems obstructive in the task of theorizing and thence countering the effect of ideology on those who actually live among its representations.

The question of the "subject" as the place toward which interpellation is directed was taken up quite thoroughly by the group of writers in Britain connected with the journal *Screen* in the seventies. The early theory of that group was intimately associated with the work of Lacan and attempted to locate, through deploying Lacan's conception of the "subject" as constituted in language, the ways in which particular texts—especially realist fiction and Hollywood cinema, which were to be seen as related modes of representation—can interpellate the subject/individual and put it in its place. It would be inaccurate to characterize the work of this group as in every way homogeneous, but its importance resides in the fact that it opened up a number of different discussions about the constituting of the subject/individual—discussions which have in many ways been resisted by the more orthodox Marxist critics such as Jameson.

An important starting point in the writing of the *Screen* group is the Lacanian notion of the "subject" as produced in language, and the accompanying recognition that there is no such thing as a "subject" before the accession to language. This is, of course, a theoretical position very different from that of Althusser whose claims about the "subject" demand that (a) it be already constituted *qua* "subject" in order to be able to recognise its proper interpellation, and (b) that the "subject" be seen as theoretically equivalent to the "individual." The Lacanian argument would be that, on the contrary, the "subject" is constituted only at the moment of its engagement with language; this has led to the view, implicit in most of *Screen's* texts, that specific forms of representation, with their own ideological function, institute and demand the "subject's" compliance with identifiable subject-positions.

One of the problems within *Screen* theory was exactly this leap from a conception of the "subject" as formed in language to the position that the "subject," because of that formation, is therefore unproblematically susceptible to the interpellations of an ideological text. In other words, a homology was established between the process by which the "subject" accedes to language or makes the transition from *infans* to "speaking subject," and the mechanism by which specifiable ideological discourses produce their effect in/on the "subject." This was the homology behind *Screen's* stress on "the construction of the subject"—as in, for example, Colin MacCabe's early statements of the way in which the "classic realist text . . . *guarantees* the position of the subject" (1974, p. 18; my emphasis). The efficacy of this "guarantee" is explained by MacCabe as the result of the text's closing off for the "subject" the free play of language. That occlusion is taken to be the same as what Lacan describes in his account of the construction of the "subject," where the operation of metaphor halts the metonymic flow of language in order to establish a divided "subject"—one simultaneously at the behest of the signified, and crossed by what of the signifier has been repressed. The assumption there is that any signifying practice, any text, recapitulates in some way the drama of the "subject's" accession to language and that it holds the same power. Indeed, in MacCabe's account from which I have just quoted, the text produces not only the compliant "subject" but also a set of disturbances in its coherence—disturbances that are homologous with the effect of the unconscious (p. 19). Couched in such an argument, there resides the following assumption: that it is a quality of discourse to produce the "subjects" appropriate to it. In this, *Screen* theory veered in the direction of an Althusserian—almost mechanistic—rigidity, despite having been originally predicated upon more strictly Lacanian principles than is Althusser's work.

The work that characterizes *Screen* did, however, make some advances on that Althusserian conceptualization of the problem of ideology and interpellation. As soon as it is proposed that the "subject" is the effect of a given signifying practice, it must then be claimed that interpellation is *various*, a function of the almost limitless production of discourses, texts, and addresses which together constitute social life. This is the thrust of the revisions which positions such as MacCabe's underwent. MacCabe himself tried to enter such a correction in a later article on "Principles of Realism and Pleasure" (1976) and the revision is elaborated when Paul Willemen, for example, reminds us that "Real readers are subjects in history, living in given social formations, rather than mere subjects of a single text" (1978, p. 48). Following Willemen's thinking, subjectivity can come to be construed as a series of moments produced in the course of social life. The "subject" need no longer be described, as it is in Althusser, as the equivalent of the "individual" but rather can be conceived as a set of variable qualities which are taken up as a way of negotiating interpellations and thus of understanding and coping with social relations. Within this more sophisticated and complex view of subjectivity, it would no longer be adequate to posit a social being as "always-already" a "subject," capable of recognising itself as such. It would seem appropriate to talk instead of an overdetermination in the "subject's" process of construction: such an overdetermination is the effect of a continual and continuing series of overlapping subject-positions which may or may not be present to consciousness at any given moment, but which in any case constitute a person's *history*. And a person's lived history cannot be abstracted as subjectivity pure and simple, but must be conceived as a colligation of multifarious and multiform subject-positions.

This different view of subjectivity is what *Screen* seems to have been advancing toward before a change in editorial staff produced what is now effectively a different journal.[2] It might be said that the virtue of the position sketched out above is that it would be able to recognize the specificity, not only of any given signifying practice, but also of singular histories. However, instead of developing such a socially specific discourse and theory, the *Screen* group proved noticeably reluctant to abandon the problematic that had been formed by the cross-fertilization of Althusserian and Lacanian thought. The inflexibility of what I called above a certain mechanistic strand in Althusser's thought was especially debilitating to *Screen*'s work.

This rigidity was attested to by a certain reluctance to consider the relationship between discourse and "subjects" as anything but an abstract one. The "subject" tends to be seen as the inevitable effect of a discourse and as *only* that effect; which is to say, *Screen*'s analytical effort was directed at establishing *a* subject for *a* discourse (and either literary or visual texts were taken to constitute a specifiable discourse). Furthermore, the device by which a homology was made between subject-positions in discursive formations and the subject/individual's entry into language also promoted a tidy cerning of the "subject." Even though the articulation of different subject-positions is not referred back to any unity of the "individual," it is instead referred simply to the unified space of the "discursive subject," dominated by its original entry into the symbolic.

This "discursive subject" resembles closely what Michel Pêcheux gives the name "subject form." Pêcheux describes "subject form" as "the identification (of the subject) with the discursive formation that dominates him (i.e., in which he is constituted as subject)" (1982, p. 114) and as that which anchors the "subject" in imaginary unified relations among itself, *its* discourse, and the discourses of social life.[3] In this view, the "subject" is immutably and always given over to the "dominant discursive formation" or language itself which is "preconstructed" as that system of meanings into which human beings are born (p. 115). In Pêcheux's thinking some kind of a universal "subject form" acts as the ground on which different subject-positions are built. But any specificity or effectivity of different subject-positions is flattened beneath the weight of a "subject" already given over to the demands of the symbolic.

As with Macherey's reworking of Althusser in the literary field, Pêcheux's re-working of Althusser in the domain of linguistics depends heavily on the notion of ideology's unified aim and provenance. But most characteristically, Pêcheux's notion of "subject form" is analogous with the notion of "the discursive subject" and contains within itself a quite complex contradiction resulting from a distinction which is nonetheless a crucial one to be made: that between "subject-positions" (what I have called the moments of the subject) and "subject form" (the destiny of the subject in the symbolic). That distinction is simultaneously opened up and elided by *Screen* theory. Insofar as the "subject's" interpellation into specific positions is dealt with, it is understood as being in every way analogous to the more fundamental constitution, namely, that of "the subject in the symbolic." And this analogy is always predicated upon the truth of the Lacanian account of psychical construction.

A prime example of this occurs in a crucial article in the passage of *Screen's* development, "The Imaginary Signifier," where the film theorist Christian Metz discusses the way in which the film spectator is pulled into identifying with the controlling look of the camera and is thereby constructed as the "subject" of the film-text. The phenomenon of identifying with the camera's look is given a full-blown Kleinian and/or Lacanian psychoanalytical explanation, in which the spectator's engagement with the film-text becomes nothing so much as an epiphenomenon of the original processes of subject-construction. Metz, in fact, thinks of the cinematic apparatus and text as a re-presenting or re-activating of primal psychical structures:

> It has very often, and rightly, been said that the cinema is a technique of the imaginary. . . . In the Lacanian sense in which the imaginary, opposed to the symbolic, but constantly imbricated with it, designates the basic lure of the ego, the definitive *imprint* of the pre-Oedipal, the *indelible mark* of the mirror-stage when man is alienated in his own reflection. . . . the subterranean persistence of the exclusive relation to the mother. . . . the initial core of the unconscious—primal repression. *All of this is undoubtedly reactivated by the process of this "other mirror," the cinema screen, which is in this sense like a psychical sur-*

rogate, a prosthesis for our primally dislocated limbs. (1975, p. 15 [translation changed]; my emphases)

Here the encounter between spectator and text becomes monumentalized as more or less a repetition. In this maneuver the category of the "subject" is given over entirely to the psychoanalytical account of the original *entry* into the symbolic. That account becomes, with all its genetic force, the privileged one to which all instances of subjectivity might be unequivocally referred.

This tendency in *Screen* received determined challenges from a number of quarters, notably from the British writers associated with the Centre for Contemporary Cultural Studies at Birmingham, and later from certain of *Screen's* writers themselves. Of the former group Stuart Hall, for example, complains that in adopting the neo-formalist approaches developed by people like Metz *Screen* succeeded in giving "'the subject' an all-inclusive place and Lacanian psychoanalysis an exclusive, privileged, explanatory claim" (1980, p. 160). Hall goes on to note what I have called the abstract relationship presumed to exist between reader and text and claims that this relationship needs to be historicised, or that it "needs a reference to specific modes of production, to definite societies at historically specific moments and conjunctures" (p. 160). One could add that it also needs a reference to the specificity of the reader's history, in which other discourses are continually active and where, consequently, an interminable series of subject-positions has persistent effect. Unless these references are made and elaborated it will be impossible to speak of the ideological presentation of subjectivity in discourse without absolutely cerning the "subject," or without putting it in quarantine outside of any social and historical determinants other than direct interpellative effects.

The crucial point here, of course, is that there is a distinction to be made between the subject-position prescribed by a text and the actual human agent who engages with that text and thus with the subject-position it offers. Clearly, any given text is not empowered to *force* the reader to adhere to the discursive positions it offers—the text is not, in Althusser's terms, a repressive state apparatus. Furthermore, a cinematic or literary text is never addressed at a reader it knows and thus can never articulate itself with its reader in a predictable fashion. It can, of course, offer *preferred* positions, but these are by no means the conditions with which a reader must comply if he/she wishes to read a text. And that is because what always stands between the text's potential or preferred effect and an actualized effect is a reader who has a history of his/her own. In other words there is, first, no necessary correspondence, but rather indeed, "an unbridgeable gap between 'real' readers/authors and 'inscribed' ones, constructed and marked in and by the text" (Willemen, 1978, p. 48). And equally, there can be no predictable or intended meaning-for-the-subject in any given text, and so it is necessary to "beware of arguing that the positions of knowledge inscribed in textual operations are obligatory for all readers" (Morley, 1980, p. 168).

The response of the *Screen* group to such observations (coming from both without and within it), was to move toward constructing a theoretical picture of subjectivity with more stress on the "subject's" social and historical place and provenance, and toward offering accounts of the way in which readers are caught in heterogeneous and contradictory positions.[4] Much of such work starts off from a certain feminist base and might be exemplified in Annette Kuhn's book *Women's Pictures* (1982). There Kuhn tackles head on the contradiction inherent in considering the relationship between "female subjects" and the institution and practices of the cinema, which is understood to be an apparatus geared toward and structured by masculine sexuality.[5]

The theoretical backdrop here is still Lacanian metapsychology and its conception of the "subject," but the book's main action is developed around Kuhn's continual insistence on the relevance of economic and social factors in the institution of the cinema. Thus a double analytical task is set: Kuhn attempts both to expose the specific ideological apparatus by which dominant cinema has historically constructed its meanings around the figure of "woman," and also to consider ways in which a feminist cinema might revise and counteract such constructions within and without the cinematic institutions. Broadly speaking, Kuhn regards dominant cinema as a device by which subjectivity is ordered and fixed, and considers that a feminist counter-cinema would be activated by textual practices invoking a different subjectivity for their readers. Taking a cue from the pioneering work of Laura Mulvey, Claire Johnston, and others, Kuhn claims that these new practices can "set up a radical heterogeneity in spectator-text relations, and finally refuse any space of unitary subjectivity for the spectator." This will, it is said, constitute a "putting in process of the viewing subject" (p. 171).

Even though Kuhn makes this distinction between, on the one hand, the "subject" as a fixed effect of the text and, on the other, a new "subject-in-process," in this work both the analyses of dominant cinema and the readings of feminist counter-cinema are predicated upon the notion that subjectivity is more or less purely and simply the effect of textual practice: a new textual practice (the institutional conditions for which Kuhn tries to spell out in the book's last chapter, which is about film production, distribution, and exhibition) will constitute a new subjectivity. The much-vaunted relevance of the specificity of social and historical conditions remains in a very real sense a secondary matter in relation to the actual textual processes which are privileged in their ability to inaugurate subjectivity.

The implicit political stance and the typical vocabulary of this view of signifying practices is very much akin to that of Julia Kristeva and the *Tel Quel* group in whose work of the sixties and seventies the struggle against capitalist ideology is to be conducted by changing the signifier, or altering existing practices of representation. The result of this project is that works of the avant-garde in any medium become revolutionary by dint of refusing to offer the security and fixity of "any space of unitary subjectivity" to the reader. The films which Kuhn champions as being part of the revolution of putting the subject in process are ones by filmmakers like Chantal Akerman and Yvonne Rainer (the latter of whom professes that "I believe in the revolution at the level of the signifier").[6] Kuhn considers these movies to be part of a "deconstructive cinema [which] sets up the possibility of an active spectator-text relation around a specific set of signifieds" (p. 177).

What Kuhn's desired spectator-text relationship theoretically elides is not the social conditions in which a text and a reader are produced (though these are secondary and scantily rendered in Kuhn's actual analyses), but rather the question of the reader's own history. A spectator of a movie like Chantal Akerman's *Jeanne Dielman* which, Kuhn suggests, opens up the "space for active participation in the viewing process" (p. 175), might well greet its three-and-a-half-hour treatment of the everyday life of a housewife with something other than the active reading that Kuhn calls for. A viewer with a history of reading other kinds of films; one having perhaps different ideas from Akerman's about what would constitute a feminist cinema; one who would simply see the movie as boring and walk out—any of these would escape or resist the supposed effect of the text. This is not to be philistine about such a movie, but rather to insist on what might seem a platitude: that a cinematic text, even one of this kind, cannot prerogate a response and cannot, therefore, infallibly construct any particular subject-position—either a fixed one, *or* one "in process."

It is, of course, not only in Kuhn's work that such a view is developed and then proposed as a pragmatic textual politics. Kuhn is merely exhibiting a tendency that is relatively common in poststructuralist thought: that of construing an avant-garde text, or one which is disruptive of readers' expectations and conventions, as a politically viable gesture in and of itself, purely by dint of its supposed ability to check and counter assured positions of subjectivity. Such a claim is typically buttressed by reference to the need to historicize artistic practice and its criticism, or to mark out the social and historical conditions of the texts. One would not deny, of course, that this work of historicization is crucial, but too often the injunction to historicize seems itself to be taken as an adequate political gesture and as a sufficient defense against the charge of formalism or abstraction. Yet what is scarcely ever taken into account, even theoretically, is the history of the reader or the human agent; thus a large part of the very crucial and complex conditions under which an audience or reader receives and responds to a particular text remains unmentioned.

Of course, if the claim is correct that the reader of a text is constituted as an interminable series of moments and of memories of those moments, it would be impossible to register, except by way of an equally interminable and vainly empirical investigation, all the passes of that reader's encounter with the text. However, it would be hardly necessary to do so, were it possible to construct some tenable theoretical propositions about the ways in which the subject/individual receives and reacts to the ideological pressure of interpellations. Instead of making claims for a "subject in process" which is finally constructed no differently from the fixed "subject" and is no less cerned, it might be useful to talk of the process itself by which subjectivity is formed instantaneously, and of the mechanisms by which interpellations either succeed or fail in constructing for themselves a "subject."

It should be understood that it is not the notion of ideological interpellation that is being put into question here: I have already argued that Althusser's sense of the permanence of ideology and his use of the idea of interpellation are exactly what need to be salvaged from his work. What is in question, however, is the definition of the "subject" where ideology and interpellation have effect. Instead of claiming with Althusser that the "subject" is equivalent to the "individual" and that both are thus the effect of ideology, I am suggesting that the state of being a "subject" is best conceived of in something akin to a temporal aspect — the "subject" as only a moment in a lived life. Along with this it can be said that ideological interpellations may *fail* to produce "a subject" or even a firm subject-position. Rather, what is produced by ideological interpellation is contradiction, and through a recognition of the contradictory and dialectical elements of subjectivity it may be possible to think a concept of the agent.

I am, of course, far from disputing the idea that subjectivity as such is always constructed within the purview of discourse, and does not exist outside of it; but, in addition to that, I am proposing that specific subject-positions, each a small datum in subjectivity, cannot necessarily be predicted as the outcome of specific discourses. This is because the subject-position that might be demanded by an interpellation is not necessarily the one which is effected: each interpellation has to encounter, accommodate, and be accommodated by a whole history of remembered and colligated subject-positions. Thus it is perfectly possible that interpellation should be resisted — that it should fail, simply. What produces such a failure is history itself, embodied in the person who lives it and who *makes* it beyond as it were the immediate and direct call of ideology. A singular history always *mediates* between the human agent and the interpellations directed at him/her. In short, even though it can be claimed that ideology is a permanent and material feature of social life, ideolog*ies* as such are not indefeasible in themselves: each of us necessarily negotiates the power of specific ideologies by means of our own personal history.

If this seems a platitude, my feeling that it bears reiteration is nothing more than a measure of the emphasis that has been placed, in contemporary discourse, on the subjection of the "subject," usually to the detriment of any consideration of the human agent's own historical constitution. Even when such an emphasis is questioned, the problem is often dealt with by removing the "subject" to another level of determination. For example, Kaja Silverman, in a footnote to an explanation of the way in which subjectivity is formed by discourse, makes mention of a viewer's possible resistance to being cerned as the "subject" of a cinematic interpellation:

. . . there are situations in which the viewer refuses to take up residence within any of the positions projected by a given text, choosing instead to activate his or her subjectivity within another discourse. Thus a viewer might distance him or herself from a given classic film by taking up residence within the discourse of Marxism or feminism. (1983, p. 291)

What is being proposed here is that the "subject" who resists somehow has the capacity to *choose* one discourse with which to counter another. Thus the "subject" is attributed a power that is, strictly speaking, anti-interpellative, and this power is derived from access to discourses which have produced a different and, in this case, contestatory subjectivity. The viewer, confronted by the interpellative claim of some classic Hollywood movie, simply decides to fall in with an alternative subjectivity.

What is interesting about Silverman's point here is that, at least implicitly, it broaches the question of a subjective or singular history: to have an alternative subjectivity ready to be "activated" supposes previous interpellation, or a former exposure to a constituting discourse. This insertion of the question of a singular history is, of course, an important addition into any argument about subject-positions. However, what remains untheorized and problematic in what Silverman says is the idea that one "subject" can be *chosen* in preference to another as a way of protecting against interpellation. The possibility of such an easy resistance to ideological interpellation would be comforting indeed. But it is very difficult to accept the proposition that subject-positions are to be construed as forming a kind of reservoir of availabilities and potentialities from which we simply choose. Who or what would be the agent of such a choice? On what grounds would a choice be made? How, in any case, does a subject-position in reserve translate into lived activity?

These questions are intended to be less than obstructive. Choice implies a *conscious* agent and it may well be that one form of resistance to a particular discourse or form of representation would be a conscious scanning and rejection of its message. Against this message might be posed the content of another discourse (Marxism, feminism, Reaganism, etc.) which is known, held as a demonstrable knowledge. Such resistances go on every day, to be sure; yet, to be posited in these terms, they have to be understood as working on a *conscious* level, at the level of the message and through particular prejudices which are themselves the effects of a history. In themselves they can actually say very little about the construction of the "subject" since they are proposed as essentially deliberate or calculated processes conducted around the substance or content of the ideological message. Indeed, it seems that it would be more appropriate for Silverman to be talking about the *content* of particular discourses rather than about the subjectivities constructed by different discourses.

My point is that, insofar as the question of the construction of the "subject" is at stake, a distinction must be made between the activity of a person (in this instance, the viewer) in response to an ideological message, and the way in which a subject-position is actually constructed in a dependency upon discursive formations. Such a distinction precludes any easy political gesture such as that of the common or garden poststructuralist variety, namely, the simple insistence that "the generation of new discursive positions implies a new subjectivity as well" (p. 199) and that the theoretical task is "the project of re-speaking both our own subjectivity and the symbolic order" (p. 283). Rather, I would suggest, the theoretical task might better be cast in terms of coming to an understanding of how the ideological force of interpellation can fail (and often) to produce a compliant "subject" for a discourse, and of asking what contestatory use can be made of that failure.

To encourage the resistances and calculations that occur at the level of a conscious and deliberate refusal of particular interpellations and the meanings they proffer for subject positionings is, of course, a crucial part of constructing a contestatory human agency. It cannot, however, do much to explicate the ways in which texts (or other apparatuses) and "subjects" interact. A notion of that interaction—other than the still persistent notion which I have been criticizing—is necessary in order to enable the theory of agency which any contestatory project requires. Certainly it is the case that the promotion of resistance at the conscious level is possible and desirable; but such a promotion—which itself would clearly have to be considered as an act of interpellation—must be able to theorize a radical heterogeneity in the subject-positions which are constituted in the human agent through interpellations. These subject-positions are continually added to by a person's experience in the social, and so the history of that experience must be taken into account before a theory of the "subject" can properly broach the question of resistance.

Of course, the two operations of resistance—the one whereby the failure of interpellations to construct a compliant "subject" is examined and used, and the second whereby conscious calculation is encouraged—should coincide in contestatory practice. Yet the stress, within current theorisation, on the subjection of the "subject" leaves little room to envisage the agent of a real and effective resistance. However much the impulse of such theoretical work might in itself be contestatory, its product is a cerned "subject" which is, by definition, a dominated one albeit with its own little bit of "freedom." A praxis of resistance, on the other hand, demands a theory of the "subject" which allows for gaps and fissures in the agent's experience of interpellative messages.

Attempting to address this latter demand I have been claiming so far that modifying the sense of the term, "the subject," or even replacing it and allowing instead for the conjoint notions of subject-positions and agency, fits better the obvious requirement that theoretical and practical projects should work together or pull in the same direction. Accordingly, I have argued that the theorizing of the "subject's" encounter with interpellation and the promotion of conscious resistance are both to be predicated upon the fact of interpellation's having taken place or having been attempted. Equally, and as a consequence, both involve the existence of a body of subject-positions which are put into play by the human agent's encounter with ideological messages.

At the same time it should be recognized that the human agent is inextricably bound up in the processes of ideology to the extent that *any* subject-position can be seen as something like a reaction to an ideologically produced message. So, even when he/she "chooses" to act "within" the parameters of a particular ideology, the human agent is still the product of ideology-in-general, and thus the promotion of calculation is still required to take into account the modalities of subject-positioning. Thence it becomes necessary to propose that "choice" or conscious calculation is possible only as the by-product of the human agent's negotiations among and between particular subject-positions. Resistance is indeed produced by and within the ideological. Where discourses actually take hold of or produce the so-called "subject" they also *enable* agency and resistance.

Chapter 3
Deconstruction

The previous two chapters have tried to describe how Marxist and "post-Marxist" thinking seems currently to understand the "subject." A major emphasis here is that an analysis of how the "subject" is constructed in relation to ideological apparatuses is a necessity for any thought which wishes radically to challenge contemporary capitalist formations. Yet such an analysis seems currently not to be in place for leftist thinking. At the same time as contemporary "democratic" societies persistently make their appeal specifically to "individuals" by way of a vast array of ideological texts and mechanisms, it is dispiriting to see Marxists continue to dismiss discussion of "subjectivity" as being too much tainted by or complicit with the old bourgeois mythologies of "the individual." As I hope to have shown, Marx's teleological "real individual," and left-wing post-structuralism's "subject-in-process" are both less than adequate for the task of conceiving ideology and its "subjects"; in turn, the "subject" which is assumed to be merely subjected to ideological interpellation is inappropriate to any conception of possible practice of resistance within western capitalist societies.

The continual struggle of Marxism to offer cogent elaborations on Marx's original analyses of capitalism, so as to make them relevant to post-industrial societies in the west, is marked. It used to be possible for Marxism to talk fairly unproblematically about social classes and about the systematic immiseration of those classes by the mechanisms of capital. But in contemporary western culture those classical divisions of class become less and less easy to recognize, and immiseration is no longer perforce the lot of working people. In America most sections of what might once have been a discernible industrial proletariat are either unemployed and disenfranchised or sufficiently remunerated in the currencies of consumer capitalism so that to talk of their potential revolutionary force is no longer anything but a naive optimism. At the same time, technological innovation has allowed the de-industrialization of western capitalist societies to proceed at an ever quickening rate; thus, the important loci for any potential collective action become more and more diffused, a new international division of labor is installed, and domestic workers take their places either as low-level managers or as low-paid employees in the various discrete units of the "service industries." The under-classes in postindustrial society no longer—if they ever did—constitute in any way a homogeneous proletariat but consist in varied and disparate (that is to say, isolated) groups, themselves divided and heterogeneous: various ethnic and racial minorities, the unemployed (including workers whose capabilities have become obsolete or young adults who are untrained), farmers and agricultural workers, the increasing number of illiterates, and so on.

In short, the changing social relations in late capitalism are scarcely any longer susceptible to most of the classical Marxist categories of analysis. It is not very surprising that thinkers such as Adorno and Marcuse, after decades of struggle, should have finished by basically abandoning the claim that twentieth-century capitalism's growth would dialectically generate the negativity and thus the resistance which would bring about its own downfall. Western capitalist formations seem to have been able to negate the threat of the proletariat by ideologically and materially restructuring both the needs and the demands of "individuals," and thus breaking up the traditional blocs of contestatory action.

In such a context the importance of ideology's effect on the "subject" is paramount. Since capitalism now consolidates its claims primarily at the level of the subject/individual, and makes its appeal there primarily through a plethora of ideological discourses, contestatory praxis requires a theoretical understanding of those discourses and their relation to the interpellated subject/individual in order to conceive of the possibility of resistances. Marxism's failure to meet this requirement, and the consequent widespread dissatisfaction with the classical components and categories of Marxism, has precipitated some kind of a crisis in radical thought. Perhaps the principal epiphenomenon in this crisis has been the tendency of leftist intellectuals to begin to turn to modes and methods of analysis which at first blush seem incompatible with Marxism itself, but which might nonetheless appear to some to respond more adequately to existing social conditions and to be helpful in elaborating a theory and praxis of resistance. In this chapter I will briefly examine one of the paths of this diversification (or rather of this escalation) in the search for more satisfying theories and concepts. My claim will be, however, that this search can be successful only if it can both (a) explicate the way in which the "subject" in post-industrial capitalism is situated in relation to the discourses of ideology, and also (b) address in a theoretically coherent manner the question of the possible resistance on the part of the subject/individual.

Even though Marx's analyses have to be revised to account for changes in western capitalism—the rise of consumerism, increasing technologization of not only industry but also of the economy itself, multi-national cultural imperialism's replacing territorial imperialism, and so on—his critique of Hegelian idealist philosophy remains in place. Indeed, in the era of poststructuralism the relevance of his attack on metaphysical thought has in a strange way been increased. Poststructuralism—by refining on one of the main emphases of structuralist thinking—has firmly and consistently appreciated the crucial role of representations and the mediation of discourses in constructing the social and in the formation of subjectivity. This recognition has led to a number of sophisticated (and severe) critiques of idealism and metaphysics in all their dispositions. In that regard perhaps the arch-poststructuralist discourse is deconstruction. With its mammoth critique of the whole metaphysical architectonics of western thought, it is often conceived as a radically contestatory discourse in the human sciences. However, I approach deconstruction here in order to question its usefulness in conceiving of or practicing resistance.

Deconstruction—or more precisely the work of Jacques Derrida—has taken as its task the undermining of what it describes as "logocentrism," or the "metaphysics of presence"—the institution and the institutions of what is recognized as the rationalist tradition of occidental thought. This task is undertaken principally through a scrutiny of the conceptual binary oppositions which are taken to stabilize the organization, construction, and ideology of literary, philosophical, and, sometimes, artistic texts. As Terry Eagleton puts it, "Derrida's own typical habit of reading is to seize on some apparently peripheral fragment in [a] work . . . and work it tenaciously through to the point where it threatens to dismantle the oppositions which govern the text as a whole" (1983, p. 133).

Stemming from, and remaining by and large faithful to the texts of Derrida himself, deconstruction has exerted an enormous—though by no means uncontested—influence on intellectual life in the last decade or so; in America especially it has found a home in major universities and has made the careers of a number of literary critics and philosophers. The initial point of deconstruction's appeal seems to be the resistance it offers in its critique of and its opposition to established and fixed modes of rationality and reading; how efficacious that opposition has been, or could be, remains in question. Thus, deconstruction's acts of resistance and its modes of oppositional critique are what is at issue in what follows.

Derrida often has had occasion to recall that the root of the word "criticism" or "critique" is in the Greek *krino*, to choose or to decide, and that criticism or critique embodies a moment of crisis at which meaning is decided. In Derrida's characterization of it, the moment of criticism in the logocentric tradition is critical and decisive because it is the point where metaphysical operations of exclusion take effect, and where the concomitant institution of reason takes place. Criticism is thus, in Derrida's pun, a process of *arraisonnement*, a mode of bringing to reason or of righting (as one would right a ship). Insofar as it proposes and practices a dismantling of that kind of exclusive and exclusionary reason, Derrida's notion of critical interpretation is an attempt to remove from critical practice, broadly understood, exactly its moment of critique. This attempted removal of the decisive moment can thus be construed to constitute some kind of an attack on reason and its foundations in the western tradition. But, of course, the practice of such a removal would therefore seem itself to have a critical function—clearly its appeal for literary critics—which is one of attack and which is predicated on a decision that something has not yet quite been brought to rights.

Derrida himself has, in fact, made it almost a point of pride to underline a certain paradoxical bind in this situation where the critique of reason is necessarily caught in the passes of reason itself, simply by dint of being itself a "critique," "attack," or "decision." Derrida's claims that one is never entirely on the outside of the metaphysical preassumptions that one reviews are his most usual way of remarking this paradox, which is then of necessity brought back into the working of the problematic now known by the soubriquet "logocentrism." Given this paradox and Derrida's decisions around it, my aim here is, first, to try to point out some of the remains of the critical moment in Derrida's work and briefly to point out how Derrida is constrained to bury those remains, specifically insofar as his decisions involve and illuminate his view of the "subject." Second, I want to examine what has sometimes been understood as the political and ideological consequences of his work.

My beginning assumption is that Derrida's work is indefeasibly tied to the problematic of interpretation, or that interpretative strategies are what is on display there; but that, of course, what is at stake for him is the paradoxical potential of an a-decisive and a-critical form of criticism or critique. Such a criticism is or wishes to be a criticism "under erasure," but it is a criticism nonetheless marked by a set of procedures which is identifiable—however mobile or provisional it might be claimed to be in theory. As simple examples, one might point to the metonymic, etymological, and catachrestical investigations which are almost *de rigueur* in Derridadaist texts; and to the related, even inevitable, variation on the "supplement" theme, or the "hymen" or "diastem" theme; not to mention Derrida's celebrated "signatures" to his texts; or even the incessant adoption and displacement of the mini-vocabulary of Austin and his vehicles.[1] These *topoi*, these tropes and their multiple dispositions and dispersions, can be said to initiate, to originate and *decide* Derrida's writing in a manner which is much reminiscent of a code for interpretation: a code which guides and produces the processional substitution of signifiers that is, by now, so characteristically deconstructionist.

Indeed, it seems to me that Derrida's mode of interpretation can be described in a relatively accurate manner by means of his own description of what he takes to be Freud's interpretative practices. In the essay, "Freud and the Scene of Writing," he investigates the metaphor of writing used in Freud's discussion of the dreamwork and its representations. He tracks down a number of difficulties which Freud apparently experiences in trying to use a metaphor of writing to explain the rendering of unconscious thoughts. Derrida notes that such a metaphor, although a common one in Freud's work, always exceeds Freud's intentions and that he thus finishes by "logocentrically" reducing the concept of writing to a regulatory proposition. Derrida concludes:

. . . in fact, Freud never stopped proposing codes, rules of great generality. And the substitution of signifiers seems to be the essential activity of psychoanalytic interpretation. Freud nevertheless stipulates an essential limitation on this activity. Or, rather, a double limitation. (1978, p. 210)

That double limitation on endless substitution as a mode of interpretation is, first, the materiality of the word which does not "disappear," in Derrida's expression, "in the face of the signified" (p. 210). In other words, even when a merely provisional "signified" is conjured up in the process of interpretation, there remains the nutty matter of the signifier which won't go away. The second limitation which Freud imposed, apparently, on his own activity concerns the absence of any original or plenary text in the unconscious which could be metaphorically rewritten in the preconscious or in consciousness itself. There is no originary text: "everything begins with reproduction" (p. 211). I want to claim that this same double limitation actually constitutes the enabling decision for the Derridadaist text.

Derrida's mode of interpretation is easily seen, I think, as a similar kind of endless "substitution of signifiers." But this endless run is always to be stopped at a certain point, or to be limited in the same way as it is in Freud. Such a point is dictated by a double proposition of (or a double faith in) the materiality of the signifier and the impossibility of locating origins. These propositions *decide* that interpretation should stop at that point where it finds itself implicated in a critical decision, or where it stumbles upon a decisive moment, a moment of critique. At those instants, Derrida allows himself to make a critical decision which stipulates limitations on the theoretically endless process of interpretation.

On that hypothesis, Derrida's reading of Freud can be followed a little further. Derrida prefaces his reading by a remark or two on his own intentions; specifically, he wants to "attempt to justify a theoretical reticence to utilize Freudian concepts" (p. 197) and also to make plain that, "despite appearances, the deconstruction of logocentrism is not a psychoanalysis of philosophy" (p. 196). It is patent that, in fact, deconstruction does have a number of theoretical procedures in common with Freud: this much Derrida himself allows. But his insistence is that the Freudian text (with its view that "nothing ends, nothing happens, nothing is forgotten" in the unconscious [p. 230]) constructs a "subject" that emerges from and remains anchored in a metaphysics of presence. Indeed, this claim is not limited to the Freudian theory of "the subject": Derrida seems to suppose that *any*

> . . . concept of a (conscious or unconscious) subject necessarily refers to the concept of substance—and thus of presence—out of which it is born. Thus the Freudian concept of trace must be radicalized and extracted from the metaphysics of presence which still retains it (particularly in the concepts of consciousness, the unconscious, perception, memory, reality, and several others). (p. 229)

So there can be no concept at all of subjectivity without a partaking in the metaphysics of presence and all its critical and decisive moves of interpretation. The double limitation that "Freud imposed" on his work constitutes those critical and decisive moments in an encoded interpretative strategy where endless substitution is halted and called back under the law—the law and its nomenclature.

Two aspects of Derrida's dealings with the question of subjectivity are of especial interest here. First, he seems in practice to ascribe both intent and effective agency to both Freud and to himself: "Freud stipulates an essential limitation" on *his* texts and Derrida supplies his own texts with the two very specific pretexts or defensive intentions which I just mentioned. In each case Derrida presumes (himself as) a certain agency of interpretative practice. And yet the second interesting aspect here appears to stand in contradiction to the first; Derrida forecloses in a quite radical—even draconian—manner on any theory of the "subject." The collision of these two features demands a quite particular interrogation: what is the status of human agency in deconstruction when Derrida has effectively claimed that there can be no possible concept of subjectivity?

The question perhaps needs some expansion. According to Derrida, Freud, working on the theory of subjectivity, is bound to a metaphysics of presence and thus to the critical history of reason and to the familiar or familial romance of decisive mastery. Derrida himself, in critical opposition, does posit the possibility of human agency—of action, intention, and the production of meaning—but still feels a "reticence to utilize Freudian concepts" and denies any theory of the "subject" (conscious or unconscious). The mode of interpretation which psychoanalysis stumbled upon—the process of endless substitution of signifiers—works so far as Derrida is concerned only up to a certain point—the point when it involves a concept of subjectivity.

And yet it should be noted that part of Derrida's reason for confronting Freud on "the scene of writing" is to make note of the similarities in the Freudian and the Derridadaist interpretative methodologies. Thus in the very course of the *critique* of Freud it becomes patent that psychoanalysis's primary modes of interpretation can be assimilated, *par derrière*, into deconstruction. The only problem is the critical moment at which the "subject" becomes actually evident, or emerges as the invention of a certain conceptual necessity: this is the moment of Derrida's criticism. For good anti-logocentric reason, Derrida *decides* that deconstruction ought to be subjectless.

In a number of places in Derrida's writing interpretative strategies akin to those that he has construed as Freud's are put into action and pose as the endless system of substitutions that Freud was unable to carry off; equally, in a number of places in his writing Derrida puts himself forward as subjectless. For example, in *Glas* (1974), those quasi-Freudian interpretative tactics are given full rein (and often with explicit reflections on the place of Freud's thought in the logic of deconstruction); in *Glas* there are also performances of "the death of the subject" through the deconstruction or dismantling of the "subject's" legal names.

However, one might be inclined to be less impressed by these displays or these Derridean performatives than by Derrida's constatives. Derrida *has* been known to constate, usually in contexts where he is unable to hide *derrière le rideau* of his performatives—for instance, in interviews. In one such interview, published in one of the London literary journals which competed with *The Times Literary Supplement* while the latter was strikebound, Derrida addresses the question of his own agential role (or putative lack of it) in interpretation:

> I am not a pluralist and I would never say that every interpretation is equal, but *I* do not select. The interpretations select themselves. (1980, p. 21)

He goes on to say that he is a Nietzschean where it comes down to interpretations. "I would not say," he says,

> that some interpretations are truer than others. I would say that some are more powerful than others. The hierarchy is between forces and not between true and false. There are interpretations which account for more meaning and this is the criterion. (p. 21)

In order to argue for and thus establish the existence of such a hierarchy of forces, Derrida decides to remove certain aspects of agency from the interpreter. Notably, he removes the quality of identity:

> Meaning is determined by a system of forces which is not personal. It does not depend on the subjective identity but on the field of different forces. . . . No one is free to read as he or she wants. (p. 22)

There is a series of problems here that I think cannot be passed over lightly. According to such a schematic code, meaning does not depend on a "subject," but it nonetheless has an agent or an operator through whom it passes. Yet that agent, bound by a system of forces which in no way depends on his or her personal identity, is capable of desire, or is theoretically (though, of course, not really) capable of reading "as he or she wants." Thus, interpretations and their ensuing or predisposed meanings, according to Derrida's logic, require the effacement of subjective desire in order to operate in a non-logocentric fashion. What is established in this absence of the "subject" and its identity, and through the erasure of its desire, is then a machinery of language which more or less goes on without us. In other words, if it is not "I" who chooses, the machinery of language and thought chooses "me," and any "I" exists only as the passive construct of a system of forces.

To the extent that the agent of the process of interpretation is apparent in Derrida's work, it is an agent whose characteristic quality is that it should be subject to, and confined to, the law of a structured metaphysics—it "is not free." In other words, it is a legal or juridical "subject," since Derrida locates the moment of subjectivity as the moment which is necessary to the operation of western metaphysics—the instance of a decisive imposition of the law of the metaphysics of presence. Derrida furthermore identifies such a legal "subject" by its characteristically having to use a legalizing signature, and by its ensuing presumption that it can hold the copyright on its own utterances. (It's ironic to note, incidentally, that many of Derrida's epigones, particularly in the United States, continue to think of Derrida himself in the terms that Michael Ryan proposes: Derrida is offered as the one "who after all still holds copyright on deconstruction" [1982, p. 108].)

This copyright-holder is, of course, the very "subject" that Derrida himself attacks decisively—for example in his reflections on speech-act theory, *Limited Inc.* (1977). This text is the response to John Searle's "Reiterating the Differences: A Reply to Derrida" (Searle, 1977)—specifically a reply to Derrida's own "Signature Event Context" (now in Derrida, 1982). Questioning Searle's right unproblematically to sign and to copyright "Reiterating the Differences," Derrida gives a nickname to Searle and to some putative co-authors whom Derrida uncovers. The nickname is SARL, an acronym in French for 'Société à responsabilité limitée'—Limited Inc. Searle and his crew are thus pulled into what Derrida calls a "contexte juridico-commercial" (1977, p. 8) at the same time as they are impugned for their "respons-abilité," or for their assumption of their ability to reply in any convincing fashion to Derrida's text. This attack on the name and its responsibility constitutes also a general attack on everyday presumptions of identity, intention, and legal status. Derrida thence allows himself to claim—irresponsibly, I would suggest—that

> It is the proper name itself which immediately finds itself split from itself. Thus it can be transformed . . . and altered into a more or less anonymous multiplicity. (p.28)

Certainly, the proper name *can* be transformed into "a more or less anonymous multiplicity." For example, the text of *Glas*, consisting largely in an extended set of transformations on the names of Derrida, Genet, and Hegel, might be considered exemplary of Derrida's attempt to undermine the legal security and fixity to which proper names contribute; or his less rigorous but frequent transformations of his own signature in a number of other texts—for example, the texts on Jabès (1978, pp. 64ff., pp. 295ff.)—might be considered an attempt to jettison his own privilege as author. The question, however, is to what extent does this investigation of the proper name of the legal "subject" actually point to ways of resistance to the "subject's" being fixed; or, to put the question another way, to what extent and to what ends *must* the proper name split from itself and become anonymous? Does the name Monsieur Divers, into which the name of Genet is transformed in *Glas*, respond to a necessity or to any pragmatic goal of resistance to the structures of "logocentric" civilization?

The answer to that question seems to me to be in the affirmative *only if* the human agent is regarded as having no other salient characteristic but that of being a *legal* "subject," a mere nominee, the signatory to a metaphysical pact with the sign and its functions of *arraisonnement*. Derrida's tactic of debarring any more complex notion of the "subject"—in particular, his "reticence" in employing the psychoanalytical theory of the "subject" and the unconscious—leaves only one "subject," which is quite specifically the legal "subject," the one with responsibilities. This "subject" is displaced in Derrida's critique of Western thought by his own invention, namely, the agent of supplementarity, the Monsieur Divers of writing. The legal "subject" is set up as being constructed without desires—certainly without cognizance of any constitutive or constitutional threat to its plenitude and legality.

Given that Derrida needs to conceive of such a nondesiring "subject" in order to establish the specificity of a subjectless process of language and interpretation, it becomes clear why he must take such serious issue with Freud and with other psychoanalytical theories.[2] It must be obvious to Derrida that psychoanalysis, for all its tendency to return to the Logos, has in fact tried to demonstrate that human agents cannot not simply or unproblematically subsist as merely sub-jected "subjects" under the law. Rather, psychoanalysis claims that the very "subject" that Derrida uses as a whipping-boy, namely the legal "subject,"is constitutionally crossed by contradiction and desire. In his moment of critique of psychoanalysis, Derrida decides to bury all the rest (*le reste* of the "subject(s)"): they would be, indeed, too substantial and too complexly conceived for *his* intentions.

What, in short, I am suggesting is this: that Derrida's view of interpretation tries to establish a kind of subjectless process which is in all essential ways given over to the force or forces of language. Such an attempt must be accompanied by a thoroughgoing criticism of theories of the "subject," even when (as in the case of psychoanalysis) such theories approach or confirm Derrida's own thought and its codes. For the purpose of his attack, Derrida characterizes the institutions of idealism as relying fundamentally upon the presence of just one "subject"—the legal one, which he also refers to elsewhere as an "empirical" subject—whatever that may be. My claim is that such a conception of "the subject" is limited indeed, but that Derrida is forced to suppress any other conception. Specifically, the *desiring* subject/individual has no place in deconstruction. Deconstruction establishes subjectivity as a mere passivity, a simple conductor of the hierarchy of semantic forces: ". . . interpretations select themselves"—"*I* do not select." This seems to be a patent eschewing of responsibility, both in terms of explaining the way in which the subject/individual acts, and in terms of making theoretically explicit what Derrida's own role in the construction of the meanings of his (and deconstruction's) texts might be.

The problems to which I am pointing here concern not so much a cerning of the "subject," but something more like its effacement. There is in Derrida's work a kind of double movement where, on the one hand, human agency is taken for granted and where, on the other, subjectivity is markedly untheorized (indeed, considered untheorizable). The supposed agent of deconstructive practice is, then, paradoxical insofar as it acts, has effects, produces texts, and so on; but still its role is passively to encounter forces which do not depend on it. Small wonder, then, that Derrida, in addition to his "reticence" in deploying psychoanalysis, and in despite of the relatively common claims that deconstructionist thinking is dialectical, has apparently been unable or unwilling to deal with a mode of thought which—for all its faults—is eager to propose that it is human beings who make history; I refer, of course, to Marxism.

After the criticisms I have made so far in this book, I do not wish suddenly to go back on the claim that Marxist analysis is in a large part inapplicable to contemporary situations, and I am not about to fault Derrida for not working within an overtly Marxist perspective. However, given that both Marxism and deconstruction hold as a crucial task the critique of metaphysical thinking, and given that deconstruction can be seen to have drawn support from many intellectuals looking for ways of solving some of Marxism's problems, Derrida's relation to Marxist thought is an inescapable topic. In the interview from which I was quoting earlier, Derrida is asked about remarks he had made in the early seventies about the necessity of a meeting between his critique of Western metaphysics and the texts of Marxism (1972, pp.53–133); his response can only be described as cynical. He claims that at that time he had been "anxious to mark the distance between marxism and what I was interested in so as to maintain the specificity of my own work"; but that now, "very disturbed by the antimarxism dominant in France. . . . I am inclined to consider myself more marxist than I would have done" (1980, p. 22).

Despite that sort of statement (which would anyway probably not promote much trust in the quality of his political commitment), Derrida has not written anything that could encourage the meeting he once appeared to endorse. Indeed, I hope to have been convincing in my argument that Derrida's view of human agency is limited in such a way that it could not be adapted to *any* oppositional politics. Deconstruction's immanent mechanism, its technologism, requires that subjectivity be construed in such a manner that it cannot take responsibility for its interpretations, much less for the history of the species. Thus it may well be that Michael Ryan, for example, is wrong in suggesting that although "Derrida is not a marxist philosopher . . . this does not mean . . . that deconstruction does not have radical implications and uses" (1982, p. 9).

Ryan is one of the Marxists who have attempted to employ deconstruction to radical political ends.[3] He claims that the political program for which deconstruction can act as a philosophical guide is something like the following:

> What is at stake, then, is a politics of multiple centers and plural strategies, less geared toward the restoration of a supposedly ideal situation held to be intact and good than to the micrological fine-tuning of questions of institutional power, work and reward distribution, sexual political dynamics, resource allocation, domination, and a broad range of problems whose solutions would be situationally and participationally defined (p. 116).

It should be remarked that Ryan's work is scarcely uncritical of Derrida's relation to the political, and in this instance he is quick to add that "only part of the above 'program' finds expression in Derrida's work"; to that one can only assent.[4] The problem, of course, is not so much with this "program"—which seems, indeed, exactly apposite for the historical phase of capitalism briefly described at the beginning of this chapter; but the problem is more a question of whether it is a programme in any way germane to or subvented by any actually existing deconstructionist discourse. The project of a "decentered" resistance must always take account of the not insignificant task of relating "plural strategies" to plural "subjects." That is to say, the task for both the theory and the practice of resistance is—as it has always been—to locate and work with the interests that both produce and delimit the human agent's actions. Such a project would have no grounds on which to interrogate and understand those interests if it were to adopt the Derridean ambivalence around the question of subjectivity.

To rely upon a form of philosophy which continually refuses to accept the role of subjective desire, and which so totalizes the structure of discursive mechanisms as to allow no space for the subject/individual to take responsibility, would be to endorse the technologism which I think is an effect of Derrida's own texts. Something of this can be demonstrated by looking at two relatively recent texts in which Derrida takes up specific political issues: "The Principle of Reason: The University in the Eyes of Its Pupils" (1983) which attempts to deal with some of the issues attendant upon the situation of institutions of higher education; and his later essay which discusses the threat of nuclear war, "No Apocalypse, Not Now" (1984).

In the first of these articles Derrida offers an analysis of the foundations upon which he claims higher education is instituted: in response to his own question about its *raison d'être* he claims that "we may reasonably suppose that the University's reason for being has always been reason itself, and some essential connection of reason to being" (1983, p. 7). This remark is followed by a reading of the meaning and history of the idea of reason. As in any deconstructive reading, once a concept has been focused upon, its "other" or its "beyond" must be brought into play. For Derrida, since the principle of reason is hierarchical, the "beyond" of reason is anarchical: " 'Thought' requires *both* the principle of reason *and* what is beyond the principle of reason, the *arkhe* and an-archy" (pp.18–19). Derrida's proposition is simply that "an-archy" is a component part, albeit a repressed part, of the institution(s) of reason, and he goes on to elaborate how this heterogeneity, this as it were "double structuring" of the institution operates socially:

> . . . the university has reflected society only in giving it the chance for reflection. . . . The time for reflection is also the chance for turning back on the very conditions of reflection. . . . Then the time of reflection is also another time, it is heterogeneous with what it reflects and perhaps gives time for what calls for and is called thought. (p. 19)

The increased exercise and nurturing of this double structure seems to be what Derrida is calling for: he even makes mention of the kind of desirable meta-institution which would provide "a place to work on the *value and meaning* of the basic, the fundamental" institution as it currently exists (p. 16). Thus heterogeneity would become the mode by which to resist the institution, and by which institutional structure may be kept on its toes, so to speak.

But it is clear that, in the terms of Derrida's suggestions, he considers a certain heterogeneity to be always built in to the institution: it has no choice but to be there. This is because the institution is regarded here as nothing much more than a machine—a discursive machine whose salient features are all *ideas* drawn from the words of Kant, Heidegger, Peirce and others. It is certainly possible to argue that universities—or any other institution—are not founded upon ideas at all; but, even if they were, there would be another important objection to make to Derrida's analysis. Within his version of the historical and discursive structuring of the universities there is no account given of human agency. For him, the operative basis of the institution is simply an idea or a structure of thought; in an almost Platonic manner Derrida construes the university as simply the material reality which corresponds to or answers to a mere idea. And the correspondence is established without the mediation of human action—it is a kind of automatic transfer conducted, without us, exclusively between the real and the ideal.

In that sense, or in the historical context with which Derrida's strictly idealist maneuver operates here, the difference between the proposed new meta-institution and the institution as it currently exists is negligible. The proposal for a strategy of resistance comes a cropper at the point where it refuses to account for the mediation of human activity and where it simultaneously becomes a repetition of the philosophical and theoretical strategies which it is supposed to resist. Of course, as noted before, Derrida is always careful to remind us that there is no getting out of the metaphysics which underlies our discourse; here, in a typical moment, he warns that "one step further toward a sort of original an-archy risks producing or reproducing the hierarchy." It is perhaps worth retorting that such a risk is in fact nothing more than the product of Derrida's refusal to provide any notion of how human agents mediate and negotiate the actual *process* by which the ideal and the real are instituted together; his refusal to recognize that the risk can be taken and the supposedly inevitable hierarchy negated. In other words, Derrida's promise of resistance cannot be fulfilled, simply because he cannot imagine *who* might effect that resistance.

This elision of the activity of human agency in the actual construction of social institutions underlines the appurtenance of Derrida's thinking to the modes of technico-idealist thinking which have always been used as the rationale—as the "reason," exactly—for the establishment of those institutions and their oppressive manners. Derrida holds no one responsible for the social history whose institutions we now inhabit; instead, responsibility is in his terms merely a question of systems, of the neutral structuring of concepts, of the history of ideas, and so on. Indeed, Derrida's work often derides the very notion of responsibility, as when he impugns Searle/SARL's attempt to persuade him to address that very question. Even where he does claim that there is a need to assume responsibility in any particular matter, it is never quite clear who might actually be the addressee of the injunction. For example, in the essay from which I was quoting above, he claims that there is "this new responsibility" (p. 16) to recognize the heterogeneous element of thought which is hidden in and by the principle of reason. Yet the form of his language in discussing that "responsibility" is entirely impersonal. The "responsibility" falls on no one in particular—not even on a vaguely defined community of scholars—but acts automatically and autonomously: "If [these responsibilities] remain extremely difficult to assume . . . it is because *they* must at once keep alive the memory of a tradition and make an opening" (p. 16; my emphasis).

This drawing away from any definition of where responsibility might fall is an inevitable symptom of a manner of thinking which deals finally with nothing but the discursive apparatus of occidental reason. Derrida has been questioned many times by both the left and the right for privileging that apparatus. The question usually comes in the form of a dissatisfaction expressed about the deconstructionist notion of a "general text" (1972, p. 82) to which all conceptual phenomena must be submitted. My argument here is not only directed against such a notion of textuality, but also against the impotence into which the notion is led unless it makes room for an active mediation by subject/individuals. Derrida's arguments continually turn back into discussions of "textuality" at precisely those moments when the issue at hand demands to be treated in a more pragmatic manner.

For example, his text on the semantics of discussions of the nuclear threat, "No Apocalypse, Not Now," deals with merely the architectonics of the available discourses of "the nuclear," without ever being able to confront what *can* finally, be called the reality of that threat.

"No Apocalypse, Not Now" conducts its argument around what is often called the "unthinkable"—the apocalypse which has never happened and which if it did, would imply a revelation of the final "truth": "As you know, Apocalypse means Revelation, of Truth, *Un-veiling*" (1984, p. 24). On the topic of revelation (which deconstruction would always hold to be an impossibility) our discourses are necessarily limited to the exchange, not of knowledge or authentic meaning, but of mere opinions and doxical beliefs. The thrust of Derrida's pronouncements seems to be that such an exchange (which he calls "deterrence"—a term which is fully exploited insofar as it carries a suggestion of deconstruction's "differance") is fixed for us since an ultimate unveiling of truth could never happen:

> But as it is in the name of something whose name, in this logic of total destruction, can no longer be borne, transmitted, inherited by anything living, that name in the name of which war would take place would be the name of nothing, it would be pure name, the 'naked name'. . . . It would be a war without a name, a nameless war, for it would no longer share even the name of war with other events of the same type, of the same family. Beyond all genealogy, a nameless war in the name of the name. That would be the End and the Revelation of the name itself, the Apocalypse of the Name. (pp. 30–31)

I quote this passage at some length, not only because it gives a good sense of the tone and texture of Derrida's discussion of nuclear war, but also because it is more or less the "apocalypse" of his article: because of the impossibility of "truth" there can be no apocalypse. This proposition is underlined by an ensuing parable about the war between God and the sons of Shem—a war which did not take place because both sides "understood that a name wasn't worth it" and chose instead to "spend a little more time together, the time of a long colloquy" (p. 31). In other words, Derrida's discussion leads to a quietist pronouncement on the inevitability of "deterrence" and a concomitant installation of the impossibility of final destruction. Once again, in an elaborate discussion of the system of meanings underpinning our talk about a genuine social problem, Derrida refuses to identify the agents of his recommendations and turns instead to a faith—a faith in the ultimate impossibility of a real referent emerging from all our talk.

The project, then, of using deconstruction to further resistance to the institutions we inhabit is often foreclosed by Derrida himself: I have given only a few instances of this, but there are many others.[5] Derrida's refusal to engage the consequences of his moments of critique (indeed, his refusal to admit a moment of critique) is perhaps the product of there being in his work no agent who might take responsibility. It seems clear that the minimum requirement for elaborating any political usefulness for deconstruction, or for deconstructive tactics, is to reinstall within it some discussion of the subject/individual as the agent within the discursive machinery of which deconstruction both treats and is part. This might have the effect of recalling deconstruction to responsibility, and of having it answer for its interpretative practices.[6]

Chapter 4
Resistance

The social sciences in the seventies and eighties have not been especially attentive to the claims of poststructuralism, nor to the deconstructionist critique of Western metaphysics; they seem, instead, to have preferred to follow their traditionally empirical route, guided by statistical sociology, ego psychology, and pragmaticist philosophies, and so on. Since this is the case, it is remarkable that the social sciences are currently—and have been for some time—riven by fierce debates about the place and nature of ideology and about the relation between social structure and the subject/individual. Even without entering too far into the specificity and the history of those debates, it can readily be seen that they take their shape in part because of the influence of the thinking of the members of Max Horkheimer's and Theodor Adorno's *Institut für Sozialforschung* or what is known as the Frankfurt School. The work of the Institut has been assimilated into the social sciences in many different ways, but in this chapter I want to consider how it has contributed to the elaboration of notions of human agency, especially in the field of educational theory.

The similarities between the work of the Frankfurt School (especially that of Adorno) and deconstruction are only just beginning to be noticed and analyzed.[1] What Michael Ryan calls "protodeconstructions" (1982, p. 76) abound in Adorno's work which, like Derrida's, is largely predicated on the notion "that objects do not go into their concepts without leaving a remainder, [and] that they come to contradict the traditional norm of adequacy" or the principle of identity in conceptualization (Adorno, 1973, p. 5). Both Derrida and Adorno, in other words, posit the necessity for a philosophy which will be capable of recognizing and employing a logic of non-identity or difference. Thus Derrida's writing is given over to a critique of the idealism, instituted in Hegel's thought, by which identity is elevated to become the very principle of the concept, and the result of which is that non-identity, "the other," is marginalized and repressed. Deconstruction's project, then, is to reinstall or recover "difference," to put it into play, posing it in a new relation to the logic of "the same." By the repeated demonstration of the alterity "hidden" within the establishment of identity, deconstruction hopes to displace the privilege which metaphysical thought gives to identity.

I argued in the previous chapter that Derrida's putting into play of "difference" meets its limitation at the point where he refuses any theory of subjectivity. Indeed, this continual refusal and its consequences lead one to suspect that Derrida is bent on having the mere *concept* of difference included within idealist thought, rather than on really displacing the privilege of identitarian thinking (cf. Ryan, 1982, p. 75). The case is somewhat different with Adorno's conception of difference and non-identity, even though both he and Derrida seem to agree to some extent in their recognition that "one of the motives of dialectics is to cope with . . . the difference that shows how inadequate the *ratio* is to thought" and that "philosophy demands a rational critique of reason, not its banishment or abolition" (Adorno, 1973, p. 85). Derrida often seems content to reintroduce alterity and difference into the space of conceptualization, without addressing the question of how the "subject" and the institutions in which it lives might thereby be changed. Adorno, on the other hand, sees non-identity as embodying exactly the transformatory and oppositional potential of dialectical thinking.

For Adorno non-identity is "the other" of Marxist dialectics insofar as Marxism's materialism has been consistently undermined by its own tendency to return to the positivity, or to the synthesizing movement of Hegelian dialectics. He claims that it is precisely the negative character of dialectics that must be maintained in order to foster the critical and liberational impulse of materialism; thus he works toward "a dialectics [which] is no longer reconcilable with Hegel" but which rather

> is suspicious of all identity. Its logic is one of disintegration: a disintegration of the prepared and objectified form of the concepts which the cognitive subject faces, primarily and directly. Their identity with the subject is untruth. (p. 145)

In this way Adorno proposes his negative dialectics as a tool by which "the cognitive subject" and the material forms in which it lives can be wrest apart, as it were. Adorno here works against the Kantian legacy which would claim that "the subject" (for Kant, a universal and transcendent category) is capable of experiencing external objects only by way of the subjective structures of cognition; thus the forms of the external world are cut to the cloth of the "subject" and cognition is a process relying upon a logic of identity.

Adorno's critique of Kant is predicated on two major grounds. First he condemns as metaphysical and abstract the transcendental "subject" from which Kant claims all individual subjective forms and categories are derived. And second, he claims that "the cognitive subject," Kant's "sovereign subject," is not fully accounted for if its role is merely to objectify and order a chaotic empirical world:

> The subject is spent and impoverished in its categorial performance; to be able to define and articulate what it confronts, so as to turn it into a Kantian object, the subject must dilute itself to the point of mere universality for the sake of the objective validity of those definitions. *It must cut itself loose from itself* as much as from the cognitive object, so that this object will be reduced to its concept, according to plan. The objectifying subject contracts to a point of abstract reason, and finally into logical noncontradictoriness, which in turn means nothing except to a definite object. (p. 139, my emphasis)

What Adorno is pointing out here, in a fairly typical moment of his negative dialectical manner of reading, is the underbelly as it were, the hidden logical aspect of the process by which "subject" and object are constructed. That is to say, he claims that the identitarian logic, in which the "subject" has to be implicated if it is to validate its concept of the object, is double-edged: at the same time as the "subject" separates itself from the object "it must cut itself off from itself." Nonidentity is thus a hidden *necessity* within Kant's view of the constitution of subjectivity.

The upshot of reinstalling the non-identical into discussion of subjectivity is a critique of what Adorno calls "peephole metaphysics" (p. 139). In its role as categorizer, and as the surrogate of the transcendent *"intellectus archetypus"* (p. 140) from which it is ultimately derived, the "subject" is *cerned* by its metaphysical task:

> Except among heretics, all western metaphysics has been peephole metaphysics. The subject—a mere limited moment—was locked up in its own self by that metaphysics, imprisoned for all eternity to punish it for its deification. As through the crenels of a parapet, the subject gazes upon a black sky in which the star of the idea, or of Being, is said to rise. And yet it is the very wall around the subject that casts its shadow on whatever the subject conjures. . . . (p. 140).

The wall of metaphysics, then, surrounds the "subject." In this sense metaphysics is, for Adorno, primarily ideology since it dictates that the "subject" is not actually free to order the world external to it: within capitalism that world already comes in "the prepared and objectified form of the concepts which the cognitive subject faces" (p.145). Identitarian logic thus compels the "subject" to be cerned by the world—a commodified world—as it is already constituted by the history and effects of capitalism. A non-identitarian logic would break that cernment, and such a logic is central to dialectic thinking. Thus, revolutionary activity and any resistance on the part of the "subject" can be mounted or maintained only by means of a negative dialectics: "Objectively, dialectics means to break the compulsion to achieve identity, and to break it by means of the energy stored up in that compulsion and congealed in its objectifications" (p. 157). This breaking apart of identity would supposedly entail the disintegration of both metaphysics and capital at the hands of a "subject" armed with the tool of negativity.

Here, however, the notion of the "subject" obviously becomes a problematic component of negative dialectics. From Adorno's statement, quoted earlier, that the "subject" must "cut itself off from itself" even while it is cerned by the procedures of metaphysical thought, the question arises as to what constitutes the "subject" before its cerning, or its implication in the processes of identitarian logic. That question has been asked in relation to Althusser's establishing a conflation of the ideologically interpellated "subject" and the "individual" (see Chapter 1). Here, it remains a pertinent one in relation to Adorno's (and, more generally the Institut's) notions of subjectivity, not least because both Adorno and Horkheimer—in *Dialectic of Enlightenment* (1972) especially—came to a somewhat less optimistic view of the revolutionary potential of negativity than Adorno had at first sketched out.

Adorno had not been able coherently to explain how the subject/individual comes by the ability to take on the burden of negativity, or how the "subject" is constructed so that it might be able to resist the lure of identitarian thought. This failure then became a central one for most of the Institut's members after World War II as they began to accept a certain pessimism about the "subject" and its revolutionary potential. Adorno and Horkheimer, in particular, faced with what seemed to be the ever more stringent ability of capital to dominate its "subjects" (faced, indeed, with what they thought of as increasing totalitarianism), gave way to the sense that, as Habermas later put it, "with each conquest over external nature the internal nature of those who gain ever new triumphs is more deeply enslaved" (1980, p. 9). It is to that "internal nature" and its constitution that the work of the Institut increasingly turned in an attempt to explain why the "subject" of postwar capitalism continued to submit to a system which demands that "he wholly identifies himself with the power which is belaboring him" (Adorno and Horkheimer, 1972, p. 153).

In the attempt to address the questions of domination and resistance at the level of subjectivity, the Institut's members paid ever increasing attention to Freud's metapsychology—conducting, indeed, a long and often painfully ambivalent affair with the work of Freud as a way of supplementing their own critique not only of Western metaphysics but also of the structures of power, domination, and ideology which serve it and which it serves. The grip, in other words, of both conceptual and material domination over the "subject" was to be explained by reference to a psychology which would add to the power of a dialectical critique of capitalism. Such a move is, of course, entirely consistent with the Institut's longstanding concern with the dialectic between "subject" and structure, or between the "individual" and the society it inhabits, and with formulating theories of transformation and resistance. However, Freud's work (not often noted for its fascination with the social dimension of the "subject") was adapted to the Institut's project only with difficulty and, to be sure, only with some radical mutations.

Adorno himself was by and large content to claim that Freud's focus on the bourgeois individual and its unconscious constitution was capable of being historicized. This is to say that, even if the "subject" of Freud's therapeutic project was peculiar to bourgeois society at the turn of the century, Freud's insights into the contradictory role of the unconscious were less easy to dismiss: early psychoanalysis provided a blueprint by which to explain the repression, exactly, of conflict and contradiction in the life of the "individual." The Freudian mechanism of repression is used by Adorno and Horkheimer mostly to underline their pessimistic sense that existing social formations — through the reification which offers the particular gratifications (ersatz ones for them) characteristic of twentieth century mass culture — conspire to assign to the subject/individual a "false consciousness" of social and personal relations. Adorno and Horkheimer regard the "subject" formed in this way as merely inauthentic:

> The most intimate reactions of human beings have been so thoroughly reified that the idea of anything specific to themselves now persists only as an abstract notion: personality scarcely signifies anything more than shining white teeth and freedom from body odor and emotions. (1972, p. 167)

The use of psychoanalytical tools to explain and critique consumer capitalism in this way is scarcely necessary unless some theory is thereby adumbrated which will allow the "subject" ways of coming to recognition of its own "inauthenticity." Otherwise the critique remains nothing so much as an elaborated reiteration of familiar notions of false consciousness, looking forward to the falling away of the blinkers and epiphenomena of ideology and to the revelation of the "individual" in its proper and essential state of freedom. Freud's work is not really crucial to this kind of thinking, and indeed legislates against it in many ways.

Adorno and Horkheimer's view of Freud's work does not attempt to alter its fundamental principles to any great extent, but only suggests the need to modify the work to make it correspond to changes in social and historical conditions. Herbert Marcuse, on the other hand, made much more explicit and problematic use of Freud in an attempt to sustain the search for an "emancipatory" view of subjectivity. Marcuse, in *Eros and Civilization* (1955), takes the psyche to be the site of what he calls "self-repression" in the "subject." Self-repression is constituted as the necessary sublimation of the sexual instincts to the benefit of the processes of labor reproduction in civilization, and Marcuse's notion of it derives from the later theories of Freud regarding the interrelation of the libido and the death drive (Eros and Thanatos). But in order to lay claim to any emancipatory potential in Freud's theory of the "instincts," Marcuse is forced to restate that relationship between Eros and Thanatos. He wants to say that both instincts are conservative and essentially passive; and that their collusion with the demands of civilization leads to what he calls "surplus repression," which becomes the condition of possibility for the "subject's" recognizing its own will to resistance.[2]

The upshot of Marcuse's position, then, is a view of the "subject" hypothesizing a kind of radical and instinctive, but imperfectly remembered core of resistance: "the primary energy of revolutionary activity derives from this memory of prehistoric happiness which the individual can regain only through its externalization, through its re-establishment for society as a whole" (Jameson, 1971, p. 113). Since that core is said to be instinctual and bound up with the forces of psychic sexuality, it is easy to see how Marcuse's ideas were consonant with their largest body of support—the student movements and their corollary social movements in the 1960s. At that time, as Philip Wexler points out, "Marcuse . . . became a hero of the new left, and his rereading of Freud was used as a philosophical rationale for a hippie, rather than more directly political counterculture." It remains the case that "no new critical theory of social psychology developed" (1983, p. 64) during this time. Indeed, what one might prefer to call his misreading of Freud (Aronowitz 1981, p. 34) in fact leads Marcuse to champion a kind of pre-Freudian "subject" whose instinctual (or biological) constitution is considered to promise a nonconflictual state or a civilization without repression.[3] This "subject," however much it might stand against the cerned or immured "subject" of metaphysics, is little more than a nostalgic fancy conceived on the ground of an almost fundamentalist biologism. Predictably, however, this kind of utopianism has found support in other areas as well; it has proved especially congenial to many an American Marxist. But in his attempt to get beyond the pessimism of which the work of the Institut's members fell foul so often, Marcuse often commits one of the other errors which seems to plague Critical Theory—it continually tries to negotiate the terms of an utopian future by reference to the plenitude of what Jameson, in the quotation above, describes as "prehistoric happiness." Marcuse never quite escapes from the notion "that something essential had been forgotten" (Jay, 1984, p. 239) by human beings within capitalist social formations; nor from the notion that this primordial aporia in the "subject's" self-realization might be able to be restored for the sake of "emancipation."

Despite the theoretical and methodological problems which attend Marcuse's work in regard to the "subject," his utopianism has been claimed to have at least "the function to preserve . . . one of his most admirable features—not to give in to defeatism" (Habermas, 1980, p. 10). However, even this debatable feature is somewhat modified by his writing in the sixties (like *One Dimensional Man*, where he too openly capitulates to the pessimism of his colleagues in the recognition that even the emancipatory potential of the pleasure principle was exploited by consumer capitalism for dominatory ends (Marcuse, 1964 and 1970). Nonetheless, his work and that of the Institut's other members has remained a crucial reference point for radical theory in both the human and social sciences, and it is to an area of work where this is especially the case that I now want to turn.

Education theory, especially as it has been thought in America, has not often been the byword for intellectual sophistication. The field has generally been dominated by either a rigid empiricism or an unquestioning technologism: certainly in its dominant forms, versions of bourgeois sociology, it has shown itself chronically incapable of offering analyses or ideas consonant with the goal of radical social change. In the last decade or so, however, a body of work has begun to appear which is not only theoretically advanced but also wittingly linked to the perceived need for a cogent analysis of the relationships existing between schooling, power, ideology, and the "subject." For the most part the theoretical frameworks drawn from the sociology of knowledge and employed in this work mark it off from the traditions of empirical sociology usually operative in education theory. Thus Wexler, for example, begins an article by summing up the effects of that mark:

> In the early 1970s we applied the sociology of knowledge to education and attacked the surface of liberal knowledge. We rejected idealism, objectivism and privatism in favor of a social and historical analysis of educational forms and school knowledge. . . . The critical models that emerged . . . included categories of Marxist social analysis, like capital accumulation, alienation, exploitation, labor process, hegemony, and even contradiction, which were new to the social study of schooling. (1982, p. 275)

Education and its practice are thus to be scrutinized by way of various Marxist and quasi-Marxist tools, and this work has its roots in the writings of sociologists such as Basil Bernstein, Michael Young, and Pierre Bourdieu, while at the same time being influenced by the Frankfurt School.

It would obviously be too immense a task to survey here the whole of this work, but some of its mainsprings can be readily identified. The aim of much of this "social study of schooling" in the 1970s is equivalent to that of the Frankfurt School's *Kulturkritik* or "cultural criticism" (Adorno, 1981, pp.19ff.). Focusing on the role of schools as what Althusser calls a state apparatus, these new education theorists have attempted a thoroughgoing critique of the way in which education both contributes to and reproduces capitalism's logic of domination and power. Thus Michael Young and Geoff Whitty, in their anthology *Society, State and Schooling*, identify two main tasks: (a) to analyze and question the relation of schools to their specific cultural and historical contexts; and (b) to understand the schools' implication in the ideological structures which they help reproduce. Importantly, both these tasks are to be carried out with a view to suggesting practical changes in systems of education (Young and Whitty, 1977, pp.1–15).

Indeed, within the new education theory the urge to change is probably the most crucial component, and the question of the resistance of the "subject" to both the disciplinary and the ideological trammels of schooling comes to be of paramount importance. Often, however, the tools employed to analyze and promote resistance are simply versions of the orthodox Marxist methodology that has been criticized in previous chapters. To take a few by no means isolated examples, Michael Young talks blithely of changes in education by which "man's common humanity could be realized" (Young and Whitty, 1977, p. 2); and Hextall and Sarup adopt a notion of false consciousness which allows them to argue unproblematically that "the way in which the world is presented and appears to us may hide the fact that these appearances serve particular interests" (Young and Whitty, 1977, p. 154).

On the other hand, the project of theorizing resistance in the "subjects" of the education process has been advanced somewhat by an increased willingness in the last few years to adopt more sophisticated theories of subjectivity and ideology. Crucial in this development has been the work of Henry Giroux whose book *Theory and Resistance in Education: A Pedagogy for the Opposition* (1983) can be regarded as almost a critical primer in education theory.

Giroux takes vehement issue with just about every existing form of pedagogical theory and joins his critique to a radical social project. His work is predicated on the understanding that the primary task now for radical educators is the construction or invention of a critical idiom and a set of critical concepts which will both address the question of the "subject's" resistance and respond to the shifting conditions of late capitalism. As it turns out, Giroux's critical idiom is in fact quite heavily indebted to that of the Frankfurt School. Indeed, the book begins with a lengthy account of Critical Theory and claims that "the Frankfurt School's notion of depth psychology, especially in Marcuse's work, opens up new terrain for developing a critical pedagogy" (p. 39). Thus, while Giroux is not totally uncritical of the Frankfurt School, its influence on his own work is deep and leads to what I take to be some of the problems with *Theory and Resistance*. However, before dealing with those and other problems, it is important to remark some of the theoretical favors Giroux does for educational theory.

What Giroux takes from the Frankfurt School is primarily a dissatisfaction with some of the more monolithic orthodoxies of traditional Marxist theory, especially in its economistic varieties. He argues, after Adorno, that struggle does not take place only, or even primarily, in the confines of the labor process; rather, the arena of struggle is ideology and culture—hence the importance of education and schooling which are singularly effective apparatuses for cultural and ideological control. Once this arena is established as the place where the dominant social forms and practices are produced and legitimated, the task for radical educators is to analyze its practice and procedures and to help locate the modes and occasions of resistance.

In the context of education theory the encouragement of resistance demands a number of theoretical gambits which Giroux carries out with panache. His first task is to sketch out the ways in which the Frankfurt School's critique of positivist reason can be appropriated to sketch out the liberatory role of critical negativity. Stressing the moment of empowerment that, following Critical Theory, he claims is immanent to negativity, Giroux envisages a radical view of knowledge which would:

(1) locate the oppressed groups in capitalist society and supply them with a discourse appropriate to their own conditions;
(2) legitimate the actual power of the suppressed cultural histories of such groups;
(3) illuminate the radical possibilities embedded in those histories; and thus,
(4) help establish the conditions for "new forms of social relations" (p. 35).

Having set out the project of his book in these terms, Giroux proceeds to a quite thorough critique of a number of areas in existing pedagogical theory. He begins with a discussion of what has come to be known as "the hidden curriculum," the name given to "those unstated norms, values, and beliefs embedded in and transmitted to students through the underlying rules that structure the routines and social relationships in school and classroom life" (p. 47). This concept of the hidden curriculum has served a crucial function in educational theory: among other things, it has allowed schools to be focused on as unique social sites serving specific ideological interests with effectiveness beyond their own walls. Giroux's complaint, however, is that even the most radical theorists of the hidden curriculum are unduly pessimistic, locked as they are into a view of the daunting efficacy of structural determinants in schools (and, indeed, in society altogether). Giroux recommends instead an investigation of the hidden curriculum predicated on the idea that structures of domination are not immutable. He claims that domination dialectically calls forth resistance, and that such resistance should be theorized, accounted for, and nurtured.

Indeed, this claim is central to his book and it reappears in Giroux's criticisms of a number of different areas of educational theory. What is known as "reproduction theory" comes under especially heavy fire on those grounds. This work, based for the most part on Bourdieu and Passeron's seminal study *Reproduction in Education, Society and Culture* (1977), proposes that institutions such as schools and the family are intended primarily to reproduce and legitimate, albeit in hidden ways, the forms of social relations needed by capitalism to sustain itself.

Giroux's suggestion here is again that social processes of reproduction should not be regarded as static structures to which human beings are purely and simply *subjected*. In Giroux's own words:

> power is never uni-dimensional; it is exercised not only as a mode of domination, but also as an act of resistance or even as an expression of a creative mode of cultural and social production outside the immediate force of domination. (p. 108)

I shall want to question exactly what Giroux means by that last phrase in the context of his dealing with ideology. For the moment, however, the necessity of Giroux's arguments should be recognized. Here, as in his later chapters on the idea of rationality in education and on the question of literacy, he makes forceful claims for a reconception of the possibilities of human action in the face of supposedly infallible mechanisms of social control. In other words, Giroux wishes to construct a notion of human agency which privileges the ability to resist those institutions of social control that sometimes seem radically impervious to change. It is in this project and in the way that Giroux carries it off across a whole range of crucial pedagogical issues that his work takes its strength. Seen in the context where educational theory has, by and large, either served the dominant culture or buckled under the weight of its dominatory claims and effects, *Theory and Resistance* is something of an advance.

I think it accurate to say that the reason Giroux is in a position to make such advances is his conscientious grappling with the question of ideology: there is no other work in the field — apart from that of Rachel Sharp,[4] coming at similar questions from a more orthodox Marxist stance — which takes ideology to be so central an issue or deals with it at such length. Giroux rightly claims that education needs a cogent theory of ideology to approach dialectically the relations between living agents and the structures they inhabit. In a reading which compares the culturalist Marxism of E. P. Thompson and Raymond Williams with the structuralist Marxism of Althusser and his followers, Giroux makes the point that neither adequately conceives the question of resistance: neither is in a position to answer the question that he quotes from Michel Foucault: "What enables people . . . to resist the Gulag? What can give them the courage to stand up and die in order to utter a word or a poem?" Giroux argues that the culturalist position has made a significant contribution to the debates about ideology by reinstalling human agency and experience as categorical tools for the analysis of social life. He is clearly sympathetic to this school of thought, even though he admits its tendency to overprivilege consciousness and experience to the denigration of (a) economic analyses, and (b) any thorough dealings with unconscious determinants. The flaws of the structuralist school — of which Althusser is taken to be the main and most culpable proponent — are more or less the mirror image of those of the culturalists. The structuralists are accused of too much privileging both the unconscious and the reproductive capabilities of capitalist social formations. My sense is that Giroux feels the culturalists to be insufficiently attuned to real material practices and the structuralists too inflexibly abstract in relation to the question of individual experience.

Obviously, the chasm between the two schools of thought has yet to be negotiated. This would seem, in fact, to be a debate with not much prospect of being resolved since there is simply too little common epistemological ground between the two sides. Thompson's infamous attack (1978) on Althusser's epistemology may be proof enough of that. Thus Giroux's attempt to bridge the gap between the two traditions and to draw lessons from each is inevitably a risky enterprise. His reason for attempting it, however, is clear enough: in line with his general argument, he makes strong claims for the fact that "ideology functions not only to limit human action but also to enable it" (p. 145), and that moments of enablement and resistance are not generally accounted for in most theoretical enterprises.

Indeed, Giroux's whole argument is built upon the conception and firm conviction that resistance already does occur and that it is part of day-to-day human practice—in schools as elsewhere. Like Paul Willis in his excellent study of an English working-class school, *Learning to Labour* (1977), Giroux seems to suggest that resistance is immanent to all institutions like schools where control and domination operate in relatively autonomous modes, but equally that practices of resistance do not necessarily function with any coherent sense of what it is that informs and necessitates them. This is a difficult issue, and one which demands a careful theory of ideology in order to be addressed. What, for instance, can be said about the fact that ideological coercion occurs with effect even in the face of oppositional conduct? Is such conduct merely ideologically "allowed"? Are its practicioners, as Adorno might have thought, merely the dupes of an ideological system that has already taken account of them or which can endlessly recuperate them?

In Paul Willis's attempts to grapple with such questions it would seem that resistance and opisitional modes of behavior are more or less undirected. They are defined by their "informality" and rely simply upon a willingness or a desire to counter an overarching mechanism of authority and control. Willis even goes so far as to say that such oppositional behaviors are not necessarily subversive but can in fact just as readily contribute to the incorporation of working-class students into the dominant culture:

> If the specificity of the institution and the vulnerability of its ideology
> help to promote certain kinds of oppositional cultures. . . . it also
> helps to disorient them into their accommodative mode by providing
> or strengthening powerful limitations. (Willis, 1977, p. 178)

Giroux's answer to such an issue is quite clearly opposite to Willis's: for him resistance *is* pragmatically tied to particular interests and needs which, historically, have been suppressed in terms of both their recognition and their fulfillment. Radical educators thus have the task of recovering the power embedded in such interests and needs; that power must then be appropriated to emancipatory social projects. This is undoubtedly the thrust of Giroux's argument and it is a strong and vital argument that needs to be made right now.

But there is in *Theory and Resistance* a residual layer of vocabulary—the result of Giroux's faith in Marcuse's call to resistance—which detracts from the force of its positive statements. At times Giroux's language seems to suggest that what might be called a "will to resistance" is simply empirically evident in the everyday lives of oppressed groups. And even though he certainly recognizes that all oppositional behavior is not necessarily to be defined as resistance, he offers very few real clues as to how such a distinction could be made or to what end. What is at stake here is a question of the *reach* of ideology, or a question of whether resistance to ideology can itself be described as ideologically determined, and this is a matter that is clearly tied to the definition of human agency. It is doubtful that there could be any theoretical justification for locating some "cultural and social production outside the immediate force of domination," to recall Giroux's phrase which I quoted earlier. It would perhaps be more accurate to argue that ideological interpellation operates at every level of human experience and at every level of the construction of the human subject. It has become difficult now to speak, as Giroux does, of "uncovering [ideology's] falsifications" since ideology ought to be seen as a permanent factor in social life; it is a structuring device which is not geared solely to the dissemination of falsehoods.

What I am pointing to here is Giroux's use of a discourse which is in some sense counter to his own arguments. However, Giroux's strength in his arguments around the issue of ideology is to locate a space for exactly a new discourse and conceptual framework. That is to say, I suspect that he would finally be able to subscribe to a different formulation of what is the task for the opposition. What is needed is no longer a theoretical truth/falsity distinction but a practice which will work the contradictions of ideology, exacerbate and exploit them in order to produce radical change:

> the symbolic realm is not really fixed and homogeneous. Precisely because what we call 'ideology' is a complex arrangement of social practices and systems of representation which are always inscribing their difference from one another, we can find a space for change. (Kelly, 1985)

Attempting to come to theoretical terms with resistance clearly will demand a recognition that its conditions are both historically specific and more or less locally efficacious. Resistance may be collective or individual, but in either case it is predicated on what Giroux often calls, after Marcuse, the "individual's sedimented history" by which his or her lived experiences, conscious and unconscious, are implicated into a whole cultural and social history. If the question of *active* resistance to dominant culture is to be cogently dealt with, some account must be given of the way in which ideology reaches into the "subject"— specifically, into the "subject's" unconscious. In other words, ideology's work in the realm of the unconscious needs be reckoned with, since resistance involves not just conscious self-constituting acts, but also the agent's individual history, conceived here as a memory which is not negligibly constituted in and as the unconscious.

Giroux's view of ideology certainly makes reference to a theory of the unconscious: namely, that of Marcuse. There is a number of problems with that work which I have argued against above. The immediate problem in Giroux's adoption of it is the tendency to promote a notion of the unconscious as simply a reservoir of repressed content. In other words, the unconscious "contains" simply that which is not known by the conscious subject. Thus the unconscious comes to be equivalent, in Giroux's lapsus, to "unconsciousness" (p. 148). This scarcely allows the drawing of psychoanalytic work into a radical problematic, as Giroux claims. Rather, it returns psychoanalysis to an older epistemology relying on a strict conscious/unconscious opposition. All the dialectical tampering in the world won't be able to remove such an opposition from its metaphysical problematic or hide the fact that it basically ignores almost a century of psychoanalytical theory.

If social theory is to deal fully with the complexities and consequences of the unconscious it needs to exorcise from its vocabulary the notions of "depth psychology" which it inherits from the Frankfurt School, and needs instead to install a more radical and flexible view of psychical determination and agency. Such a view would minimally require a conception of the mediating function of the unconscious. That is to say that the unconscious, as has been claimed in more recent and more complex psychoanalytic theory than Giroux draws on, must be seen as the site where social meanings and practices are negotiated *prior to* and *simultaneously with* any activity of the conscious agent. This involves abandoning the idea of an area of fully conscious and knowledgeable activity discrete from the unconscious. Only armed with such a theoretical notion will social theory be able to account for the complexity of individual receptions of ideology and ideological formations, and thus be in a position to construct more than merely rhetorical notions of resistance.

It should be apparent that my remarks here are addressed not only to Giroux's work in pedagogy but equally to the area of radical social theory to which *Resistance and Theory* is intended to make a contribution. Giroux's book brings that work to the point where new questions need to be asked in order to promote a further understanding not just of schools and educational practices but equally of capitalist social formations in general. Giroux is especially strong in his insistent demand that the place of individual agency now be examined in order to subvent resistance and appropriate it to a wide range of emancipatory projects. Preeminently necessary to these aims is an understanding of ideology and its relation to the unconscious. With the current—indeed, continual—reopening of the question of ideology, its modes, functions, and capabilities, comes a necessary return to the question of the multifarious modes and positions which people adopt, or are made to adopt, within social formations. The "subject," after all, is perhaps most easily defined as the place where ideology takes its effect (Hirst and Wooley, 1982, pp.118ff.). Thus, to account for human agency and its actions—resisting or passive—in the face of ideology, social theory must begin to apprise itself of what psychoanalysis has to say about their shared problematic—the place of the "subject" within structures of power and domination.

Chapter 5
Unconscious

It does not, of course, go without saying that psychoanalysis has something to offer to explicitly political theories of "subject" and agent, or to theories of ideology. Indeed, as has been noted earlier here and often elsewhere, psychoanalytical theory tends to do nothing so much as construct a notion only of the "subject's" subjection to ideological pressures; furthermore it is often understood as being not only heavily pessimistic, but also idealist insofar as it does not make explicit the possibility of a dialectic between "subject" and social and ideological structures. However, without too much revision, psychoanalytical theory can be used to expand upon exactly the mediating function of the unconscious which I mentioned at the end of the previous chapter and to sketch out some idea of the efficacity of human agency within the structures that psychoanalysis has come to know as the symbolic realm.

In a piece of work designed to recapitulate and defend his formulations around the notion that the unconscious is structured as a language, Lacan makes an important distinction between *sign* and *signifier*. This distinction is crucial in that it relates to a point I was making in an earlier chapter: namely, that there is a difference—not usually sufficiently operative in work that uses psychoanalytical theory as its base—between the actual construction of the "subject" in the realm of the symbolic and the ability of a given subject/individual to read ideological signs and messages. Lacan begins thus:

> Signs are plurivalent: doubtless they represent something for someone; but the status of that someone is uncertain. . . . This someone could

finally be the whole universe in as much as what circulates there, so we are told, is information. Any centre where that information is totalised might be taken for someone, but not for a subject. The register of the signifier is instituted on the fact that a signifier represents a subject for another signifier. (1966, p. 840)

First of all, it is clear that for Lacan, as he differentiates between the sign, which means something for someone, and the signifier which has no communicative message to bear, any question about the field of language itself leads immediately into a question about the place of the "subject." For Lacan, the dialectic between the "subject" and language (the field of the Other, as he calls it) is constitutive. The point he makes in this passage is, I think, that the subject/individual who receives information, who trades in meanings (the reader, spectator, or social agent) is to be located in the register of the *sign*. The specificity of Lacan's notion of subjectivity, on the other hand, resides in the "subject's" being subject to the signifier. The "subject," therefore, is to be distinguished in this way from a "someone."

What seems to me important about this notion of Lacan's is that it allows us to grasp that the "subject" is *not* that which corresponds exactly to any living, active being; rather, the "subject" is proposed here as in some sense only an *attribute* of such a being. It should, nonetheless, be pointed out that Lacan's distinction is intended to enable him to locate a fundamental ordering of the "subject," or what Miller will call a "structure of the structure" (Miller, 1977, p. 34) of the psyche in its subjection to the signifier; whereas what I want to stress here is that any such structuring must be seen as only flighty and provisional — even if it is a recurrent structuring, or a continuous ordering of the "subject" in specific moments and according to specific discourses and modes of interpellation.

The important difference between the "subject" as Lacan deals with it and any "subject," a "someone," that is supposed to be capable of activating itself, is exactly the unconscious. Some explanation and interpretation of the terms of Lacan's conceptions of the unconscious and the "subject" are in order here, since they will be used to help construe my argument.

Lacan is at pains to stress that the unconscious is not the cause of the "subject," nor is it the simple "circle of that which does not have the attribute of consciousness," but rather it is "a concept forged on the trace of what operates to constitute the subject"; and what operates to constitute the "subject" is the field of the Other, language itself. It is, then, language that in this sense is taken to be "cause of the subject" (Lacan, 1966, p. 830) by dint of being the "subject's" Other. Exactly *between* the field of the "subject" and the field of the Other, and imbricated into both, is the unconscious. The opening and shutting of the unconscious in the activity of a lived life (to be perceived in dreams, slips, jokes, as much as in neuroses or psychoses) "gives the two domains [subject and Other] their mode of conjunction. . . . The unconscious is between them as their active break" (p. 839). The activity of/at that break is to be regarded as constituting a kind of surface in motion where the "subject" is, exactly, *articulated* in its relation to language.

Lacan thus formulates the unconscious as the "edge" (p. 838) at which the "subject" is structured in relation to the symbolic. It is interesting to see that, insofar as it can be read as a topography, this formulation entirely does away with the visualization of the unconscious as somewhere behind or underneath consciousness; does away, to be sure, with any residual suspicion that the unconscious is equivalent to "unconsciousness." Rather, Lacan places the unconscious between the "subject" and the symbolic, as the edge where they are conjoined. This is precisely the emphasis that is omitted in Kaja Silverman's attempt, which I described in Chapter 2, to account for resistant readings where, in order to conceive of an agential resistance, she has to install (counter to her otherwise consistent arguments) a "subject" that does without this *mediation* by the unconscious. For that matter, it is the same emphasis that is elided in Althusser's account of ideology where there seems to be a direct imposition of the ideological interpellation onto the "subject" (and, as has been seen, onto the individual at the same time), without any interference from the unconscious.

At different points so far I have been suggesting (not altogether explicitly but also not quite tangentially) that the urge, currently *de rigueur*, to historicize one's analyses—that is, to follow the Marxist imperative of always stressing the historical and social conditions of production above all else—is insufficient on its own as a way toward understanding the articulation of the subject/individual and the social formations it inhabits. One reason for this is exactly the way in which it tends to foreclose too quickly upon any viable notion of the unconscious. At the same time as there is a need to *specify* social and historical conditions, there seems to be no virtue in taking such specifications as the theoretical last word, especially if that means discarding other theoretical contributions, such as that of psychoanalysis. If I have taken issue with a number of different accounts of the "subject" in its relation to ideology and social structures, this is because they seem to exemplify the tendency to forget exactly the theoretical work of the unconscious (on which they often build) as soon as they have to deal with the questions of resistance and agency.

The difficulty of accounting for agency without returning to some notion of the cerned or conscious subject/individual is, of course, not to be underestimated. Indeed, it has been often complained—for example, see my discussion of Anthony Giddens's work below—that most frequently the attempt to "decenter the subject" has had as its cost the inability to theorize action. However, what *can* be said is that the term the "subject," in so much as it is understood in a psychoanalytical sense, is fundamentally at odds with such a reinstallation of a cerned "subject." If anything comes out as an injunction from the work done on the "subject" in the Freudian/Lacanian mode, it is the necessity of taking into account the way in which human action, however defined or to whatever social determinants it is said to be submitted, is *never not mediated by the unconscious*. Furthermore, the very existence of the unconscious precludes the presumptive celebration of any unary self capable of accounting unproblematically for its actions, let alone for its motives or its constitution. Such a self is always a lure—it is the "individual," undivided and unique—and should not be smuggled back into analysis as the unavowed presupposition to any theoretical work which has as its goal an understanding of how people might change the orders they inhabit.

I mean here simply to stress the importance of Lacan's situating the unconscious between the "subject" and the symbolic, and of his characterization of this "edge" as being an "active break," something which cannot be passed over in practice (discursive or agential). This is the definition that Lacan relies upon when he makes a number of claims, including when he says that "the unconscious is a concept forged on the trace of what constitutes the subject" (which is, as we have seen, "the Other . . . for the subject the place of its signifying cause" [1966, p. 841]). The unconscious might in this way be seen as a kind of resting place for language on its way to the "subject," but importantly it is a place where meanings are not negotiated, only signifiers. It is with that sense foremost that Lacan proceeds to conclude that the unconscious is structured as a language—the unconscious as discourse of the Other—which produces the "subject." As Lacan says, "we are 'speakings,' which is a word that could substitute for the unconscious" (1977c, p. 49).

From this starting point Lacan constructs an account of the relation between "subject" and Other consisting in two fundamental movements or operations, the first of which is figured as an alienation. To describe this alienation he employs a Venn diagram:

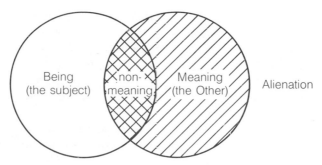

The diagram is used to explain how the "subject" is caught in a dialectic with the Other; any conceptual attempt to stabilize or transcend that dialectical passage would involve a sacrifice of one of the parts. Thus:

> We choose being, and the subject disappears, escapes us, falls into non-meaning; we choose meaning, and it only survives shorn of the part of non-meaning which, strictly speaking, constitutes the unconscious in the construction of the subject. In other words, it is meaning's fate, as it emerges from the field of the Other, to be for a large part of its field eclipsed by the disappearance of being which has been induced by the very function of the signifier. (1977b, p. 211, translation changed)

What this difficult passage conveys is exactly the interference effected by the unconscious in relation to both "subject" and Other, or to both being and meaning. The unconscious, as the active break between them, separates them irrevocably so that "the subject is born divided, because of being born with the signifier. The subject is that sudden event which, a moment before, was nothing" (p. 199, translation changed).

To receive the full force of this formulation is, I take it, to recognize a process which occurs in moments. That process is one of alienation, to be sure, in which the "subject" is formed as a result of, articulated with, yet divided from a process of signification. Of course, Lacan is attempting to account here for the *original* genesis of subjectivity, a kind of once-and-for-all structuring of the "subject" in relation to signification. Thus it can be complained that he conceives of the symbolic order as not explicitly ideological, given that ideology must be understood as having specific historical modes and interests. But the structuring process of the "subject" in language can be (and, of course, has been) understood as relating to historically specific interpellations without necessarily foreclosing on the notion of the unconscious as "edge"; and without making an inflexible claim to the effect that each interpellation functions as a form of repetition or as a renewed activation in the "subject" of a primary and more basic structuring event (that is, the entry into the symbolic). This is not to say that repetition should be regarded as an irrelevant category. Rather, it should perhaps be seen as an attribute of the unconscious mechanisms of such a sort that its substantive effect, its particularity in lived existence, would be as unpredictable as the effect of a text or any other ideological interpellation on the subject/individual and its actions. The most that it would be possible to talk of would be preferred (or better, *proffered*) subject-positions in the case of texts and interpellations, and tendencies and compulsions in the case of the unconscious.

If this seems like playing fast and loose with the metapsychological account of the unconscious, I would claim that it is not quite so far from Lacan as it might appear at first sight. I am trying to sustain Lacan's notion of the peculiar position and constitution of the unconscious, but I also wish to understand his description of the "subject" in its broadest possible terms—that is to say, in terms which will mark the "subject" as resilient and as temporally provisional in relation to the unconscious, although still inextricable from it. Thus I am suggesting a view of the "subject" as a momentary relation in the living being to the unconscious and thus to the social as it is metaphorized in its description as a set of signifying practices. The history of these moments, indefeasibly linked to the history of modes of production but not entirely determined by it, constitutes the history, *not* of the "subject," but of subject-positions among whose arrangement there is no conceivable equipollence of elements.

Lacan's effort to deal with what he sees as the second operation in the construction of the "subject" can help in grasping the way in which those different subject-positions, the different *subjects* of the subject/individual, are bound together in their disymmetry and heterogeneity. This "second operation" is what has come to be known as the process of suture. Lacan himself uses the term suture to refer to what is in effect the closing off of the unconscious from the two domains of "subject" and other. This is a process whose prime function is in aid of an inoculation of the unconscious. Lacan characterizes it as a "pseudo-identification" (p. 117) taking place as "a conjunction of the imaginary and the symbolic" (p. 118) and calling for the establishment of a presumedly coherent "I" in discourse. Suture, according to Lacan's explanations, is the way in which the "subject" at one and the same time separates itself from, or disavows, its construction in the field of the Other, and simultaneously erects itself in the garb of coherent "subject." Lacan here manipulates the French verb to separate, *séparer*, to expound this process: *séparer* meaning simply to separate, divide, distinguish; *se parer* meaning to adorn oneself, deck oneself out; and both senses are subsumed under an etymological pun on the Latin *separare* stressing "the *se parere*, the *s'engendrer*, the *to be engendered* which is involved there" (p. 214). Equally involved in this complex pun is the notion of parrying—how the "subject" deflects the effects of the unconscious.

Thus the moment of separation is when the "subject," seeing itself appear in the field of the Other (and here Lacan's celebrated essay on the mirror-stage is the main reference [1977a, pp. 1ff.]), responds to the signifier which dominates it:

> By separation, the subject finds, one might say, the weak point in the primal dyad of the signifying articulation. . . . In the interval between two signifiers lies the desire that is offered for the subject to find in its experience of the discourse of the Other (1977b, p. 218, translation changed).

This interval represents for the "subject," not a meaning or a communicative message sent from the field of the Other, but exactly an absence, a lack which Lacan calls a *manque-à-être*, a lack-in-being in the "subject." Presented with the gaps and divisions between signifiers, the "subject" fills—sutures—the gap with an imaginary function: "because it can parry (*parce qu'elle pare*) this moment of lack, an image comes into play bearing all the price of desire" (1966, p. 655). Thus, as Miller puts it, "Suture names the relation of the subject to the chain of its discourse . . . it figures there as the element which is lacking, in the form of a stand-in" (1977, p.25–26).

This stand-in is that with which the "subject" decks itself out (*se pare*) in order to "parry" the self-separation or the lack that constitutes it. Lacan is explicit that this is a function of the imaginary. The imaginary – what I would call the plane of the "subject's" *self*-cerning – operates to construe for the "subject" the sense of plenitude or lack-of-lack which is a necessity for the ego and its functioning.

Lacan speaks of that stand-in as the *objet petit a*, a term which does not usually get translated in English editions of his work. The *petit a* (small a) stands for *autre* (other) and the *objet* (object) *petit a* is that image which, for the "subject," or on the "subject's" side of the dialectic between "subject" and Other, fills the gaps in the discourse of the Other. Although the *objet petit a* is a crucial part of Lacan's theories, all that need be said about it here is that, as fantasy, as stand-in, it allows the "subject" to construe itself as coherent in language. Its index, as it were, is the speaking "subject's" "I" in discourse. The "speaking subject" is thus marked by its own pretense or its own illusion that it has no effective unconscious – a disavowal which subvents the ability to act and speak at all. The "I" that speaks is presignified in language as identical to itself in its enunciatory act. Thus the "speaking subject," having been sutured, having decked itself out with an "I" that may speak, "is strictly cut to the measure of the enunciatory subject (*sujet de l'énonciation*) and is made to cover it over, or rather to suture it" (Milner, 1976, p.43). Thus suture is the mechanism by which the "subject" is closed off from the unconscious, or the unconscious is closed off from the "subject," in the effort to produce a coherent representation for the "I" which may engage in the production of meaning (that is, may engage at the level of *signs*.)

Thus, in relation to a "subject" that is presumed to be able to choose to activate its subjectivity, it may be seen that the very expression "I choose" is problematic. The "I" who chooses is, if I may say it this way, itself the product of a certain interpellation in the symbolic. In the act of enunciation, "I" is both the mark of an alienation, and also the garb or the disguise that disavows that alienation.

It is easy to see at this point how tempting it is to suggest that new forms of subjectivity can be formed through new forms of discourse, or that work done on discursive formations to change them is tantamount to opening new pastures of subjectivity. If Lacan's schemas, and their extension by writers like Miller and Milner whom I have been citing, are correct, they constitute fairly convincing arguments about what occurs between the "subject" and its language at the level of the unconscious. However, the suggestion that the "subject" is determined by language should not (a) be extended into the argument that the "subject" is a "subject" of absolute dependency and complete determinacy; nor should it (b) be assumed that a conscious manipulation of discursive formations can produce *intended* subject-positions. Both these arguments effectively ignore the place of the unconscious *between* "subject" and Other; each argument effectively immobilizes both "subject" and language. In the rush to "always historicize" (Jameson, 1981, p. 9) there is a tendency to ignore the fact that the processes of the construction of subjectivity and the establishment of a unary speaking "I" are themselves both historicizable, and both actually effect a history—the history of the subject/individual. By way of an emphasis on the possibility that the processes described by Lacan might be regarded as a set of continuous and changing rearticulations or re-formations of subjectivity, this other history can be brought back into consideration.

Of central relevance in this history is, of course, the fact of representation, or the way in which the subject/individual is represented to and for its ego. I take it here that the ego has the function of eliding in certain ways the very history of the subject/individual, and that the ego operates by virtue of and in conjunction with a position in language that is most obviously indexed by the "I" of discourse.

What seems to me of interest here is not primarily or not so much the assumption, routinely assailed by poststructuralism and by psychoanalysis especially, of an illusory coherence in the "I"; but rather that the definitional characteristic of the plenary and unary "I" is the way in which it is enabled to enjoin a certain epistemological tradition in the West. That tradition, assailed under the name "Western metaphysics" by Derrida and others, rests largely upon the claim that the "I" that speaks can be presumed to be coterminous with—or nothing but—the enunciator of the knowledge of "individuals."

This is to point out that the epistemologies subventing traditional representations of the coherent subject/individual in discourse can no longer be regarded as *simply* the extensions and products of a necessary psychical subjection to language. Rather, they must be implicated back into their socio-historical specificity. This is another way of saying that psychoanalytically informed explanations of the relationship between "subject" and other cannot be taken as if they were the last word in the theorizing of subjectivity, but must always be brought back round to a historicizing discussion of the ideologies and institutions (and thus the interests and practices) upon which subjectivity is predicated and which it serves. And yet by the same token, neither is this historicizing account of structures and ideologies to be thought of as the last word about the "subject." Thus any view of the sub-jection of the "subject" must be inspissated by taking into account singular histories. Only if this dialectical thickening takes place is it possible to see the way in which the agential elements of subjectivity, formed in and by the contradiction of subject-positions and by conflicts of self-interest and ideology, are themselves historical and historicizable. But such a project is not well served by any motion to cern the "subject," or to regard any particular subject-position as indefeasibly linked to its supposedly appropriate epistemology. Epistemologies, after all, are abstractions, whereas subject-positions are the components of a lived life.

The epistemologies that have reigned in the West, and the interests that have underpinned them, at least since Descartes, are open to examination through their changing relationship to discourses and social formations; that much would seem obvious, and such an examination is supposedly the project of, for example, Foucault's work.[1] Importantly, epistemologies act as brokers for specific social formations. Although they may be described dialectically as both construing the nature of the social and also existing as the product of the social, their efficacy resides in the fact that they are by and large hidden, while they yet remain as systems to which recourse is made for legitimation of particular social programs. For a simple example, an epistemology that privileges something like "human nature" can remain as a *post factum* device to explain the immutability of social formations. With each such epistemology comes its commensal "subject," or the stand-in "I" that is invented to hold it down and fix a relation to discourses and to the social. Most remarkably in the Western tradition such a "subject" is endowed (as if by a kind of wish-fulfillment) with the very qualities of fixity and coherence that are, in fact, the ones most crucial to a cohesive and effective (i.e., dominatory) social organization. Such an "I" apparently needs must know what it is doing and saying.

My claim here is that such a stand-in must, on the contrary, be recognised as *variable* even at the point where it most "knowingly" and "deliberately" takes on the burden of its own illusions. In other words, a satisfactory account of the "subject" will have to address the fundamental instability at the heart of the epistemological project of lining up an appropriate "subject" for every discursive practice. That instability is the contradiction whereby the "subject" of/in a given discourse comes to be described as both the dupe of that discourse and also its knowing agent. With a different emphasis, it can be suggested that human agency must not be confused at all with some kind of knowledgeable submission to discursive or epistemological formations, but rather ought be seen as the condition of being exactly in contradiction to such formations. Only with that emphasis does it become possible to think agency as something other than a discrete, internalized quality of the "subject's" knowledge and to begin to conceive it as a disturbance in self-certitude and epistemological cernment.

Onto the epistemological and discursive terrain occupied most trenchantly by what the social sciences tend to regard as a "knowledgeable subject," psychoanalytical theory has, of course, thrown a few stumbling blocks. Psychoanalysis has insisted that the privilege granted to such a "subject" is misplaced and that the hold of the ego is not only precarious but also indefeasibly and complexly tied to structures of misrecognition and repression. However, psychoanalysis seems to have had but little resonance in that field of inquiry — orthodox social theory — which traditionally most often assumed the "knowledgeable subject" as an *a priori*, even empirical, category. That is to say that social theorists have been chronically content to let the epistemology in and around which they worked have its certainty and its confidence in the notion of knowledgeable social actors. The claim of psychoanalyis has been, to put it briefly and crudely, that to posit such a "knowledgeable subject" is to foreclose on the complexity of the subject/individual's relation to its own construction and by extension to the social.

Nonetheless, there can be no doubt that psychoanalysis has had its effect on that orthodox mode of social science. Indeed, an investigation of the history of social theory in this century (or since Freud) might show that the foreclosure of the complexity of subjectivity occurred partly in reaction to psychoanalysis's irruption into the intellectual arena. It has been the tendency of modern social theory to move toward a model of human agency and social structure which allows for, indeed relies upon, a privileging of determinant social formations and which neglects the question of the subject/individual's constitution. That is, as if in reaction to the fact that psychoanalysis has been posing the question of unconscious human activity and has thus been rendering problematic exactly the category of the "knowledgeable subject," twentieth-century social theory and philosophy has almost given up the field, retreating instead to increasingly mechanistic descriptions and explanations of the social actor. The work of Talcott Parsons, known as functionalism, could be taken as being emblematic of such a retreat.[2]

So, as psychoanalysis and social theory have flourished in isolation from each other during this century, each has adopted its own somewhat dubious *Weltanschauung* by way of compensating for that estrangement. Psychoanalysis, for its part, has looked to a universalist schema for its theory of the social: psychoanalytical theory and its insights are more often than not merely inserted into an overarching and ahistorical conception of the social which can provide little hope for radical change. Modern social theory, for its part, insofar as it has even attempted to look for a theory of subjectivity, has moved toward a mechanistic and pragmaticist psychologism: the "subject" for modern social theory is often a rather too neat conjunction of powerful social determinants and a prosaic, nay, passive self-awareness. Indeed, the "subject" is ultimately construed there as little more than a compliant *obj*ect designed to fit into the structures which can apparently be described satisfactorily enough by empirical research.

But now contemporary social science is in the rather paradoxical situation of thinking it necessary to move back to its pre-modern roots in order to reinstall some notion of the "knowledgeable subject" and in order to rectify the urge of this century's social science toward a mechanistic and monolithic determinism. Such a task — that of countering a social science in which "human beings are not treated as knowledgeable, capable agents" (Giddens, 1982, p. 199) and in which social or institutional structure seems to reign supreme — runs the risk of failing to learn the lessons of social thought's own recent history. That is, social theory can be justly considered reckless at this point if it refuses to acknowledge the necessity of a theory of the unconscious in any discussion of the dialectic between structures and agents. Yet, even while the acknowledgment is made, such a theory is what is significantly missing from the work of even so careful and forward-looking a social scientist as Anthony Giddens.

Giddens is undoubtedly correct when he claims that we not only have to "avoid any account of socialisation which presumes either that the subject is determined by the social object (the individual as simply 'molded' by society)," but we must equally reject any account "which takes subjectivity for granted, as an inherent characteristic of human beings, not in need of explication" (1979, p. 120). Giddens's work thus recognizes, at least, that a theory of the unconscious has a place in the social sciences—and in this he differs not only from his more empiricist colleagues, but also from influential thinkers such as Winch (1965), Louch (1963), or Oakeshott (1974), each of whom attempts to account for human agency in terms of "subjects" who are for the most part knowledgeable about their own motives and who can happily construe intentions for their meanings.[3] Giddens himself, on the other hand, is able to accept and make an argument for the possibility that "meaning is constituted on the level of the unconscious as well as that of the conscious, whatever the dislocations that might exist between the two" (1979, p. 122).

For Giddens, the need to theorize the place of the unconscious arises when human agency is considered in terms of what he calls a "reflexive monitoring of conduct as a chronic feature of the enactment of social life" (p. 39). In this formulation Giddens seems to owe something to Michael Oakeshott's definition of human agency as an "intelligent engagement concerned with responding to understood situations" (1974, p. 97). For Oakeshott, human agency is always the product of a dialectic between an agent's "understanding" and his (Oakeshott always uses the masculine pronouns) "reflective intelligence" (p. 23). Oakeshott thus necessarily posits a "subject" whose actions reflect, more or less unproblematically, its own "knowledge" about itself and about its contingent circumstances. Clearly, for him, unconscious agency has no place. What Oakeshott's definitions of action and agency rely upon is a fairly traditional view of self-knowing and consciousness and a concomitant—indeed, inseparable—understanding of ethical and moral signification. The result of this kind of argument is the erection of a human "subject" whose actions are predicated upon what seems like a total inability to act *without* self-reflexive "knowledge." Such a knowledge, if proposed as a condition of human agency, again forces out the notion of the unconscious as a locus of mediation for action and utterance.

It is this sort of thinking that Giddens claims to be correcting. Whereas Oakeshott quite explicitly repudiates the notion of the unconscious (a list he gives of the psychological terms most important in the social sciences does not even include the unconscious [p. 21]), Giddens is drawn into deeper water by his own recognition that forms of unacknowledged or imperfectly rendered reflexive monitoring both can and do exist in the life of the human agent. Nonetheless, the necessity for a theory of the unconscious does not detain Giddens for very long. As soon as self-regulation is established as an immutable feature of conscious everyday life, it turns out that the unconscious can be explained away as nothing more than a source of hidden or distorted self-awareness: "the actor in some sense 'knows' what is in his or her unconscious, although not discursively . . . a 'bar' of repression only allows the gaining of discursive awareness in distorted form" (1984, p. 6).

From this it becomes clear that the unconscious for Giddens, far from acting as a mediating locus between structure and agent, is merely epiphenomenal. Its effect is obfuscatory: it merely makes more difficult the knowledge that the actor can have of his or her intentionality and activity. In other words, if it were not for the inconvenience of the unconscious, intentionality and self-knowledge would be perfectly well informed. This view of the unconscious as nothing more than an obstructive mechanism that functions merely to produce distortion and imperfection in conscious practices is, of course, exactly consistent with what Giddens describes as "a 'stratified' model of personality" (1979, p. 123) in which "conscious" and "unconscious" functions derive from states of "consciousness" and "unconsciousness," respectively. Here, the unconscious is again viewed more or less simply as a storehouse of repressed content or as a mere barrier blocking awareness. It has no structuring function but only an inconvenient blinkering function. It thus remains recalcitrantly pre-Freudian in the sense that it is, implicitly at least, posited as the locus of "unconsciousness."

At whatever point the social sciences attempt to validate the "knowledgeable subject" as the *sine qua non* of their theories and descriptions, or as soon as they subsume the notion of the unconscious under the primacy of conscious knowing and acting, they construct or repair one of the main beams in the epistemological architectonics of the Western tradition. This is to say that, if the unconscious is left as an entity merely suspended from consciousness, or is submitted to the possibility of some kind of full consciousness or awareness, any theory or model which attempts on those grounds to explain human conduct within a social system must necessarily rest upon two major assumptions, each of which must be called into question.

The first of these, as I was trying to describe it in slightly different terms above, is the assumption that there could exist, one day, a kind of self-regulating human "subject" which would in itself combine a sentience (albeit determined by the social environment) with a fully conscious activity (which may be exerted in and upon that environment). The underlying faith here is in the possibility of a *balance*, or of exactly a *ratio*nality. The second assumption is that such a "subject" would be intrinsically part of some social totality which could be described as purely a sum of its social parts, or as some kind of pure dialectic of determining social forces and active human agency. Here it is the notion of totality that is important and questionable: it is as if the social were to be understood as a complex but finally solvable calculation, with a neat whole number as its sum. Against these assumptions, the notion of the mediating function of the unconscious and of constitutive contradictions in subject-positions allows much more for the imbalance and the ragged relation between the social and the "subject," between epistemological and discursive force and the "subject's" constitution.

Both of the assumptions discussed above can, I think, be described as symptomatic. Not simply are they the evident epiphenomenal tenets of the social sciences in general, but they are also almost paranoid symptoms of a desire for models and theories which can point to a nonconflictual stasis. Optimally, both the human "subject" and the social structure in which it lives will share the other's qualities of balance and wholeness. In this regard then, it is hardly surprising that the form of psychology which has most frequently been adopted into the social sciences is ego psychology, with its stress on the possible resolution of conflictual drives in the psyche and on (in some cases more peremptorily and popularly than in others) the ideal of the healthy and whole—I would say, wholesome—human "subject."

These desires which I am describing as symptomatic—the desire for social totality and for the plenitude of the human "subject"—subvent the methodologies used currently in the human sciences as much as in the social sciences, and they bespeak the presence of exactly those epistemologies which are at the core of our local intellectual traditions. It is to the question of the silent operation of those epistemologies and to the question of the "subject" that comes along with them that I wish now to turn and to address what I described above as the unstable contradiction around the notions of "subject" and agent in epistemological formations.

Chapter 6
Paranoia

To survey the way in which "subjects" and theories of subjectivity are construed within specific methodological forms in academic discourses, I want to look at an area of study where questions of epistemology and of the appropriate "subject" for epistemology are not just being continually worked and reworked but also necessarily and especially foregrounded; I wish to illustrate the entrenchment of particular forms of thought, in relation to problems of the "subject" and of epistemology, within the discourses of anthropology.

Anthropology today falls somewhere in between the human and the social sciences. Its "hard" scientific aspect—the collecting of data and empirical evidence, statistical research, linguistic analyses, for example—is nearly always carried out to the accompaniment of its traditional humanism. The scientific anthropologist works day to day in a disciplinary field which is beset by questions of epistemology and interpretation and by concomitant philosophical questions about the relation between observer and observed, about the constitution of ideologies and methodologies, and so on. Indeed, anthropology faces in an especially poignant manner many of the issues which are crucial to intellectual activity today. I want to comment on some of these issues, in relation to the "subject."

Part of my discussion here will be about the use of narrative in the human sciences, because narrative is an especially privileged device for anthropology (which discipline often both collects its data and presents its findings through narrative representational means). Equally, narrative can be considered a classic and almost fundamental mode of representation within various of the human sciences, such as history, philosophy, theology, and of course literature. It is perhaps for this reason that there is a remarkable move in these and other areas toward an assumption of many of the methodological (and, specifically, interpretative) problems which currently engage the interest of literary critics and theorists.

Disciplines such as anthropology, history, philosophy, psychology, and the emerging field of cultural studies are all tending right now to "literarize" their practices. What I am pointing to might be illustrated in the work of a historian like Hayden White, an intellectual historian such as Dominique LaCapra, by Richard Rorty in philosophy, or by Clifford Geertz in anthropology.[1] The tendency is to regard, in an unprecedently intense manner, the objects of knowledge in these disciplines as being susceptible of "reading." This is not "reading" in an older, more metaphorical sense (as one would read facial expressions, for example), but in the sense that the activity of knowledge-gathering and interpretation is now subjected to the process of reading as it has been explicated and theorized (and to some extent regulated) in literary theoretical practice. At any rate, the objects of each discipline are now often considered as primarily *textual* phenomena.

The history of what may loosely be called literary theory (strangely little of it being specifically concerned with literature) and of its seepage into other disciplines is, of course, long and complex. Suffice it to say about this history that an anthropologist, a philosopher, or a historian now provokes no surprise by dealing with writings by structuralists like Todorov or Genette; with deconstructionists such as Derrida or de Man; with "culturalists" like Barthes or Fredric Jameson; or even with Lacan's version of Freud. Such thinkers as these have been adopted into various fields, not just because their work might address the specific objects of those fields, but more because it has a particular thrust. First, it has encouraged the abolition of what it often takes to be idealist and/or humanist ideologies and methodologies. This it has done primarily by questioning an increasingly apparent stasis in humanist thinking: namely, the methodologically and pragmatically settled unity both of the objects of knowledge and of the observing or interpreting "subject." In unsettling the latter unity, of course, Freud and to some extent Lacan are of special importance. Second, and following on from the first effort, this work has made claims, in various modes and directions, for both the primacy and also the intrinsic uncertainty of processes of signification in the study of any cultural practice. In this regard, the point of reference is often deconstruction (at least, the word "deconstruction" is often used, even if the practices it describes actually bear little resemblance to or have little in common with deconstruction proper).

Through these efforts and claims there has emerged an anti-humanist and anti-idealist notion of the *text* and this notion has been allowed to expand its frame of reference to include all signifying practices, all cultural processes: the world and its inhabitants are now fully textualized. Where once the "reading" of any cultural object or practice would have produced its exegesis or explanation in a very general and loose sense, it now produces a cultural text which is then opened to the disunifying and undermining reading of the poststructuralist. For example, history itself is now commonly taken by a historian as a purely textual concern wherein no fact is self-evident and where even so basic a concept as "the event" is subjected to epistemological and methodological scrutiny; history may now be conceived as a kind of conglomeration of texts, and thus as being full of the aporias, disjunctions, and fissures which we have been taught to discover in all texts.[2]

What, in short, we are seeing in the traditionally defined and conceived academic fields is the textualization of all objects of knowledge. All traditional practices of accounting for (or simply accounting, quantifying) reality are rendered problematic and are interrogated as to their epistemologies and ideologies. More generally, the institutions of the academy and their practices have been submitted to the much-vaunted hermeneutical suspicion of the post—modernist era. It might be added here that the overall consequence of this privileging of textual and methodological doubt is the bringing into question of all epistemological formations insofar as they can be regarded as being imbricated into the ideologies and ideological apparatuses of Western social formations. This is supposed to be, for example, the effective instance of Derrida's work, as I noted in Chapter 3—even if Derrida is manifestly in retreat at the moment from the critique of ideology that his work once suggested, and even if he increasingly retreats into the escapism of purely irresponsible textual play.

Derrida's example is not unique, of course. Very often the effect of this postmodern or poststructuralist questioning is the kind of whirling stasis and low-grade nihilism of which he seems now to be merely the avatar. Equally often the effect is a political quietism resembling nothing so much as the political aloofness of precisely those institutions which one had assumed were the objects of attack. In this sense the "know-nothing" attacks on poststructuralism from overtly traditional discourses are, ironically enough, overanxious and misplaced: poststructuralism often seems to have abandoned any of the oppositional efficacy it might once have promised and tends now to settle willingly and snugly into the very institutions it seemed once to threaten.

Happily there are, however, stronger versions of the poststructuralist critique of ideology and epistemology. The work of Paul Hirst and Barry Hindess, for example, claims still that epistemology is itself an ideological device which presignifies a relationship of sameness and difference between objects and the discourses in which they appear. In their view, epistemological formations consistently fund the effort of humanist ideology to find in the putative empirical object the guarantee of both scientific objectivity and subjective plenitude. In their work they examine—in order to reject—the human and social sciences' constant epistemological *point de repère*, namely, the assumption that the order of reality and the order of concepts are ultimately non-discursive and reside in "experience" or in some ideal subjective "consciousness" (Hirst and Hindess, 1975; Hirst, 1979).

This kind of anti-epistemological argument claims that there is always a certain arbitrariness in the relation (traditionally supposed to be a fixed relation) between any specific intellectual (and discursive) order and the material order it wishes to deal with. This is more than a familiar post-Saussurean (i.e., poststructuralist) reference to the arbitrariness of the sign. It is a recognition that signifying practices themselves do not allow the claim or assumption that there can be a balance or a *ratio* between observer and observed—and this by dint of the inability of the "subject" or the language user to take on the fixed position of "knowledgeable subject," or to know completely or unproblematically. Moreover, this is an argument claiming that the object of any given discursive practice is nothing other than the construct or the production of that discourse and is specific to it. There are, in other words, no knowledge processes *in general*. Such a claim refuses one of the fundamental grounds of rationality as it has been hegemonically defined and suggests that there can be no object or real to which any and all discourses can commonly refer. My own argument would wish to add to this latter claim the necessity of considering the place of formations of subjectivity in the construction and operation of epistemologies and methods, since the dismantling of their rationality immediately opens up again the question of what rationalism has always marginalized, namely, desire and agency.

Even though certain forms of sociology and social theory still cling to a simple empiricism, and even despite the almost Kantian voice in American pragmatism which would claim, in ways reminiscent of Dewey, that a well-intentioned or honest and thorough observation of appearances might be sufficiently circumspect a methodology, it has been a long time now since the object of knowledge in any intellectual or methodological system could really be taken as some raw, unproblematic, and accessible referent. By and large, empiricism has been threatened by the mixed forces of hermeneutics and the more generally efficacious privileging of textuality and semiotic analysis. However, within the tendency to textualize the object of knowledge, some problems remain; specifically, a smuggled empiricism still very often finds its way beneath the very flux of textuality. It is quite familiar in liberal humanism, for example, to suggest (with the help of the lengthy philosophical question of appearance and reality, and through the modern linguistic philosophy that I would take to be a progeny of that debate) that the object of knowledge is still fundamentally *there* and available for us, but that it is our means of apperception and explication which are problematic. This is a quietly empiricist view which can be found to guide much of the traditional understanding of literature, and which may perhaps be taken as an informing characteristic of modernism itself. It is a view which finds one of its theoretical expressions in the movement of Dilthey's "hermeneutic circle" and the phenomenological scurryings of such as Gadamer and Ricoeur. There, at least residually, the object of knowledge is still veiled by—rather than *produced* by— the discourse that trains its sights upon it.

In anthropology the hermeneutic circle has been re-entered by influential figures such as Clifford Geertz. The interpretative problems that such a perspective is intended to salve are perhaps best summed up in Geertz's grave and humane question regarding "one of the significant mysteries of man's life in culture": the question of "how it is that other people's creations can be so utterly their own and [yet] so deeply part of us" (1983, p. 54) – "us" presumably being anthropological fieldworkers who engage their subjectivities in a culture other than their own. This question, which Geertz's work seems always to find most discomfiting but which it seems just the same strangely unwilling to pass beyond, is a problem only insofar as it resides firmly in the hermeneutic circle and installs an implicit epistemology and "subject." The mystery of the object for the hermeneut is, in fact, entailed in the internal logic of his/her own discourse, since the hermeneut will not recognize that discourse's productive capacity extends to the object of knowledge itself.

The hermeneutic project is shot through in this manner with a kind of bad faith, designed, I think, to claim both the empirical substance of discourse's object and also the humane mystery and innocence – the cleanliness – of interpretative procedures. Indeed, in that dual project can be perceived exactly the symptoms of a paranoia: the paranoia of a humanism that wishes to maintain its rights on a reality which it will yet not recognize as its own offspring or construction. The integrity of the hermeneut's interior process is defended as the only morally proper constitution; the integrity of the outside, the other, is to be tolerated but not owned (in either sense of that word). Analogously, what is crucial to the paranoiac is the dual ability to objectify or *realize* a reality and yet to proclaim the "subject's" innocence of its formation. In this sense, it is possible to see Geertz's continually weighty and weighed utterances about the double-bind of the liberal humanist as typical, and as symptomatic of a paranoid dual passage between self-affirmation and self-defense. Of this paranoid hermeneutic bind Geertz observes, for example, that "though this is not precisely the most comfortable position, nor even a wholly coherent one, it is, I think, the only one that can be effectively defended" (1983, p. 41).

This dual mechanism does not quite deserve to be glorified under the name of a dialectic, hard as it presses to be understood as such. If it were to be considered a dialectic, it would necessarily be as a purely idealist one still yearning for its *Aufhebung*. In its avowedly difficult, even impossible search for an unthreatening and secure position for both "subject" and object it offers nothing more than a kind of holding operation. Tactics of this sort have a tendency to revert to the most abstract of epistemological categories (of which Hegel's spirit might be the archetype) in order to fend off the threatening and destructive gap between the architectonics of discursive formations and social reality. Indeed, this may well explain Geertz's own recent retreat to the notion (borrowed from Lionel Trilling) of "the moral imagination" (pp. 36–54, for example). This abstraction allows for the ethical transcendence of that which it hides behind itself—namely, the humanist's fundamentalist (even common-sensical) dyads of same and other, whole and part, and so on. These dyads are terms not, of course, of difference but of a foreshortened idealist dialectic still attending to the yet-to-come possibility of its own resolution. Geertz's rapprochement of the two components of the dyad—most notably in his own and topographical dyad of the local and the global—awaits its resolutory term by which the dialectical geography will be finally illuminated. At the same time as, in his words, "we seek to turn [the two terms], by a sort of intellectual perpetual motion, into explanations of one another," "we" anticipate a kind of synchronicity, a "simultaneous view" (p. 69) whereby the global and the local will be grasped in their commonality and in their thus peculiarly conceived specificity.

What I would claim is that, however much Geertz and all the other hermeneuts in anthropology and elsewhere might stress the simultaneous and dialectical connection and disjunction of self and other (local and global), the fundamental category which they long to reach is that of the whole: "we" hop back and forth between parts, uncomfortably and with little satisfaction, until a totality (which is, of course, already presignified as a possibility, as a possible category) can be brought properly into focus as a result of our patient and humane attempts to "reduce the puzzlement" (Geertz, 1973, p. 16).

Geertz's stance is on one side of what many have recognized as a fundamental problem within all humanist epistemology. This problem resides in the pitting of one final mode of explanation against some other one: either we are constrained to refer all evidence and interpretations to the claim that they belong to or contribute to some holistic sense of the order of things—to what I would call a *general knowledge*—or we are bound to recognize that the evidence and our best interpretations do not allow us to generalize—where it takes all sorts, or where a theory of *general relativism* takes over. These apparent alternatives are perhaps not so different as they might at first sight appear, since in the long run even the most rampant relativism logically needs must refer itself to either a finitude (a conceivable totality) or to a holistic notion of truth (which is a truth considered as the sum of its parts). Thus both have in view a conceivable totality.

In a way, then, both these two principal modes in humanistic explanatory epistemology have entered the lists carrying the same favors. Both partake of and help to constitute a familiar occidental epistemological category which is that of *the conceivable whole*. Holism, the search for some universality, however devolved, is firmly predicated upon two ideal possibilities which are linked: first, upon the possibility of interpreting a series of parts (e.g. the elements of a culture, or the variations between cultures) into or through a *set* which will be said to include all series; second, upon the possibility that the observing or interpreting "subject" is already in a sense "tuned-in" to the conception of a whole by dint of its own subjective qualities (which possibility Geertz intends by this notion of "the moral imagination").

If both these predicates are taken into account, it can be suggested that the humane complaints of a Geertz are not *only* (perhaps, not so much) an anxiety about the evident lack of holistic descriptions and theories of the other, but importantly too an anxiety about the "subject's wavelength," or about the moral qualities—the coherence and plenitude—of the "subject." It is, at any rate, the case that both predicates are funded by a self/other distinction which, even if it almost daily becomes more reflexive and thus more troublesome for the humanist, is at the ideological root of the human and social sciences. It perhaps cannot be stressed sufficiently that this categorical *imperative* is an ideological device and a symptom, a duality by which everyday life is reproduced and in which it finds its constitution(s). As Geertz, my whipping-boy here, consistently demonstrates, that duality is under threat. It is, of course, always unstable and often recognized to be such; but within the gap which produces that instability, the concept of the whole always comes as subvention, as epistemological support and guarantor. We live, to put it baldly, in a humanist culture which is "holocentric," and whose discourses variously and to varying degrees betray not only the hegemony of the desire for holistic explanation, but also the faith (albeit a sometimes shaken or shaky one) in the correlative "whole" human "subject," the model for and purveyor of whichever particular epistemological formation it is *obliged* to, or which cerns it.

The general problematic under consideration here is, then, clearly an ideological one; thus it brings up very general questions about modes of representation, methodology, and subjectivity. In the traditions of the West, it is most often assumed that there can exist an analytical and descriptive discourse which will "work" equally well, whether it is brought to bear on twentieth-century Bali or nineteenth-century America. The deployment of such a paradigmatic assumption is the crucial problem for liberal ideologies and methodologies, since it provokes the kind of interpretative impasses which can be found not only in the work of anthropologists like Geertz but also in the work of historians like White or LaCapra—and even in that of Michel Foucault, which is often assumed to offer ways out of problems of this traditional variety. What, of course, is at stake there is exactly the area which Foucault himself claims to deal with: the historical specificity of discursive fields of power, authority, and domination. It is clear, equally, that the proper locus for investigations of the significatory and epistemological operations of power and authority is the field of representation; a proper account, for example, of the epiphenomenal changes in the representational strategies of anthropologists could not be separable from a history of the West's exploration, exploitation, and colonialization of other parts of the world, nor from the postcolonial emergence of new forms of cultural and economic hegemonies and indirect military imperialism.

According to James Clifford, some anthropologists have responded to these latter developments and to the ensuing general crisis in representation by adopting what he calls (from a Bakhtinian and vaguely post-Marxist perspective) "paradigms of discourse, dialogue and polyphony" in place of the older hermeneutical models (1983, p. 133). Clifford regards this response as a replacement of the humanist's tendency toward monological holism by a dialogic or a heteroglossia. This response is proposed, in a loose way, as an attempt to rectify the modes of representation that have been endemic to the human sciences. Nonetheless it is difficult to agree that "dialogical" or "heterogloss" textualization of the object of knowledge in the anthropological encounter is in any way less of an attempt to recover the putative "whole truth" of discourse than is the most naturalistic of empirical practices. This is to say that the adoption of a polylogue for representing the process of knowledge-gathering, whatever its impulse and whatever its carefulness, often remains a strategy of mimesis. Consequently, it fails to question the fundamental epistemological decisions of its cultural heritage. Indeed it might even be suggested that, in adopting what amounts to a strategy of *dramatizing* the cultural encounter, such work reproduces a representational mode even more fundamental and fundamentally ideological than mimetic and strictly narrative naturalism themselves. In other words, there is not much to choose between the older, narrative forms of anthropological accounting, and the newer "dramatic" ones.[3]

Still, the importance of returning to an examination and critique of those hegemonic modes of representation which we tend to think of as sufficiently natural cannot be underestimated. Their political, ideological, and epistemological appurtenances must be made clear. It is perhaps also quite crucial to add to this call the proposition that such an examination can take place only in the recognition of the importance of the passage of language (representation) through and in the subject/individual. Here the question of the pre-eminent anthropological mode of representation, narrative, has been addressed mostly with the help of contemporary narratological theory. However, narrative theory has been slow to consider the relation of narrative to the construction of subjectivity. Equally it has by and large failed to address very effectively the relation of narrative to social formations.

That latter failure has been experienced, I think, because of a persistence on the part of most narratology to attempt to discover or invent the *total* system of narrative's construction and functioning. All kinds of writers on the function of narrative (but also on the function of art more generally) refer to a certain utilitarian role which it is said to play inside what is crucially pre-established, presignified as a social totality. From Collingwood who conceives art as an antidote to some corruption of community and communal consciousness, to Benjamin who sees storytelling as a way of preserving the integrity and wholeness of particular social relations, to Lukács where the novel and the epic are differentiated by dint of their differing abilities to reflect the unified or totalized nature of social life, through to humanists like Bettelheim for whom storytelling is a way of acceding to the full meaning that resides somewhere beyond the reduced and alienating conditions of social existence, the specter of a pre-existing and pre-signified social whole maintains its presence. In a twist on that familiar way of thinking, Fredric Jameson makes holistic claims for narrative when he suggests that narrative functions to anneal imaginarily the contradictions which any social totality suffers from and wishes to cover over.

Jameson's approach seems to me to be merely the latest statement of the epistemological procedures I have been discussing. In his analyses and speculations Jameson consistently refers narrative back to some kind of social totality because, as he claims, the urge to totalize is fundamentally part of our ideologies and epistemologies. Thus far, one can agree; however, the logic that brings him to his consequent recommendation—that we ought, then, in the interests of social change, always be guided by a vision of such a totality—seems strange. Social change of the radical sort which Jameson champions is surely and sorely inhibited by such a submission to dominant conceptualizations.

Crucial to the vision of that totality's maintenance, says Jameson, is the insight that "all narrative must be read as a symbolic meditation on the destiny of the community" (1981, p. 70) and in such a way that "meditation on social classes and political regimes becomes the very *pensée sauvage* of a whole narrative production" (p. 34). This is not Jameson's only reference to the work of Lévi-Strauss: in support of his general proposition that artistic production both constructs and contributes to various forms of social totality (or, as he often states with approbation, to various kinds of utopian guiding vision), he draws upon Lévi-Strauss's reading of the graphic art of the Caduveo. Lévi-Strauss has claimed that this art compensates for Caduveo society's institutional or constitutional disorder by serving as "the fantasy production of a society seeking passionately to give symbolic expression to the institutions it might have had in reality" (1971, p. 76).

It is clear that here, once again, the notion of a pre-signified social whole (either a supposed or an actual one, either a hallucinated, utopian whole or one which is constructed in reality) informs the view of artistic production. This holistic urge enters specifically and loudly into the place where the liberal hermeneuts were loathe to admit its presence: that is, it enters the threatening breach between the terms of a contradiction in the real. Although Jameson pursues full-tilt a vision of the ways in which a viable Marxism can be constructed within the bounds of bourgeois American culture, his propositions betray an epistemology that is the same as (though in many respects more circumspect than) that of his liberal antagonists. Perhaps the best indication of the theoretical implications of his holistic stance is that he is led to posit that a utopian or holistic longing is as it were natural to what he calls "humankind" and is thus to be found embedded in *any* ideological system—including one such as National Socialism (1981, pp.287–88). In that sense Jameson seems aware, without being aware, of the truism that the totalizing impulse is not unconnected with totalitarianism. Indeed, my point here is exactly that: even Jameson's putatively contestatory Marxist discourse is built upon the pre-signification of a totality and thus remains firmly imprisoned within the traditional epistemological assumptions of the Western world.

The hallucinatory or delusional function that narrative is made to fill when it is construed as the imaginary resolution of contradictions within an already signified social whole is familiar enough. The form of narrative by which we are most usually surrounded in capitalist society is what is known as "classic realism," a mode associated mostly with the nineteenth-century novel but which is also apparent as the dominant manner of narratives as various as Harlequin romances and Hollywood entertainment and movies. The primary interest of this mode of representation for literary and cinematic theory seems to be, as I have discussed already, its setting into place of particular forms and relations of subjectivity. Specifically, the classic realist text is understood as an attempt to install the illusion of a plenary and controlling producer (the authorial "subject"), and also to create in the reader the particular subjectivity or subject-position appropriate to the consumption of the text. It can be seen, as I suggested earlier, that the subject-positions which seem to be most overtly offered by the text are the ones which are in a sense necessary to it in carrying out its ideological task. This does not mean, however, that the ones on offer are the ones which are actually effective — the history of the reader or spectator has more to say about the matter than that: the text's consumer is not always and infallibly a "subject" for the text. The problem with the view of art's resolutory function, as held by Jameson and Lévi-Strauss, is that it cannot account for such variations or resistances. Not only does this lead to the establishment of logically suspect notions of the whole (what kind of holistic theory is it which cannot account for its parts?), but also encourages the elision of the reality of individual histories.

It is, of course, precisely against any suggestion of the importance of those histories that Marxist theory has often worked. They are part of the mythology of bourgeois thought for Marxism and constitute one of the reasons why the quite opposite concept of totality has been so often touted as a fundament in Marxist thought, especially in this century. Lukács had claimed that "what is crucial [in Marxist thought] is that there should be an aspiration towards totality" (1971, p. 198) and that it is precisely its holistic impulse that distinguishes Marxism from all other philosophies; inevitable and obvious qualifications and corrections notwithstanding, Lukács's admonition has remained the watchword for Marxism in general. There are two surprising things about this fact. First, it might have been expected that Marxism, given the tenets to which it adheres in all its forms, would be funded by a less Hegelian notion of the logical relations existing between part and whole. Second, Marxism has had little difficulty in tracing the history of the concept of totality to any number of pre-Marxist thinkers as various as Vico, Spinoza, Montesquieu, Rousseau, and Kant, yet it seems to have gone along for the most part ignoring its own similarity to the very holistic epistemologies which it has opposed.[4]

Holistic inquiry into art, however sophisticated, careful, or even camouflaged it may be, encourages an elision of the reality of individual histories in two ways. First, its analysis privileges a mostly speculative and certainly abstract relation of the work of art to the social—and this only within the context of a social whole which must be pre-signified. There the places of individual producers and consumers are subsumed under the need to consolidate or reinforce a theoretical view of the systemic mechanisms of the whole. (One might ask, quite naïvely, to what extent the producers and consumers of Caduveo graphic art or of nineteenth-century novels can ever be said to be party to, or agents of, the ideological function their art is supposed to fulfill.) But second and equally important, holism arises from and continues to fund an ideological and epistemological economy which characteristically requires of its agents a "full" subjectivity (often with an underbelly of blocked awareness—what the social scientists call unconsciousness) which it *presumes* and employs in the maintenance of juridical social relations.

Furthermore, these two modes of elision (if I may state myself so) require each other; they are indeed commensal. They both point toward a situation in which they would be the same as each other for all epistemological intents and purposes. Earlier I suggested that they are also symptomatic of a paranoia, and it is to an explanation of that statement that I now want to turn, still alighting on questions of narrative and subjectivity.

Narratology has for some time been making use of a fundamental distinction between the *discours* and the *récit* in narratives. The *récit* or simply the story, can be described as the linear elements of a history, or as the basic set of events in a narrative's passage. *Discours*, on the other hand, is the logic of the story, the linguistic organizational parameters to which the material of the *récit* must be submitted. Thus the *récit* is produced within this logic that is called *discours*. Narratologists will claim further that the *récit* is only ever a fictional construct since the linear events of a history have no possible objective description: rather, they are wholly subservient to the logic of the *discours*. The reality of the *récit* may or may not be doubted (although it is the effort of classic realism—and of many readers, probably—to leave as little room for doubt as possible); but that reality must always pass through a discursive organisation which is controlled by a consistent and guaranteeing "voice." Such a voice acts as a kind of ichnographic presence above the text and is perhaps better called the text's controlling metadiscourse, since the *discours* itself can be assigned to any number of other intra-narrative elements (narrator, chorus, etc.) which might operate in any number of different ways (direct speech, *style indirect libre*, etc.).[5]

The import of this distinction between *discours* and *récit* is that it allows us to see two things in particular. First, it helps establish that the *récit* is not innocent; which is to say that any formulation of events is immediately susceptible to questions about the place of its controlling origin, about the intent of its over-arching metadiscourse. Second, it reveals the submission of narrative to a controlling but often hidden "subject." The place where that "subject" is most often hidden—where it thus appears most "natural"—is perhaps in an apparently straightforward chronology in which, say, historically data are tabulated into a sequence. So even a narrative consisting in the sequence, "Pope Pius II, 1458–1464; Pope Paul II, 1464–1471," for all its apparent objectivity, is controlled, is discursively organized, and is thus not innocent so far as the narratologist is concerned. It is controlled by assumptions which in a very real sense *precede* and pre-signify the *récit* itself; and which also bespeak the presence of a controlling "subject" of discourse. These formations echo the larger epistemological couplet of social totality and unified "subject."

It is the place and nature of this controlling "subject" that I wish to take up here, especially since its characteristics are reminiscent of those perceptible in the building of paranoid fantasies and hallucinations. My argument will be that this controlling "subject" in the narrative is far from being suitable for helping to promote claims that narrative imaginarily resolves contradictions in the social; and that it is far from being the unified "subject" such claims needs must build upon. Rather, I will suggest that an examination of this "subject" will underscore the instability, even the impossibility, of the epistemologies which it inscribes and by which it is itself inscribed.

Of course, paranoia has often been used—and often very loosely—as a point of reference for explanation of particular social forms and practices. One thinks immediately of Ruth Benedict's celebrated work *Patterns of Culture* (1959), where the notion of a paranoid social mechanism is used to explain the so-called malignity of the cultural practices of the Dobu and the Kwakiutl (and where Benedict is, incidentally, astute enough to propose that paranoid and megalomaniac *mechanisms* are not absent from Western cultural organization either). Paranoia has also been used to describe—inevitably—the vagaries and idiosyncrasies of American political life. In film studies the cinematic apparatus itself is sometimes regarded as the effective technological counterpart to paranoid perceptual mechanisms. Most usually, however, paranoia is of merely thematic concern. Even though paranoia and paranoid fears are often played out and played upon in narrative film (one has only to think of the film noir, or of horror movies) criticism has concentrated on the substantive rather than the discursive or structural dimensions of such movies. The structural connections between paranoid subjective mechanisms and narrative itself are rarely considered. Equally, in literary studies the narrative-paranoia connection is studied only for its most general thematic yield. My intention here, then, is to look at the way in which paranoid structures are characterized in psychoanalytic theory and to try to relate those descriptions to some of the typical traits of narrative procedures.

Freud's dealings with paranoiacs were obviously limited, since paranoia is a psychosis, not a neurosis, and thus it properly resides beyond whatever curative possibilities psychoanalysis might claim for itself. Psychoanalysis, Freud states, relies upon the neurotic's assailing his/her internal resistances during and as a result of the analytical session; so it relies upon personal contact with and intervention by the analyst. The difference between the neurotic analysand and the paranoiac is that the latter has already bodied forth "in a distorted form precisely those things which neurotics keep hidden" (Freud, 1958 [1911], p. 9) and which have to be discovered or invented in the course of the cure. In other words, paranoia is always already a full-fledged system of symptoms which will refuse to recognize the analyst's interpretative strategies; it has no internal resistance to overcome. Everything in paranoia is up-front, so to speak. This does not mean, of course, that the paranoiac is not subject to repression—far from it—but merely that the "talking cure" does not constitute a way through to those repressions.

It is this relative lack of efficacy in analytical procedures that dictates that psychoanalysts not treat paranoiacs—even though psychoanalytical readings of paranoia are indeed possible and in fact proliferate. Signally, Freud himself is of the view that "readings" are exactly the point here and accordingly he takes most of his insights into paranoia from the narrative autobiographical account by Daniel Schreber of such an illness. Freud claims that the written account of this long illness is as useful as (if not more useful than) a personal dialogue, simply by dint of its having been able to represent the patient's reflective understanding and careful systemization of his own symptoms. The written text by Schreber is a kind of preterition of all the interpretative strategies that would otherwise be made available by the analyst. Indeed, as Lacan has suggested, paranoia itself is already an interpretation. But an interpretation of what? That might be the best question to ask in order to enter the complexities of the paranoid mechanisms.

Paranoia involves a disturbance in the relationship between the subject and the reality it perceives. With paranoid symptoms, the perceptions of the world beyond the body which the patient allows himself or herself are entirely at the behest of an internal economy (or what is imagined as its inside). That internal economy is predicated upon the "subject's" primary narcissism and constitutes what Lacan knows as the imaginary, the set of images, figures, and identifications in which the "subject" seeks a guarantee of its totality. The narcissistic effect in the imaginary is itself, of course, libidinal in character, involving the attachment of the sexual drives to chosen imagined objects. The imaginary, in other words, is the place of libidinal attachment. In paranoia, the libido is turned upon the ego itself so that, in a loose sense, the paranoiac's object-choice is his/her own ego. Freud suggests that in such a case anything perceived as noxious within the ego (in the interior, as it were) is then projected onto external objects: the "subject" thus endows the external world with what it takes to be its own worst tendencies and qualities. According to Melanie Klein, an analyst who regards this process of projection as a normal step in the development of the ego, the "outside" thus becomes the place of what she calls "the bad object."

This projection is undertaken in order to maintain the fiction, exactly, of a wholeness and wholesomeness in the "subject's" internal economy. In other words, the fictional delusion of goodness and plenitude, going by the name of "I," demands the expulsion, the destruction even, of the "subject's" own impropriety and division. What is interesting here, of course, is that the very fiction designed to anneal this division fundamentally relies upon it and, to an extent, exacerbates it by making the inside and the outside distinct repositories. Not surprisingly, this projection onto the external—a veritable *production*—creates a fictional universe which is threatening to its creator: it is full of the bad things against which he or she must clearly defend. For the "subject" here the obviousness of the need for defence has its correlate in the fixity and obstinacy of the outside world.

The symptoms of paranoia are thus what Lacan describes as a series of "objectifying identification[s]" (1977a, p. 17). They are the price paid for the strongest possible construction of discrete self and other, of separable inner and outer worlds. But however perfect, hygienic, and secure this system may seem with its cerning of both inside and outside, its fictional methodology (if I may call it that) returns against the "subject." As Freud points out, the paranoiac's delusional conceptions of reality "make demands on the thought-activity of the ego until they can be accepted without contradiction. . . . [these are] interpretative delusions" (1962 [1896], p. 185). Such interpretative strategies, delusional or not, nonetheless constitute the real, lived world for the paranoiac and subvent the double movement which is characteristic of paranoia: the shifting from fantasies of malignity and catastrophe emanating from the outside, to the continual vindication and aggrandizement of the "subject" itself.

What seems to me important about these paranoid symptoms here is that in their projective mechanism they both defend and alienate the ego. Projection defends the ego insofar as it demarcates it, gives it an impregnable border with a vigilant border patrol; it also alienates it insofar as it cuts it off from its own production (that is, its fictional world), so that the ego can refuse to acknowledge the factitious nature of the world it has created. Here, of course, I draw my analogy with the hermeneutic epistemologies of humanism where the observer's wholesomeness prevents the recognition that the viewed world is actually its own product, a doubled image of itself.

The case, then, with both the paranoiac and the humanist is that this image is constructed in such a manner as to stress and vindicate the "subject's" adroitness and flexibility in manipulating the world to its own ends. The division of the "subject" (the division it *makes* and the division it *is*) is thus hidden for the purposes of a mastery. In this mode the paranoiac and the hermeneut cern themselves—and consequently *con*cern themselves with the outside world *only* in the service of the plenitude and security of their attachment to their own ego. Paranoiac delusions, then, are delusions of interpretation and fictionalization, formed to protect the ego from any alteration which might make it unwholesome, unlovable. Thus, as Freud points out, these delusions prevent the "subject" from registering (or protect against its registering) "self-reproaches."

My analogy, of course, is meant to be nothing more than suggestive—one wouldn't wish to certify anyone in particular as clinically psychotic in that sense. However, what I am proposing is that a connection may be made between the interpretative strategies of the humanist and those of the paranoiac, and the connection is being stressed in order to draw a merely structural analogy. In other words, there exists a kind of "metaparanoia" in humanist practices. The "subject" in these practices, as in paranoia, is an interpreter, unable and/or unwilling to recognize the condition of its own interpretations as constructs, fictions, imaginary narratives. Such a "subject" not only constructs the order of reality in which it wants to live, but also has to defend itself against the otherness of that very world. The mode in which this is conducted is quite simply that of objectification. Paranoia is a kind of archetypical objectifying device, an arrangement by which the "subject" produces and interprets its world and then reconciles its own putative and defensive coherence with what is established *a priori* to be an objective formation. The device is *claustrophilic*, having vital interest in the security and comfort that can be derived from its own fundamentally unnegotiable closure of the categories, self and other.

And yet the importance of these symptoms for what I am proposing is that they absolutely depend upon an initial opening of those spheres, an opening which is the threat they themselves are designated to ward off. The discomfiture of a Clifford Geertz, for example, with having to think through the dialectics of the otherness of the other, as it were, is actually a symptom of the fundamental instability of the hermeneutic closures upon which humanism depends and which it demands. That discomfiture is registered as primarily a threat to the self, or the "subject." But unless both the solidity of the "I" and the alienated construct of the external world are to collapse, the threat cannot be squarely confronted or openly avowed: the threat is thus always thrown off, sent into the cernements of the hermeneutic circle, there to spin in relative innocuousness while the observing/interpreting "subject" continues to regard itself as being in "the only [position] that can be effectively defended."

This much said, it should now be possible to return to the question of narrative and substantiate the claim that this fundamental representational mode supports and nurtures the epistemology and traditional methodologies of humanism, as well as its invention of the other and its cerning of the "subject." Narrative, like paranoid mechanisms, is clearly involved in the construction of a particular kind of reality which serves a particular ideological function, whatever its exact nature or parameters. That reality in classic occidental fiction need not be of any connection or similarity to a "common-sense" description of reality, but need only be verisimilitudinous: it is bound to produce what Barthes calls "the effect of the real." Indeed, it often turns out to be the most "imaginative" sorts of fiction, like science fiction or popular thrillers, which are most consonant with the traditions and aims of classic realism. Like the delusions produced in paranoia—which could be seen as themselves an unhappy parody of imaginative fiction—the imaginations of fiction need do no more than *function as*, or produce the effect of, a passable world; and its characters, the people inhabiting such worlds, are required to do no more than attain the status of the "fleeting-improvised-men" whom the paranoiac Schreber saw around him (Schreber, 1955, p. 43).

Equally as important as the realistic effect is the task that both classic realism and the paranoid narrative have of constructing a fixed and reliable "subject" who will in a sense endorse or stand behind the fictions as their guarantor. That "subject"—what I have called the "subject" of the metadiscourse, functioning like the paranoiac's ego—controls the intention and interpretation of the world it has created in such a way as both to protect its own coherence and autonomy and also to fulfill the juridical demands of the symbolic system in which the utterances may be understood. Indeed, it is the desired fate of both paranoia and classic realism to be construed as interpretations of an already existing world, even though the world they both create is their own. The possibility of such a construal going awry, of its not happening, is foreclosed in both modes by what I've called the claustrophilic tendency: in their very form and passage both seek the closure of that which they have opened. They seek the end of the story, the horizon of interpretation, the end of "the puzzlement," the arrangement by which all interpretations can be circumscribed and whereby the "subject" can revindicate its control which, ideally, should never have been in doubt. And equally they seek to conceal the very moment of control, the megalomaniacal moment at which the world is made and the ego secured.

This is, evidently, a quite bald, but I hope not unsuggestive, rapprochement of the processes of paranoia, classical narrative, and humanist epistemology. I do not intend to draw anything but the broadest homologies; I certainly do not intend to be constructing relations of synonymy among these things. I have merely been suggesting several things, which are all connected. *First*, that the supposedly objective world (the other) which any given discourse confronts need not—indeed cannot—be construed as a general, totalizable reality. It is the discourse itself which constructs the object, and the object is specific to that discourse. *Second*, that such an other object is not constructed for nothing; its function is to ensure the security of the "subject" of the discourse and to vindicate the wholesomeness of the same. This suggests, *third*, that since the "subject" is beholden to be the "subject" of the discourse (failing which it cannot communicate or satisfy the legislative demands of a discursively formed social organization), the "subject" needs must have an interest in the construction of the object. But that, *fourth*, this interest is "metaparanoid" in nature and so the object that it constructs must appear to meet the conditions of a general, shared, and objective reality. It is for this reason that the "subject" claims it as such.

With these suggestions in mind I'd like to return to the questions and criticisms I was raising, some pages ago, in relation to the totalizing tendencies of both the human and the social sciences. What seems to me to be at the root of the urge in those areas of study to totalize is finally this "metaparanoia." The urge, of course, takes its funding from an ideological and epistemological imperative which wants to establish (a) that a correspondency exists between discourse and the objective world, and (b) that there is an unimpeachable "subject" which resides in, feeds from, and guards that correspondency. In stressing the paranoid aspect of this ideologically sanctioned arrangement I am hoping merely to find some leverage by which to remove, or even just budge, the pretensions to what I called earlier general knowledge. Roland Barthes once labeled such pretensions the aspirations of "*the* paranoid discourse," namely, science (*scientia*) itself (1975, p. 90). Barthes, indeed, had more to say on the matter:

A good proportion of our intellectual effort now consists in casting suspicion on any statement by trying to uncover the disposition of its different levels. That disposition is infinite, and the abyss that we try to open up in every word, this madness of language, we call scientifically: "enunciation." It's this enunciatory abyss that has to be opened up first, and for tactical reasons: in order to break down the self-infatuation in our statements and to destroy the arrogance of our sciences. (p. 70)

Chapter 7
Autobiography

The "tactical reasons" for wanting to break open "the enunciatory abyss," and for underscoring the mediating gap between the "knowledgeable subject" and the "I" that speaks, seem to me to have never been quite fully enough engaged in the discourses of the human sciences. An interrogation of the very grounds of utterance, methodology, science, subjectivity, and so on, and an attempt to displace the epistemological certainty of the speaking "I," seem by now to have installed a critical force which is given over to, exactly and merely, interrogations and displacements. The apparently acceptable norms and codes of contemporary critical and theoretical discourse seem in the late 1980s to have deprived intellectual discourse of its critical edge; what replaces the edge is a critical *turn*, a whole little tropology. We are now at the heyday of that deprivation's effect and at the point of an intellectual *pas*. All around us the new right becomes more and more powerful and cynical, liberal humanism is almost psychotically anxious, and the left more displaced than it has been for many years. The question of the "subject" in this conjuncture is crucial since what is taken to *be* the "subject," the "I" that speaks a given discourse, reflects, as it has always been taken to reflect, specific epistemologies. Wherever the "I" speaks, a knowledge is spoken; wherever a knowledge speaks, an "I" is spoken. This is the dialectical mechanism of a certain *presumption* of the "subject": that is, a "subject" is presumed to exist, indexed as an "I" and loaded with the burden of epistemologies, wittingly or not.

It is clearly not an accident that the modes and effects of that presumption are now investigated almost exclusively, if ceaselessly, under the tutelage of the human sciences — a term with ever increasing currency since its transplantation from the continent. But the term might be said to belong, finally, to a system of faith by which exactly this presumption of the human "subject" and its knowledges is made. Thus, "human" refers always to a "subject" that speaks the *scientia,*" the possibility of a knowledge concerning that "subject" (or, con-*cerning* it). Thus the human's science is not construed as anything other than the point of intersection between "subject" and system. Knowledge comes to seem more and more disembodied, separated from the human agent who is exhorted to turn, simply. Knowledge is no longer *of* the human agent, but is "merely" a detachable quality or feature of the subjected "subject." In such a situation, the agent disappears and is replaced by a "subject," or by simply the notion of a "subject." Indeed, the concept of the "subject" is perhaps best understood today as that which is imported for the task of arbitrating or standing between "human" and "science," between agent and knowledge, and hiding both. The "subject" is thus an abstraction, the place of a more or less formalist operation of the human sciences.

Ironically, one of the thinkers most directly responsible for the installation of the concept of the "subject" into everyday critical vocabulary is Lacan, who in fact proposes no such cerned or abstracted view of the subject/individual. His work not only lays the ground for a more mobile view of subjectivity, as I have suggested, but also lays bare some of the pretensions and mistakes inherent in adopting the-subject-as-concept, or in presuming the "subject":

> There can be no science of man, because science's man does not exist, only its subject. . . . You know my long-standing repugnance for the appellation "the human sciences," which seems to me to be nothing but a call to servitude. (1966, p. 859)

Lacan goes on to suggest that what he calls "modern logic" acts as a legitimating device for a science that erects the concept of the "subject" in such a way as to keep it "internally excluded from its object" (p. 861). This, he says, is the mechanics of structuralism, for example, which he impugns through a discussion of Lévi-Strauss for its revalidation of the traditional scientific tactic of making the "human" and its "science" into reflections of each other (pp.861–62). Lacan attempts to recall, or reinstate, into the discourses he is attacking the notion of the

> subject of the signifier. . . . This subject, carried by the signifier in its relation to another signifier, is to be severely distinguished as much from the biological individual as from any subject of a psychological evolution that can be subsumed as the subject of understanding. (p. 875)

Thus, the project of opening up the enunciatory abyss, in Barthes's terms, entails not only the destruction of categories such as "the knowledgeable subject," or "the individual," or "man," but equally important it has as its aim the returning of a differently defined knowledge to its proper and designated user, the human agent. The signifying "subject" as Lacan describes it is quite simply the "subject" that can be fitted into a view of effective human agency; that is, Lacan's "subject" can be read as the particular intrication of knowledge, discourse, and history in the constitution of a materially and historically specific human agent. So with the attack on the "knowledgeable subject" must come the hope of an *unpresumed* subject, an agent whose knowledge and discourse—and thus whose activity—are no longer cerned, no longer the separate spheres which divide "subject" from structure.

Roland Barthes's writing is almost unique among the multitude of voices in contemporary theory for its attempt to represent such an imbrication of "subject" and "knowledge." To try to describe fully that writing, or the passage of its explorations of subjectivity in relation to one cultural artefact after another, one discourse after another, is beyond the scope of these pages and might be, in any case, a redundant suppletion.[1] It is a writing that begins in the 1950s at the vanguard of structuralism in literary studies and ends in the 1980s as a plangent diatribe against the dominant epistemologies and methodologies of our time; along the way it touches upon literature, film, photography, painting, fashion, music, advertising, and just about every other recognizable form of cultural object. The oeuvre is an eclectic and vertiginous tour of our cultural institutions, an astonishing attempt at formulating and exhibiting what Barthes called a *mathesis singularis*, the registration of all the varied and contradictory "knowledges" that social discourses offer to the "subject."

What needs to be said about that work here is that its often stated aim is the decomposition or the denaturalization of bourgeois culture in all its forms and structures. At its beginning, in books such as *Writing Degree Zero*, *Mythologies*, or *The Fashion System*, all written before the end of the sixties, it attempts to critique the underpinnings of contemporary culture through analyses which rely, albeit inconsistently, on particular systems of thought (historical materialism, psychoanalysis, linguistics, etc.). But later the project is continued with an almost total disdain for all and any of those systems: the *mathesis singularis* becomes unmoored from any such pretended certainties and proceeds as a more or less explicit investigation of the nature of the subject/individual in relation to social objects and formations. It becomes, indeed, a personalized treating of "l'Intraitable dont je suis fait"—the untreatable, the imponderable that constitutes me (1980a, p. 153). Nonetheless, this "subjective" investigation always clearly takes as its opponent the epistemological structures and methodological systems which we inhabit.

It is this antagonistic relationship that I want to look at here, particularly insofar as it brings up a number of questions concerning the political efficacy of what might seem to be, in Barthes's instance, a merely subjectivist rebellion against monolithic modes of thought. The texts on which I want to draw most are three of Barthes's later books, each of which might be considered as autobiographical:

Roland Barthes par lui-même (1975), *Fragments d'un discours amoureux* (1977b), and *La Chambre claire* (1980).[2] What will be particularly at stake in my discussion is the way in which Barthes's attempt to represent the self, or to *write* the "subject"—its autobiographical investigation—is indefeasibly bound up with a critique of the "metaparanoid" modes of knowledge and conceptualization of self and other, about which I commented in the previous chapter.

In his influential essay "Autobiography as Defacement," Paul de Man suggests that "autobiography . . . is not a genre or a mode, but a figure of reading or of understanding that occurs, to some degree, in all texts." This, he says, is because a "specular structure" is established as soon as a writer "declares himself the subject of his own understanding" (1979, p. 921):

> The specular moment that is part of all understanding reveals the tropo-
> logical structure that underlies all cognitions, including knowledge of
> self. (p. 922)

De Man's point here is that autobiographical texts, like all cognitive artefacts, are of necessity submitted to a tropological runaround which precludes any certainty, any knowledge outside the structural constraints and limits which have made it appear possible. The article in which these propositions appear attempts to demonstrate through Wordsworth's *Essays upon Epitaphs* the supposed "linguistic predicament" into which the autobiographer therefore must fall—to be rescued only by death, silence—when confronting the series of receding mirrors that constitutes, exactly, self-reflection. For de Man (and arising from his brand of criticism which might best be described as an "existentialist deconstruction") the autobiographical project is a privileged kind of impossibility, always given over to uncertainty, undecidability, and, finally, to death—all inscribed within the very structure of language, which he calls "privative" (p. 930).

De Man's pessimistic—deterministic, even—view of the double-bind of the language user ("Autobiography veils a defacement of the mind of which it is itself the cause," he says [p. 930]) might be taken as an extreme example of how the devolved structuralist (i.e., poststructuralist) tropologia points to nothing but impossibilities, to nothing if not the resigned shrug of the academic. The situation he describes is one which is in a sense undeniable: the complex questions of the relation of "subject" to language at any given moment in any particular kind of discourse are quite daunting. However, reducing them to a specular metaphor—the "subject" cerned within the focused rays of light between mirrors—and to a constant movement of undecidability—the perception of a certain *vertigo* of the "subject"—is designed, I think, to foreclose upon the very political and epistemological possibilities which can be glimpsed when the autobiographer like Barthes explicitly attempts to shatter the mirrors, or break the apparently fixed specular relation between "subject" and knowledge. In other words, wherever a refusal of the boundaries of the specular relation is at least suggested and worked upon, or where the powerless subjection of the spoken and specularized "subject" is questioned, then the demonic resignation of the tropologists can be countered. Whereas for de Man, autobiography (and thence, implicitly, all the epistemological processes open to us) is subsumed under the trope of "prosopopeia," the continual inscription and reinscription of masks which is circumscribed by and which serves merely to remind us of our own mortality, it would seem that Barthes's "autobiographies" attempt to write a way through that impasse in a manner which refuses the absolutely specular bind which de Man establishes.

In deciding to write about himself in the three later texts I've mentioned, Barthes makes some crucial observations about the nature of the "I" that speaks. Generally, the autobiographer has implicitly seen him/herself as the whole and coherent human being who underwrites, subscribes to the possibility of a knowledge about the self; the view of language that is involved there is one where language is little more than a vehicle capable of carrying a reflective knowledge. In such autobiographical places the reader is offered some kind of cohesion of the writing "subject" which is guaranteed by the writing signature, by the name which is attached to the text. The reader is asked to submit to a fiction which is then legalized. Barthes, on the other hand, consistently refuses the validation of that legally recognizable self. He professes, in the third person, that

> he feels bound up with any writing whose principle is that the subject is only an effect of language. He imagines a vast science, into the utterance of which the knower would finally include himself—this would be a science of the effects of language. (1975, p. 82)

The inclusion in this "science," in this knowledge, of the knower him/herself is totally different from the kind of static and hermetic relay of mirror-relations in which de Man thinks the writer is caught. It speaks to the possibility of a mobile and continual process of knowledge and its inscription. This process is accretive or ever expanding and, thus, open to the inscription of a changing history of the subject/individual. It is that continual process that Barthes's work registers, all the while recognizing not only the pull of interpellation in any of the objects of his study, but also the perhaps even more conservative pull—the temptation and the lure—of the imaginary.

An autobiographical narrative, a writing of the story of the self, is like any other discursive arrangement in that it is subjected to a necessary organization in terms of *discours* and *récit*. From the distinction between these two elements it can be suggested that there can be no "subject" of the story, the *récit* (that is, no "subject" unproblematically or cohesively a product of the life of the autobiographer). The "subject," after all, appears only when the *récit* is uttered, enunciated from the place of language. In other words, the *récit* can only be represented in the discourse's organizing parameters. Any specific mode of organising is, of course, pressured by the historical, the ideological: the subject/individual

is cerned by being offered particular modes of organization for particular historical and ideological purposes.

The "subject" of the *discours*, the "I" that speaks, is immediately not available
as the "subject" of the *récit* but is rather the organizing "subject," different from
the putative or desired "subject" of the *récit*. This split corresponds to what structural linguists describe as a division in any utterance between the "subject of the
enunciation" and the "subject of the enounced": "I" does not talk about or correspond to "I": rather, "I" talks about "me." Inscribed, thus, in the formal structures of utterance is the "enunciatory abyss" that Barthes is intent on opening up,
where the "I" that speaks constitutes an enunciatory subjectivity and the "me" that
is absent constitutes the "subject of the enounced." Such a non-self-possession in
the speaking "subject" is familiar insofar as it is constitutive of the very gap which
is inscribed at the roots of our tradition and which it has been the continual task
of the epistemologist to anneal. From Augustine's "I am not what I was," through
to logical positivism and on into the pop psychology of the last few decades, for
example, the consistent ideological effort of epistemological procedures has been
to "rescue" the subject of the enunciation from its distance from the enounced.

However, it is clear enough that, when Augustine writes "I am not what I was,"
for example, not only are the two different "I's" in fact admitted to be separated
or discernible, but that also a third "I" emerges—the "I" that would be prefigured
or desired by the moral and ideological operation of trying to maintain the coherence (the wholeness) and the propriety (the wholesomeness) of the ideological
subject (in the case of Augustine, the proper "subject" of Christianity). This third
"I"—if I can crudely call it in that way—is the one which is elided in de Man's
pessimistic account of the specularized motions of epistemology. For de Man,
there is "subject" and there is object, and never the twain shall meet, since the
"subject of the enunciation" can never stand in the place of the other except by
the illusion of the mirror. What de Man symptomatically ignores (symptomatically, I mean, in that this is a signal to the moral and political blindness of his
brand of deconstruction) is the third "I" that is the intended moral effect of a closing down of the enunciatory gap. That third "I" is the cerned and complete individual which will be called upon to hold in place the circuit of guarantees obtaining between "subject" and knowledge. It is, in fact, the ideological "subject."

In traditional autobiography the appearance of the third "I" is a crucial instance
of the ideological force of the discourse, by which the intended moral "subject"
guarantees its *own* knowledge by virtue of its provenance in a life lived ("what
I have learned . . . ," and so on). Indeed, in the autobiographical mode the "I"
that speaks typically becomes a kind of *de facto* third-person pronoun, supposedly
having full objective possession of that which it views. This effect is most clearly
operative, obviously, in an autobiography like that of David Hume which is actually written in the third person. The force of such a guaranteeing "subject" cannot
be underestimated; and thus autobiography itself cannot be underestimated as a

privileged form of ideological text wherein the demand that we should consist as coherent and recognizable "subjects" in relation to a particular knowledge appears to be rationalized. Indeed, even though it is clearly correct to say that autobiography involves a process "that occurs to some degree in all texts," de Man's truism should not be allowed to divert from the *generic* power of autobiography to construct and legitimate a "subject" which will guarantee juridical social relations.

De Man's (properly poststructuralist) separation of the two "I's," and his refusal to think about the place where they collude, can be taken as a cipher of the tropologist's quite negligent attitude toward this future "I"—the third, moral "I" of our metaparanoid tradition. Roland Barthes, on the other hand, is concerned specifically to attack both the cohesion and the propriety of that moral construct. If the human agent is constituted by many effects of being a "subject" or, more simply, *is* many "subjects," and if each of these "subjects" is remarkable by virtue of its particular relation to the "I" that speaks them, then that "I" is always itself an imaginary construction upon which no moral third term can be erected. To say this is to repeat in different terms what Barthes contemplates in his book on the image (on photography, exactly), *La Chambre claire* (1980a). Noting, importantly, that photography enables people to see themselves for the first time outside of the specular mirror relation, Barthes describes the tension between the desire to be the proper and coherent *ideological* "subject" and the sense of its actual fictionality:

> It would be nice if my image—which is mobile, jostled and jolted through a thousand photos of me at different times and at different ages—could coincide with my "me." . . . But in fact it needs to be put another way: it's my "me" that won't coincide with my image; because it's the image that's stodgy, immobile and obstinate (which is why society relies on it), and it's "me" that's flighty, divided and dispersed so that, like a cartesian diver moving in a jar, it won't hold still. (pp.26–277)

Barthes clearly rejects the conflation of the ideologically fixed "subject" (fixed in the image and depended upon by "society") and the human agent's experience of that "me." Barthes is concerned, then, with the transgressive effect of the agent upon the solidity of the ideological "subject" and stresses the lability of the relationship between a lived life and its ideologically attuned representations. Not that the "subject's" "me" ever escapes fixity in a certain sense, but that the nature of that fixity—its content, perhaps, or the vagaries of its own history—is in constant change. That is, even if the "subject" establishes certain forms of consistency or repetition by way of its imaginary identifications (and here it is understood that the demand that such identifications be made is a fundamental interpellation), these are continually vulnerable to the registration of ever renewed and contradictory interpellations. The quoted passage in fact very well illustrates the tensions between the ideological demand that we be one cerned "subject" and the actual experience of a subjective history which consists in a mobility, an unfixed repertoire of many subject-positions.

For Barthes there is in this mobility, in this inability to make cohere all the jostled and jolted "subjects" that he is, a certain pleasure – the pleasure of being the place of transgression in relation to the cerned subject we are presumed to be. This pleasure is, indeed, the thematics of Barthes's work and is variously named and demonstrated, but is most often referred to as *jouissance* (enjoyment, orgasm, or, as it is sometimes translated into English, bliss; there seems no reason, however, not to translate it as jouissance, a word which does exist in English). Jouissance for Barthes is to be distinguished from, but dialectically implicated with, *plaisir*, pleasure. Whereas *plaisir* relies upon the fixity of the "subject" within the codes and conventions it inhabits, jouissance is specifically transgressive and it marks the crossing by the human agent of the symbolic codes which attempt to keep us in place as one "subject." Jouissance comes to be understood in Barthes's work as exactly the effect of a multiplicity posed against the monism that is our social cement.

One way in which Barthes terms this dialectical conflict is in *La Chambre claire* where he says that his readings of photographs cross two moments. On the one hand, there is a *studium* type of reading which entails pleasure and where that pleasure is dependent upon the viewer taking up the subject-position proffered by the photograph. This pleasure is, in a sense, one of identification with the law – a phallic pleasure, one might say. On the other hand, there is a *punctum* type of reading. The *punctum* reading involves the sense of a subjectivity inscribed athwart of the "subject's" identificatory urge. In other words, and reductively, the *studium* is read through codes and sets in place the fixed, ideological "subject": whereas the *punctum* does not respond to those codes and displaces the cerned "subject." Codes, of course, never allow us to speak our desire; they are intrinsically totalitarian in that respect, since they take our place and speak *for* us; the *punctum* problematizes such a *presumption*.

This distinction is, of course, not to be understood undialectically. What Barthes describes is exactly a tension, a jostling even, within the subject/individual's constitution and experience. This is an explanatory schema which corresponds in more than a loose way with Julia Kristeva's distinction between the *symbolic* and the *semiotic* where the fixed and prohibitive rationality of the symbolic is what upholds the law, and where the semiotic is the fragmentary and quite inconsistent crossing of the symbolic.[3] It is not a question of there being two discrete modes in some sense "available" to the subject/individual; rather, both modes might be considered as intertwined. Both, certainly, are in their way the effect of interpellations. The crucial point, however, is that the schema allows room for a theoretical resistance to the solidity of externalised image in the symbolic. Where the symbolic appears to demand the establishment of a clear and cerned "subject," it in fact operates by means of a multiplicity of demands for differing and various subject-positions. These subject-positions cannot neatly overlap and produce the cerned "subject" that would be the ideal citizen, but leave gaps and contradictions which help constitute the subject/individual's history and which are indefeasibly part of it. What I am calling Barthes's autobiographies wish to embrace those lacunae in the construction of the fully and properly interpellated "subject."

The pressure, then, to construct a uniform self is itself multiform, demanding different "subjects" at different times—but demanding, exactly, always a subjection. The social order, Kristeva's symbolic, represents itself *for* the "subject" within signifying practices of all sorts. Barthes conceives of subjectivity as exactly an infinite and infinitely mobile collection of subject-positions in cahoots with given discourses but never entirely given over to them. And it is in the "never entirely" there that Barthes discerns the semiotic or resistant force of jouissance, foreclosing on the presumption of any identary "I." Such an "I" would, in any event, be nothing more than a fictional representation, a colligation and a suturing of a collection of imaginary identities. Thus, for Barthes, to talk of writing "The Book of Myself" immediately necessitates a caveat: "This should all be considered as if spoken by a character in a novel—or by several, rather" (1975, p. 123). In other words, the "me" can be written only as if it were somewhere else:

> Today the subject apprehends itself *elsewhere* and subjectivity folds back in upon another point in the spiral—deconstructed, disunited, deported, unchained; why should I no longer speak of "myself" when "my" self is no longer "one's" self? (p. 171)

Clearly the acceptance of the jouissance of this splintered subjectivity, of the almost celebratory dispersal of subjectivity, must call forth a relation of the "subject" to the external world which will be different from that metaparanoid relation established in and guaranteed by the unary "subject." This is the political question that Barthes's work is always at the edge of, and which it never quite seems willing to answer. In this respect it might seem representative of that thinking in which it is rooted, namely, structuralism. In general one might think of structuralism as having failed to deliver on its very lucid and insistent oppositional promises, and yet of its being almost totally superseded by the critical dances of poststructuralism as something of a loss. At this point it's perhaps still possible to return to some of structuralism's important impulses and ask whether any of them can even yet be recuperated. Accordingly, it is important to recognize the contestatory impulse of Barthes's early work (his continual effort to "decompose" bourgeois culture is, of course, commendable; equally, his lucid perception of the links between cultural objects and forms of subjectivity is admirable); but it is also important to ask to what political demands can his work be linked?[4]

This latter question is a difficult one, made more difficult by at least one aspect of Barthes's method: he often seems to trivialize the force of the ideological. Indeed, that is one of his main tactics against it. By deploying the notion of jouissance he seems usually to attempt to deprive the social of its overarching ability to remove the subject/individual into the trammels of ideology and power. Jouissance is often—perhaps too often—the subjective response by Barthes to a real powerlessness and to a kind of abjection; it can become a celebration which merely kicks a little at the prevailing order in an almost infantile rebellion. It is thus legitimate to ask to what extent Barthes succeeds in anything but a purely personal guerrilla warfare. Indeed, his final work on photography is so "personal" that it exists, he says, as a memorial inscription of his mother's death, and his "own death is inscribed there; between the two [deaths] nothing but waiting; I have no other resource but in the irony of saying I have nothing more to say" (1980a, p. 145). But even so, this kind of personal text always addresses a social context, even if only to celebrate glimpses of being "voluptuously relieved of the responsibility of being a citizen" (1980b, p. 34). And this is perhaps the best case that can be made for Barthes's later work: it has the ability to at least glimpse moments where the ideological hold is barred.

The person who foregrounds the moments of inefficacy in ideological structures is, for Barthes, one who submits the power of social structures to reduction and ridicule. It seems that this power does not have to become—as it often does become for more overtly political discourses—the bad object onto which the human agent's aggressive emotions are simply projected; rather, it can be ridiculed and trivialized as the *doxa*, defined as:

> public opinion, the majority spirit, the petit bourgeois concensus, the voice of the Natural, the violence of prejudice. We can call *doxology* any way of speaking that is adapted to appearance, opinion or practice. (1975, p. 51)

Barthes's strategy here is to characterize the *doxa* as a more or less monolithic and cumbersome mechanism against which the subject/individual can pose the mobile pleasurable experience of being a *para*doxical "subject." Thus parrying the *doxa*, the subject/individual's jouissance is set off against doxical solidity and immobility which, although overbearing, is seen to be full of its own contradictions. Barthes's oppositional writing project, then, is to reveal instances of a new and paradoxical subjectivity where the symbolic's hold is not total. This means opening up the *doxa* and opening up language itself. The *doxa*, representing itself in the reigning set of discourses, is the arrogant system which offers itself as "the fundamental science of the real: fantasmatically endowed with an ultimate power, that of deadening or checkmating language itself, reducing any utterance to its residue of reality" (pp. 57–58). The discourse of the *doxa* can thus be seen to be always repeating itself, generalizing itself, wearing itself out, and its privileged trope is the stereotype (Barthes reminds us that *stereos* means solid).

Against the solidity of that system Barthes is concerned to posit the nuisance of his own powerlessness and jouissance which are constructed in the gaps of the supposed solidity and coherence which he inhabits. This intrusion or nuisance has the effect of opening the "enunciatory abyss" and "casting suspicion upon any statement by trying to reveal the arrangement of its different levels." Barthes's project is distinguishable from that of literary deconstruction in that his work always returns, not to the level of the trope, but to the level of the human agent who is writing or reading: in this resides his conviction that, when the enunciation is decomposed, then not only is the *doxa* threatened or decomposed, but also the horizon of the subject/individual's relation to the social comes into view.

I say "comes into view," but with some ambivalence. Purely linguistic rebellions do not much suffice nowadays. In the context of late capitalism there is a temptation to fall into a certain despondency when considering new forms of subjectivity. Barthes readily admits this difficulty in his writing. Yet he institutes that problematic exactly at the core of his work and endows it with a certain value: so much of a contestant, he might claim that the very fact of the project's difficulty should be enough to make it recognizable as needing to be done. At this stage in our history the relations between "subject" and language, between the ego and its imaginary, or in short the relationships that are taken to subvent the networks of ideology and power, are urgently in need of attention and disruption of whatever kind. And for Barthes, writing is the activity which most clearly confronts, in its accosting of the enunciatory abyss, in its impossibility and its paradoxical nature, exactly those relations. Furthermore, *writing oneself* demands an appeal not only to the symbolic — the system of signs used to keep us in place — but also to the imaginary where we seek the reflection of our plenitude.

Barthes's concern in *Par lui-même* is clearly to find a way of escaping that realm of the imaginary, to continually displace the identifications that settle there and fix us. One of the most obvious ploys he uses is to write his book in fragments — all *discours*, no *récit* — and to operate within those fragments the widest possible variation of personal pronouns. The writing subject constantly shifts between I, you, he, we and the initials R. B., while also consistently returning to analyze and reflect upon the effects of such displacements. What is at stake here is not simply Barthes's own effort not to allow the imaginary any stability, nor simply the effort to prevent the reader from making each utterance refer back to a unified enunciator. Rather, it is a question of offering something else: the history of the fragmentary construction of fragmented subjectivity in a theoretically infinite language. Barthes demonstrates here the process whereby he, as "subject," comes to be crystalized at certain moments and then to be diverted, cast adrift again (*dérivé*, to repeat one of the book's most often used words). In this manner Barthes proposes the activity of writing as not some expression of presignified or determined instances in a life, but rather the process of language's constructing a momentary subjectivity *for* the human agent who always, by contestatory and resistant use and reception of language, emerges as the place where contradictory discourses are marked. The project is perhaps best summed up by Barthes's own insistence that "in the field of the subject there is no referent" (p. 60).

This is not to say, of course, that the "subject" has no history or real existence (any more than Barthes's famous essay on "The Death of the Author" [1977a] denies the existence of real people writing). Rather, what is proposed is a new plot, a new *discours* which enacts the agent's relation to the "I" that speaks and to the imaginary. There is no referent to be *historized* (if I may refloat an archaic verb which means to relate as history, to narrate), but there is a continual process of *historicization*, the ever renewable representation of instances of subjectivity and situation across time. To adopt a saying of Jean Louis Schefer's, the one possible *récit* is that of the extension of time across the body. That is the only authentic history of a human being that might possibly be grasped, but only insofar as time and body can be grasped *momentarily*, forever given over to the "subject's" impossible position as "subject of the enunciation."

The body, of course, will itself change, and it never coheres as an image except insofar as the "I" narrativizes it and forces it to fit into a given discursive organization. Barthes plays with this image of the body throughout *Par lui-même*. The events of Barthes's life or the *récit*, the extension of time across the body, the events that could perhaps be historized, can be given only as a series of photographic images that themselves reflect the change in the body and that produce a wonderment in the "I" that looks at them now. Barthes compares photos of himself taken in 1942 and in 1970:

> Surely I never looked like that? How would you know? What's this 'you' that you might resemble or not resemble? Where would you find it on what morphological or expressive plane? Where is your real body? You're the only one who can't see yourself except in reflections, in images . . . you're condemned to the imaginary. (1975, p. 40)

The final sentiment there—that we are condemned to the imaginary—could act as the locus of all that is problematic and difficult in Barthes's last works. While it is still the effort of *Par lui-même* to resist the stasis of the imaginary register, his *Fragments d'un discours amoureux* and *La Chambre claire* embrace much more some version of the imaginary lure. The first of these books, *Fragments*, offers an instance in a series of fragments, a series of figures, scenarios of a surrender to the imaginary where the "subject" willingly attempts to perform the consistency of the imaginary—that is, where it is in love. The solitude and the social marginality of the *one* who is in love are given as products of the imaginary where it is indeed of one's own "self" that one is fond. In this book Barthes thus tries to illustrate the massive difficulty of a person in love.

Written in fragmentary form across a set of motifs and figures that do not cohere, the book plays out the tension between "subject" and imaginary, where imaginary coherence is undercut by the momentaneous array and changing disposition of subject-positions at the same time as the imaginary pulls toward a homeostasis or a constancy in relation to the other (the loved one). The tension appears quite simply as the pain of the lover, amply attested to by this moving book, but it is still tempting to read that pain as a kind of allegorical representation of the impossible relation of the human being to the demands of the social.

However, this book does run the risk of foreclosing on the ideological subversion that *Par lui-même* was able to approach. This is in part explicable by the fact that the lover's situation is posited as a unique one: the lover is excluded from the doxical world where the plenary "I" normally finds its haven. *Fragments* is in fact a repertoire of the effects of a dialectic of exclusion and inclusion, of the lover's being at once excluded from a social world where love would be the current obscenity (1977b, p. 210), and being included in an imaginary relation to just one other. But even as the book proposes a certain fixity of the *amoureux*, where the imaginary takes its solipsistic pre-eminence, the doxical demands of the social world are refused. Thus what the book presents in the way of fixed subjectivity is exactly a fixity of the imaginary, a kind of freezing of a particular imaginary mechanism. What is missing from the investigation of the imaginary in this book is the *jouissance* that marked the earlier book: here there is only a *pleasure,* dependent entirely on the other and thus on imaginary identifications. But it is, to be sure, not a paranoid freezing of the "I"—doubtless because the autobiography entertains no narrative as such.[5]

The same kind of pull toward the acceptance of imaginary stasis is to be found in Barthes's final book, *La Chambre claire*, which confronts the content of the imaginary with the good object par excellence, the mother. That is to say, the book deals with photography and the imaginary ostensibly, but with the death of Barthes's mother actually. It is also inscribed "In homage to Sartre's *L'Imaginaire*" and seems to constitute finally some kind of defense of the imaginary against all the "I's" that are constituted in the act of reading images. It is a book that is in part content to gainsay all those "I's" by adopting a comfortable and comforting position in relation to the imaginary.

It is, of course, not irrelevant in this regard that in the last teaching of his life, at the Collège de France, Barthes described his discourse as like the "comings and goings of a child playing beside his mother, leaving her, returning to bring her a pebble, a piece of string, and thereby tracking a whole locus of play around a calm center."[6] The suggestion here is that the attempt to deliberately fail the legislative demands and commands of the symbolic entails the establishment of a voluptuous and subversive relationship to the mother. If *La Chambre claire* seems, on the one hand, to be a literal playing out of that necessity as well as a memorial to Barthes's real mother, it must be seen at the same time as a deliberate rejection of mastery and a valorizing of fragmentation, loss, insecurity, and the jouissance that is concomitant with them.

Even here, where there is a kind of decadence in Barthes's later career, or a certain kind of falling away, the aim of his early work to decompose the culture is still evident but in transmuted form. All the ideological social demands made on the human being are conceived to work against that oldest of taboos in patriarchal society, namely, enjoyment of the mother's body. Barthes's final works are explicitly cast in sexual terms such that the site of the maternal is the site of resistance to all the codes and conventions which are paternal. The law of the father stretches, indeed, to every cultural doxa, language included. For Barthes, as he says in his inaugural lecture at the Collège de France, coded language itself is inherently fascistic. To counter it Barthes in most of his career privileges the kind of text which "imposes a state of loss, discomfits . . . unsettles the reader's historical, cultural, psychological certainties, the consistency of tastes, values, memories, and throws the relationship to language into crisis" (1973, p.25–26). At the end of his career, by contrast, the place of the mother has been espied as the very locus of resistance. Not surprisingly, then, one of his posthumously published essays, on Stendhal, explicitly deploys an opposition between France as *patria* and Italy as *matria*: it is in the *matria* of course, that he feels "relieved of the responsibility of being a citizen."

What this trajectory constitutes is, I think, something profoundly uneasy to *judge*. That is, there is a certain impossibility in bringing to bear upon that work of Barthes's all the doxical manners which the work has effectively denounced. Suffice it to say that, even though one's political qualms about Barthes's individualism, his romanticism, even his dandyism, might grow stronger as his work progresses, two things remain importantly present: first, the project of being the agent who "simultaneously and contradictorily participates in the profound hedonism of all culture . . . and in the destruction of that culture" (1973, p. 26) or the almost loutish agent of "the subversion of every ideology" (p. 54); second, the ceaseless concern with a tension within the "subject" that is at once agent and also many "subjects," and with the human being who is able simultaneously to "enjoy the consistence of the 'me' (there's his pleasure) and the pursuit of its disintegration (there's his jouissance)" (p. 26).

Both these elements of Barthes's work are, I think, worthy of attention on many scores. There exists today, in many a circle, the sense that nothing could be more bourgeois and more useless than this kind of investigation and account of the subject/individual's import. The claim that any attempt to dismantle the age-old social/individual dyad is ill served by further stress on the individual is a common one.[7] However, Barthes's push toward the assumption by the human agent of his/her own history (which is the history of subject-positions continually changing, being cast adrift, being constantly buffeted by history and their own histories and never being coincident with either) by and large does effect an erosion of that dyadic monolith. By recognizing that the two terms, social and individual, are not simply imbricated one on top of the other, but are each determinants for the other, Barthes's writing embodies in itself a resistance. To point out that this writing ends up in a kind of despair, in this waiting for death of which he talks, might not be a damning criticism. That despair can be seen as a fatigue brought on by a consistent countering of that version of the "individual" proposed by the doxa and entrenched firmly in everyday ideological practices from advertising to fashion, politics to psychology. But importantly, Barthes has written against the abstract and metaparanoid construals of the "subject" as entertained by the discourses of science and traditional forms of epistemology. Indeed, the aim of his work is to undertake the exhausting process of writing "à découvert"—writing without cover, open to the skies, not shadowed by any presignifying system (1975, p. 106). So this may be a fatigue coming from the incessant attempt to work through any self-proposing truth or any doxical position, and from trying to relate the actual oppressions and repressions which constitute human social life. In these senses, Barthes's work is attractive and scarcely negligible.

And yet the political questions remain to be asked of Barthes since this despair arises more or less directly from some of the features I have already mentioned, and could indeed be said to form them: Barthes's individualist guerrilla attack on the social; his apparent faith in the efficacy of linguistic resistance; the fall of his last writing into the comfortable lure of the imaginary; the signs of decadence and dandyism which Barthes seems to have cultivated. These features have to be seen as a significant retreat from the investigations of the "subject" that I have been proposing elsewhere in these pages.

A telling indication of the tensions between, and the implications of, all these strands of his writing might be seen in some words from the last pages of *La Chambre claire*. Barthes ends this, his last book by suggesting that the photographic image is now so generalized in our culture that

> it completely derealises the human world of conflicts and desires in the pretence of illustrating the world. What characterises so-called advanced societies is that they currently consume images rather than beliefs. . . . [It is] as if the image produced *a world without differences (an indifferent world)*, from which nothing can spring except here and there the cries of anarchisms, marginalities, individualisms. . . . It's up to me to choose: I can submit the image to the civilised code of illusions, or I can use it to confront the awakening of unmanageable reality. (1980a, pp.183–84; my emphases)

In its almost elegiac humanism (the complaint against consumer society's dehumanizing effects) and in the lapse into fairly crude allusions to the hoary problem of false consciousness, this passage gives plenty of ammunition to the view of Barthes as despairing and even decadent individualist. At the same time, however, a couple of other aspects of the quotation seem more positive. First of all, the words that I have emphasized seem to me to stand as a warning against the whole ethos of poststructuralism. Perhaps the most important problem with our current theory is the way in which its breaking down of identitarian logics and cerning discourses tends easily to open out onto precisely the world without differences to which Barthes refers here. Such a world is not only logically but also morally "indifferent." If this passage can be read at all as a premonition of the tropological irresponsibility of the kinds of theorizing that have taken hold in the years since Barthes's death and which he notably failed to adopt, that surely is something positive. By the same token, the unambiguous taking of responsibility in the phrase "It's up to me to choose (*A moi de choisir*)" can be usefully contrasted, for example, to what might be called the technicist resignation and irresponsibility of Derrida when he claims that meanings choose themselves (see Chapter 3).

In this passage Barthes stands at the edge of an "unmanageable reality" that can be interpreted as the horizon of what I called, at the beginning of this chapter, our current "critical *turn*, a whole little tropology"; and I read him as resisting it. Nonetheless, the tone of this passage is still very reminiscent of the complaints of Adorno against mass culture—and reminiscent, too, of the tone of resignation that attaches to the later work of the Frankfurt School. The writing of the Institut's members had tried consistently to develop a theoretical and dialectical account of how resistance to what Barthes here calls "the civilised code of illusions" might occur. But, as I suggested in Chapter 4, their view of the "subject" failed their attempts. Here Barthes, even having investigated quite fully and with some theoretical rigor the question of subjectivity, might still be said to fail in something like the same way. One noticeable feature about the passage I've quoted is that it makes allusion to the *studium/punctum* ways of reading photographs. Throughout *La Chambre claire*, as I noted, these ways of reading were not to be regarded as in opposition to each other: dialectically linked, they in fact sketched out the terms of a nondualism. Here, however, Barthes throws them against each other, and their conflict is to be mediated by the "subject's" will: "It's up to me to to choose." Equally, the terms of the choices are loaded. The "subject" only has access *either* to a familiar world of "illusions," *or* to some "unmanageable reality."

Faced with the strictly political project of taking responsibility (displacing images in the aid of beliefs), Barthes refuses to make his choice. And even as he refuses, he nonetheless returns the "subject" to some putative control, without specifying the limits on that control (or indeed on the choice). That is, the "subject" becomes endowed once more with that particular power of choice which closes down and even reneges upon the dialectical and processual methodology which had been so impressive in Barthes's early writing.

It is interesting in that regard to note that the history of his work corresponds in a rough way with the stages of the developmental formation of the "subject"

of which Melanie Klein speaks. Klein, of course, is one of the many psychoanalytical thinkers upon whom Barthes has drawn at one time or another. Klein maintains that the earliest form of the ego in the child can be described by reference
to the mechanisms of paranoia. At that stage the predominant psychical process
is projection: persecutory anxiety is intense and the world is rudimentarily split
into "good objects" and "bad objects," which are kept as dissociated as possible
by the "subject." The stage following the paranoid stage is what Klein calls the
depressive position in which the splitting of good and bad objects is attenuated
and a semblance of balance is achieved between hostility and security in the libidinal economy. This stage is marked by the child's establishing a secure good
object—usually the mother—onto which both good and bad cathexes are made.
This position is called depressive because it is accompanied by the affects of both
fear and guilt in regard to the good object—fear and guilt in case the good object
should be destroyed or used up either by the child's hostilities or by its greed for
sustenance.[8]

Barthes's writing does seem to follow the path of that much of Klein's theories.
His work constitutes a movement away from the persecutory anxieties of what
I have called metaparanoid structures and toward the supposedly more stable
economy of the depressive position. It is remarkable that his writing also shares
the specific terms of Klein's suggestions: he moves from disenchantment with the
arrogance and paranoia of knowledge, toward the establishing of a good object
in his dead mother. The coincidence is perhaps too pat to be exploited much further, but it is worth mentioning that the third developmental stage which Klein
describes is one of reparation, where guilt and anxiety are resolved in the birth
of what Klein calls a mature human being. Of course, Kleinian psychoanalysis
is directed toward this mature "subject," or toward the coherent identity that is
the goal of all ego psychology and which is the cerned "subject" of all ideology.
It is perhaps not too fanciful to see in the despairing end of Barthes's writing a
collapse into the familiarly comforting and fixed image of the "subject." With that
collapse the oppositional moments and impulses of structuralism finally die out.

Chapter 8
Semiotica

So something goes awry in Barthes's project, or rather something changes in his effort to continually champion what has become known as the decentering of the "subject" and to undermine "doxical" structures. The story of Barthes's engagement with the linkages between the usually dyadic terms, individual and social, can be seen to become increasingly pessimistic and even desperate. Of course, this kind of passage from the radical desire for subversion, resistance, and change toward an emotional kind of self-resignation in the face of the perceived impossibility of such change is hardly an unfamiliar one. It is the narrative of the failed radical and can be seen in the stories of writers like Adorno, for instance. It could even be one of the genotexts contributing to the relative disarray in much leftist thinking and strategizing.

Barthes's importance here resides simply in the fact that his work, from its inception in the contestatory discourses of structuralism, has revolved around questions of subjectivity, but does not seem susceptible to being described as post-structuralist. Even if he falls back finally onto the relative security of a version of cerned subjectivity, he nonetheless has mounted a challenge to all putatively contestatory work through his recognition of the necessity of inserting the component of *singularity* into all analyses of resistance. In the context of his inability to sustain the oppositional character of his own earlier work, it becomes all the more crucial to elaborate ways of conceiving the dialectic between cerned subjectivity and oppositional agency in such a way as to privilege resistance.

Perhaps it is the very extremity of Barthes's earlier positions which renders them problematic. His desire to attack the rigidity and arrogance of social structures by posing against them the "subject's" own lack of cohesion often embraces whole-heartedly the extremes of theories of the "decentered subject." A shibboleth of structuralism, the "decentered subject" often turns out to be an all-or-nothing proposition. Taking his cue from the psychoanalytical theories of subjectivity that were at the nub of critical debate in the late sixties and the seventies, he makes the case for the radical inevitability, or the structural necessity, of decenteredness: the "subject's" accession to language and symbolic structures *necessitates* its fundamental division or its status as what has become known as the "split subject" or the "subject-in-process." Barthes's ultimate return to a version of the cerned "subject" is perhaps an indication that he can only view the "decentered subject" and the cerned, doxical "subject" as logical opposites, with no mediation between them being possible or desirable. As I tried to suggest at the end of the last chapter, this is perhaps not quite a stable opposition for him; nonetheless it exists and has its consequences.

The "decentered subject" has been taken up with more of an abandon by some contemporary theorists than by Barthes. It can be objected to this that any adoption of a version of subjectivity which stresses only its split condition is fundamentally a reactive procedure, leading to precisely the vision of in-difference which Barthes held back from but of which contemporary theory seems excessively fond. The "split subject," in other words, is perhaps nothing so much as the flip side of centered or cerned subjectivity and is both historically and conceptually dependent upon it. In that sense neither the decentered subjectivity of much structuralism, nor its in-different heir in poststructuralism is what I am proposing in this book. While it is absolutely crucial to attack dominant ideologies and epistemologies of subjectivity — theories and systems of representation wherein the "subject's" subjection is maintained through an elision of its active and oppositional components — it would be far too hasty merely to counter those homogeneous versions of the "subject" by some vision of total heterogeneity. An account of subjectivity which recognises what I have been calling the colligation of multifarious subject-positions would appear to be a more flexible one insofar as it allows us not only to take seriously the "subject's" interpellated positions and the permananence of ideology, but also to conceive of the possibility of resistance through a recognition of the *simultaneous* non-unity or non-consistency of subject-positions. Such an account is intrinsically more dialectical than the either/or construction of which one can suspect Barthes.

Perhaps a more promising approach onto the terrain which Barthes covers is that of his erstwhile colleague Julia Kristeva, whose work will be the topic of this chapter. Kristeva has been a figure of major importance in literary, feminist, and psychoanalytical theory for nearly twenty years now. From the beginning of her involvement in what has been called the structuralist revolution and in the rise of semiotics, she proclaimed the same necessity as that from which Barthes begins: the inclusion of a theory of subjectivity in any discussion of language and

representational systems. Thus her work has been largely concerned with the notion of the "speaking subject." This emphasis has led her in many directions which
are relevant to the issues I have been raising and will raise. But especially I am
interested here in Kristeva's attempt to construct a properly dialectical view of
subjectivity – and one which will pay regard both to the construction of subjectivity and also to the political consequences of the notion of the "subject." It has
become increasingly unclear over the last few years whether or not her attempts
in this direction have actually been sustained, let alone successful. This is because
her work as a practicing psychoanalyst appears to have sent her into a subjectivist
impasse not unlike the one that I've been describing Roland Barthes as submitting
to. However (and as with Barthes), I will argue here that many of Kristeva's
earlier investigations and interventions are still of great importance, especially
in light of her own more recent work and that of poststructuralism more
generally.[1]

In an essay first published in 1971, Kristeva lays out the bases of much of her
thinking when she claims that the strength of Roland Barthes's work is its investigation through literature of the intersection of subject and history. This "intersection," she says, is where "the ideological tearings in the social fabric" (1980a, p.
93) can most readily be glimpsed. Such an emphasis on the privileged position
of literature for such a project (especially "avant-garde" literature) is a constant
one throughout Kristeva's work: the text is consistently seen as a special case by
dint of its considerable freedom relative to other systems of social representation.
Literature is the place where the legalistic or fixatory structures of the social (always seen as signifying systems and therefore as in some way analogous to language and dependent upon the "subject's" accession to the symbolic) confront the
repressed or marginalized processes of language and subjectivity (those which
correspond to what I have been calling the contradictions through which human
agency can be glimpsed). These latter processes, Kristeva claims, always constitute an excess in relation to whatever juridical (or doxical, as Barthes would say)
demands might historically hold them in check. In other words, the processes of
literature's system are uniquely placed to illuminate and question the ideological.

This view of the text might immediately appear to be somewhat similar to
Macherey's or even to Althusser's. Macherey, for instance, with the same stress
on its linguistic aspects, talks of the text as something arising from a specific ideological matrix which it displays or offers as a kind of knowledge:

> Mingling the real uses of language in an endless confrontation, it con-
> cludes by *revealing* their truth. Experimenting with language rather than
> inventing it, the literary work is both the analogy of a knowledge and a
> caricature of customary ideology. (1978, p. 59)

However, Macherey's ensuing emphasis is on the *use* to which this form of
knowledge about the social might be put in the service of a Marxist science of

the literary text. Although for Kristeva the text does offer the same kind of "reve-lation" (a display of conflicts and contradictions which illustrate "ideological tear-ings"), her attempts at explaining it are more concerned with the psychoanalytical structures which, she says, produce and underpin those confrontations. For Macherey the result of the text's peculiar contradictions and lacunae is a baring of real contradictions and thence of the social struggles conducted around them. For Kristeva it is important to discover how texts engage and rely upon certain processes in the "subject's" relation to language. If the ideological, in its represen-tations to the "subject," operates a hold that is alienating but finally incomplete and in itself contradictory, then literature becomes the site "where this alienation and this blockage [of the subject] are thwarted each time in a specific way" (1980b, p. 96).

Considered in this way the text comes to constitute something like a border-line or an interface between the demands of social and subjective existence. Thus throughout her work Kristeva will propose the text as a kind of laboratory in which the experience of subjective *limits* can be viewed and dissected. Her admi-ration for Barthes's work is due to its having been able to locate and describe in texts what she calls "the secret motor" of the "Christian-capitalist era" (p. 97) – namely, the peculiarly contradictory constitution of the "subject." Of course, Kristeva's version of the "subject" has to be seen in the light of its origins in Lacan's work where the accession to language, the oedipal moment, is posed as the beginning of subjective alienation and as the moment when desire arises (see Chapter 5). For Kristeva the text registers the modes of subjective oscilla-tion between desire and the law. In that sense the "subject" itself can perhaps then be described as something like a mediation, as a securing image standing between its own unconscious desires and histories and its submission to the ideo-logical.

Already this notion of oscillation and mediation takes Kristeva a certain dis-tance away from Barthes's work which, as I suggested, is not necessarily or al-ways so dialectically informed. Kristeva wants to see the "subject," this "secret motor of history," not entirely as sub-ject to and dependent upon the ideological, nor as entirely free. Her "subject" is *both* "repressed and innovative." In literature its birth in and its struggles with this tension become distilled:

> 'Literary' and generally 'artistic' practice transforms the dependence of
> the subject on the signifier into a test of its freedom in relation to the
> signifier and reality. It is a trial where the subject reaches both its limits
> (the law of the signifier) and the objective possibilities (linguistic and
> historic) of their displacement, by including the tensions of the 'ego'
> within historical contradictions and by gradually breaking away from
> these tensions as the subject includes them in such contradictions and
> reconciles them to their struggles. (p. 97)

This dialectical view of the "subject" and of the text as its privileged habitat is the ground and warrant for the methodological step for which Kristeva is probably best known: her introduction of the paired terms *semiotic* and *symbolic*.

Kristeva's use of the term "symbolic" differs from Lacan's, mostly by virtue of being used in relation to the other term, the "semiotic." Lacan's symbolic seems to be defined as the realm of language itself and thus as the order which constructs every "subject." Within Lacan's ultimately monolithic and overarching symbolic order Kristeva discerns not only what she calls its thetic dimension (its encratic and legalistic, even paternal, aspect), but also another. This is the semiotic, conceived as the excess of language as it threatens the repression in the "subject" which is demanded by the "subject's" submission to the thetic. The semiotic is defined, then, through the language of psychoanalysis as being an only partially socialized supplement to the symbolic order. That is, it is linked to a kind of residual, pre-oedipal aspect of subjectivity. Kristeva makes the case that the semiotic is the effect of the bodily drives which are incompletely repressed when the paternal order has intervened in the mother/child dyad, and it is therefore "attached" psychically to the mother's body.

Kristeva's semiotic and symbolic are not posed in contradistinction to one another. They both have a part in the construction and constitution of the "subject" and continually cross each other to the extent that together they render "signification as an asymmetrical but double process" (1974, p. 80). In that regard, it is the particular function of literature "to introduce, across the symbolic, [the semiotic] which works, crosses it and threatens it" (p. 79). Kristeva establishes these two terms in a pair so that, even though the symbolic is dominant in conscious activity and in everyday life, neither is not present in signifying practice. Their pairing and their necessary co-presence entails that neither can ultimately be thought of as "in control" of any utterance, or of any "subject." There can be neither "an absolutisation of the thetic . . . [nor] an undoing of the thetic by the fantasy of an atomising irrationalism" (p. 80).

This schema works to produce a dialectic in which the symbolic and the semiotic aspects of any utterance, and thus of the "subject's" constitution, impose limits on each other. It is scarcely correct to read Kristeva's early work as if it automatically championed or envisioned the irruption of the semiotic into symbolic rules and structures (even though this may be true of her more recent work). In fact much of what she says is concerned to specify in some way the constraints placed on the "subject" by this pair of terms. She claims that in the "subject" there is always a "heterogeneous contradiction between two irreconcilable things" (p. 80) which will allow her to talk about a "sujet en procès": the "subject" not only in process, but also as it were on trial, put to the test as to its ability to negotiate this contradictory tension.

There is for me a worryingly easy slippage, in all that Kristeva says, between the processes of textual construction and the constitution of this "subject-in-process" (1980b, p. 135). It could be argued that in a sense the one is proposed as the reflection or expression of the other—a complex variation, perhaps, on more familiar materialist aesthetics. But, of course, Kristeva's justification for what might seem to be not much more than an analogy is to be found primarily in Lacan's conception of the imbrication of "subject" and language: her reliance on Lacan is clear when she says that it is this "heterogeneity . . . known as the unconscious [that] shapes the signifying function" (p. 135). But it would not be true to say, on the other hand, that Kristeva's theories stand or fall with Lacan's. Just as crucially they are related to other regions of psychoanalytical theory. For example, the notion of the semiotic owes something to one of the ideas that occasioned debate between Freud and the early Freudians: namely, the notion of the so-called archaic concentric drives which analysts such as Ernest Jones proposed as specifically feminine in order to counter the phallocentric theories of infantile sexual development offered by Freud himself. Kristeva, however, does not specifically subscribe to Jones's concomitant suggestion of a discrete feminine development, but rather extends Freud's bisexuality thesis and suggests, through her examination of the partial symbolization of such pre-oedipal drives in signifying practice, that both the concentric and phallocentric drives are crucially part of the construction of both male and female "subjects."[2]

But Kristeva's view of this interrelation of language and subjectivity is predicated not only along psychoanalytical lines. One of the clear fundaments of her work (though it is not often dealt with by her commentators) is in Hegelian and Marxist dialectics. First of all she adds an emphasis which is usually absent in psychoanalytical thought when she recognizes that both language and the "subject" can and should be seen in their varying historical forms and in direct relation to the historical conditions of existence of those forms. This insistence satisfies the demand for historicization that is crucially part of her materialist program. The theoretical possibility of such a historicization has, however, to be worked for: language, the "subject," and historical conditions are not simple terms susceptible of being easily read off from one another. The necessity of theorising their interconnectedness through dialectical thinking, however, is what Kristeva attends to. Thus she necessarily begins with Hegel's notion of negativity.

In his *Phenomenology of Spirit*, for example, Hegel sees negativity as the mediation between self and other. It is the concept which describes heterogeneity itself in the dialectic or process of self-consciousness; and thus it is what enables self-identity (the same) to distinguish and distinguish itself from the other. Equally (dialectically), the other can be defined as that which is distinguished from the self by the mediation of negativity. Kristeva proposes that for Hegel heterogeneity is the force of a certain excess within the process of the "subject's" forging a conceptually unified and securing schema of self and other; and that such a force is more or less synonymous with "liberty" or "freedom." Heterogeneity figures in the dialectic as negativity:

negativity . . . can be thought of as both the cause and the organisa-
tional principle of *process*. Distinguished from nothingness and also
from negation, negativity is the concept which represents the indissoluble relation between an 'ineffable' movement and its 'singular determination': it is mediation, that which exceeds those 'pure abstractions,' being
and nothingness. (1974, p. 101)

Kristeva thus establishes an approximate synonymy between these concepts
(heterogeneity, negativity, and freedom)[3] and argues for their function as a disturbance across the constitution of fixed notions of self and other. She then claims
that "the Hegelian conception of negativity already prepares the ground for the
possibility of thinking a materialist *process*" (p. 102). Thus, in Lenin, for instance, negativity is established as a material force and as the "necessary and objective linkage between all aspects, forces, tendencies, etc., in the domain of
given phenomena" (p. 102).

This strikes me as an all-important emphasis. First of all, this is the component
of the materialist dialectic which Kristeva wants to preserve: the principle of heterogeneity become objective process. Negativity is established, by virtue of its
excessive relation to the two major poles of Hegel's thought, as the very vehicle
of the semiotic, as an objective force which will threaten and destabilize the conceptual unity of Hegel's identitarian logic. And also, it is important that negativity
be claimed as an objective process because its mediating function will guarantee
that a determinable, and dialectically determining, linkage exists between self and
other. Without such a linkage the very possibility of the "subject" using language
to refer to the other is foreclosed upon. This is both the function and the benefit
of what Kristeva calls the forgotten fourth term in Hegel's dialectics.[4]

Some of what may well be Kristeva's most important suggestions derive from
this reading of the dialectical tradition and from her reasserting of this fourth
term. In particular two claims stand out. First she points out that

as the logical expression of objective processes, negativity can only
produce a subject-in-process. In other words, the subject constituted under this law of negativity can only be a subject crossed by negativity.
(p. 103)

Thus the required connection is made between negativity as a principle of thought
and language and the "subject's" actual constitution. She complains, however, that
the standard materialist dialectics, despite its recognition of the importance of this
process of negativity in relation to the "subject," has managed "to retain only one
element — the subject's subordination, as a unity, to socio-natural processes" (p.
103). This has been a major theoretical error because it means that Marxism
effectively has placed negativity always *outside* the "subject," recognizing only
a sub-jected social entity.

This failure of Marxism to take account of negativity in its dialectical role as linkage between the social and the actual "internal" construction of the "subject" leads Kristeva toward what is perhaps one of the most successful attempts there has been to supplement materialist dialectics with psychoanalytical thought. The concept of negativity finds "its materialist realisation [only] when, with the help of Freud's discoveries, we dare to think negativity *as the very movement of heterogeneous matter*" (p. 105). This is what Kristeva tries to do in her relating of negativity to the notion of the "subject-in-process." This leads to a second important formulation wherein she assigns a description to this objective process of the heterogeneous. The heterogeneous matter of which she speaks is, of course, language, "the border between the subjective and the objective, and also between the symbolic and the real. . . . the *material* limit against which the one and the other are dialectically constituted" (1980b, p. 107; my emphasis).

If only because of this "subject"/other relationship and its mediation by the material, concrete processes of language, Kristeva's "sémanalyse" (that is, at least, her work in the seventies) seems to me to constitute a decided challenge to other forms of both poststructuralist and materialist thought. Not only is her thinking elaborated by means of a convincing dialectics, it also manages to pay due attention to the way in which subjectivity is both constructed and lived. Kristeva has managed to take the question of the "subject" into, as it were, the embrace of materialist dialectical thought. Her affirmation that the "subject" is not just "repressed" but also "innovative" is a crucial one, especially since it is made to counter the view of subjectivity as a mechanism of pure subordination and to avoid the epistemological problems of either abstracting the "subject" or eliding it altogether.

These two operations are for her the ones conducted on the "subject" not only by most of the previous tradition of historical materialism, but also by deconstruction, and by the kinds of semiotics against which she is able to define her own "sémanalyse." In relation to deconstruction, for example, Kristeva makes the observation that "by wanting to block the thetic . . . [it] abjures the subject and is obliged to ignore its function as social practice"; Derrida's *différance* is, in other words, "a neutralisation of productive negativity" (1974, p. 130). It seems to me that this criticism is essentially just, and consonant with what I was arguing in Chapter 3. But, in any case, its articulation in Kristeva's work serves to emphasize her sense of the importance of negativity per se. In deconstructive logic, this "neutralization" of negativity is an attempt to undo the link which negotiates between identity and otherness as the mark of their indefeasibility. This negative link necessarily subvents all properly dialectical thought since it is the factor which guarantees the simultaneous movement between self and other and confirms the possibility of reference. That is, construing language as the concrete "form" of negativity, Kristeva affirms not only the possibility but also the necessity of maintaining language's referential function — without such a relationship to the other, the "subject" could have no access to or practical knowledge of either itself or the material world. Language thus must remain the edge or the mediating border where relationships between self and other are negotiated; and to ignore this is to foreclose on the possibility of acting on and changing the structures of the social.

Kristeva's criticism of deconstruction, conducted around this characteristic abnegation at its core, accompanies her arguments against some other forms or strands of semiotics. In an article which attempts to define the field and the object of semiotics in the mid-seventies, she remarks two distinct "types" of semiotics. The first she sees as

> an attempt at formalising meaning-systems by increasing sophistication of the logo-mathematical tools which enable it to formulate models on the basis of a conception (already rather dated) of meaning as the act of a *transcendental ego*, cut off from its body, its unconscious, and also its history. (1973, p. 1248)

Such a semiotics, perhaps typified at that point by the work of Umberto Eco, can indeed be seen as a kind of techno-rationalist enterprise insofar as it claims for itself the status of a science in quest of an objective description of "the social existence of the universe of signification" (Eco, 1977, p. 317). Thus "scientific" semiotic investigation is something like a marriage between, on the one side, the most dogmatic forms of historical materialism and, on the other, bourgeois science. And it's interesting to note that such a marriage is actually quite a stable one — except that its respectability demands the suppression of questions of the "subject" and of any notion of human agency. Kristeva's arguments for the inclusion of the "subject" and its constitution in semiotic analysis would prevent semiotics from becoming yet another strategy of "objectivity" and "rationality" whereby the "subject's" repression is once more guaranteed and the agent's innovative activity is once more proscribed.[5]

So far, then, I have been arguing that Kristeva's "sémanalyse" is of crucial importance for its introduction of the notion of the "subject" into a carefully theorized materialist context, for its investigation of the tensional dialectic of the subject (the mutual constraining of the semiotic and the symbolic), and for the attempt to concretize this dialectic. Especially, I have wanted to say that her reworking of dialectical thinking to the end of elaborating justifications for this concept of the "subject-in-process" offers to supply at least the ground for a materialist view of the "subject" *and* of human agency. The semiotic/symbolic prevents another recourse to a notion of the "subject" which is entirely passive.

None of this is to say that "sémanalyse" is free of its problems or that it should escape critique. For example, Kristeva's typically poststructuralist view of the materiality of language has often been objected to, and even dubbed "idealist" for apparently hypostasizing language. I'd suggest that such criticisms are less appropriate to Kristeva's work than to that of Barthes, for instance, or to the general run of poststructuralist theory which Kristeva herself criticizes (semiotics, deconstruction, etc.). There is certainly a risk in such work that, to paraphrase a suggestion of Eagleton's (1978), if language is taken to be in itself material this can entail the loss of distinction between language and its referent; that is, the referent in the world can become de-materialized. However, Kristeva's stress on the character of language as one historical and social practice among others seems to me to forestall this objection. Kristeva recognizes that, in Janet Wolff's words, linguistic signs and systems of representation "are *only* material insofar as they originate in material practices, and in their concrete appearance in texts; as systems of signification they are not" (1981, p. 65).

It might in part be as a response to the necessity of locating language in the way that Wolff suggests that Kristeva enters what I take to be another problematical argument. To say that language as concrete negativity is a practice in the social is not, as Stuart Hall has argued, "tantamount to reducing all practices to the single practice of Language" (1978, p. 120). But it is true that in order to avoid being convicted of such a reductionism Kristeva has to be able to make distinctions and be able to specify the nature of particular practices. In addressing that necessity she is led to establish artistic texts as a privileged locus in which the "form" of negativity can most easily be seen and where the tensional play of semiotic and symbolic structures can be most conveniently investigated. The justification for giving what amounts to a pre-eminence to artistic production is thin in Kristeva's work. She seems often to fall into the ideologically familiar view of the text as in some way more free, more innovative than all other discourse of practices. Of course, a case could be made for such a position without necessarily reinstalling the old humanist ideologies of literature and art; but such a case would be most effective if made in relation to what appear to be thoroughly constrained forms of artistic production, such as classic realism or Hollywood cinema. Kristeva, however, makes the case mostly in relation to avant-garde texts like Joyce's, Céline's, Mallarmé's, Artaud's, and so on. As soon as this kind of text is approached a contradiction comes to haunt Kristeva's work. That is, avant-garde texts (at least as Kristeva construes their domain) mark a distance between themselves and the question of referentiality which Kristeva has otherwise fought to retain.

This championing of avant-garde textuality becomes, as I take it, a symptom — perhaps even a cause — of what has happened to Kristeva's work in the last few years: the practices of the avant-garde have become increasingly posed as the emblem of the only kind of linguistic and thence political dissidence possible in relation to the symbolic. This happens as Kristeva turns her emphasis away from the mutually constraining dialectic between the semiotic and the symbolic, and toward a revindication of a putative priority and primacy of the semiotic. That is to say, she begins to expand the psychoanalytical basis for the semiotic/symbolic coupling and locates the semiotic much more determinedly in the pre-oedipal where it is assigned logical and ontological priority over the oedipal symbolic. This move is designed to foreground the resistant quality of the semiotic, but at the same time it "individualizes" that force, makes it transhistorical and largely removes it from the closely worked historical and materialist dialectic of the earlier work.

The fullest rationale for prioritizing the semiotic is to be found in Kristeva's *Pouvoirs de l'horreur* (1980a). This book begins with an attempt to describe something which, in the first subheading of the first chapter, is to be "neither subject nor object," but which turns out to be not negativity either. This something is what Kristeva calls "the abject"—the mark or even the expression of the crossing of the symbolic by the semiotic in the "subject" and in language. Psychoanalytical theory operates (and has operated in Kristeva's work) with its primary attention on the relation between self and other, "subject" and object. But Kristeva now claims that this emphasis is insufficient insofar as it forgets that the object as such can be recognized only by the ego—and even then only after the imposition of symbolic law in the formation of the "subject." She criticizes this forgetting, arguing that the manifestations of the semiotic, which she has tracked and located in her previous work, are in fact residual signs of something prior to the ego and thus of something that cannot be properly recognized by the constituted ego, but can only be very partially represented in the "subject." The "subject" thus experiences the abject in a way beyond or prior to object relations and thus beyond the psychoanalytical description of the "subject's" desire.

The abject is something that "disturbs identities, systems and orders. Something that does not respect limits, positions, rules. The in-between, the ambiguous, the mixed" (p. 12). But it differs from Kristeva's earlier notion of the semiotic in two crucial ways. First, it is the mark of the painful difficulty for the "subject" of being constituted in the semiotic/symbolic dialectic: it is the moment when "the subject, tired of its vain efforts to recognise itself from the outside, discovers that its impossibility is its very existence [*être*]" (p. 12). In this sense the abject is the recognition of psychical pain and thus contains an element which the semiotic did not.

Second, and related, the experience of the abject can be constituted as pain, difficulty, impossibility because it arises from the "subject's" registering or remembering its existence prior to the oedipal moment. The pre-oedipal is the object of the "subject's" primary repression; thus its "return" is traumatic. But in positing such a return, Kristeva is led to reify the existence of the *content* of primary repression. The sense of this can perhaps best be illustrated by reference to the following passage:

I picture a child who, having ingested his parents too soon, becomes afraid "all by himself," and in order to save himself rejects and vomits up everything that he is given—all the gifts, all the objects. He has, or

could have, the experience of abjection. Even before things actually *exist* for him—even before they can be signified—he ex-pells them, dominated by his drives, and he lays claim to his own territory by establishing the abject as its borders. . . . What he has ingested instead of his
mother's love is a void. (p. 13)

This passage installs the abject as a function of the child's relation to the mother's
body. It is this relation which is repressed at the moment of the child's access to
language. But in Kristeva's version here, language can be taken up "only on condition that [the subject] continually confront this 'elsewhere,' this repressive and repressed weight, this ground of an inaccessible and intimate memory: the abject"
(p. 14).

Thus the abject is akin to the semiotic—but the semiotic become a reification
of the "subject's" relation to the mother's body. This relation is then posed as the
condition of access to language. Kristeva repeats this emphasis, this prior conditioning of the "subject" by the abject, in a number of moments. Abjection is said
to register "the experience of loss logically prior [*préalable*] to both being and
object" (p. 13); it relies on the existence of "the Other who precedes me and pos-
sesses me, and who by this possession makes me exist. A possession anterior to
my future" (p. 18); it is the mark of a separation "before the beginning" and it
"confronts us with our most archaic attempts to mark ourselves off from the
maternal entity" (p. 20).

Kristeva goes on to study what she sees as the symptoms of abjection in the
history of the Judeo-Christian tradition—of which the avant-garde text is apparently the present-day expression. Her aim here is to locate simultaneously both
the preconditional status (the logical priority) of the semiotic and also the painful
history of its imperfect repression and its struggle to be expressed in the symbolic.
In other words, she attempts to chart a kind of privileged history of dissidence
in which the symbolic law represses the very condition of its own possibility. The
immediate effect of this history is to idealize the semiotic because of its having
been repressed and demeaned, and in sympathy with its pained attempt to reach
even partial symbolization.

This entails the undoing of the carefully theorized dialectic that had previously
obtained in the semiotic/symbolic pairing. The two now become much more distinct and separate; they constitute a dualism which is all the more clearly
delineated by the struggle between its two terms. It seems to be a struggle which
could be won, whereas previously it had been not so much a dualism as a simultaneous inscription and mutual regulation. In other words, the dialectical link of
negativity has been removed, with the result that the political impulse of
Kristeva's earlier work necessarily changes. Instead of replicating the formula I
quoted earlier (there can be neither "an absolutisation of the thetic. . . . [nor]
an undoing of the thetic by the fantasy of an atomising irrationalism"), Kristeva

seems to work toward a kind of quietism where the previous potential of the semiotic's transgressive force of the semiotic is embodied in the abject as desperation and ineffectiveness. The specifically disruptive effect of the forgotten fourth term is forgotten once more.

The trajectory from the earlier view of the semiotic to its reification in the symptoms of abjection is not totally dissimilar to that of Barthes—although it's still true that Kristeva does not embrace any version of the cerned "subject." Rather, she clings to a version of the "subject-in-process," but it is now imbued with a kind of pessimism and deprived of its theoretical connection to real political struggle. This change in Kristeva's theory has been accompanied by her disillusionment with various kinds of political discourses, and also by an increased emphasis on the value of individuality and its inappropriateness to concerted political effort.

One of the marks of this change is her ability, in *Pouvoirs de l'horreur*, to write quite rhapsodically about the fascistic work of Céline. She calls his World War II trilogy "an apocalyptic music" (1980a, p. 179). She sees his writing as "a tune without notes . . . the consummation of Everything and Nothing into style" by which the individuality of the "subject" is opened to "these non-states, neither subject or object, where *you* is alone, singular, untouchable, unsociable" (p. 159). The abjection of which she sees these texts as the concretization is thus given over to a vindication of pure subjectivism. Even Céline's notorious anti-Semitism is brushed off lightly: it is, apparently, "like other people's political engagement— indeed, like all political engagement, insofar as it installs the subject in an illusion that is justified only socially—a *garde-fou*" (p. 160). It ought to be sufficiently clear from these quotations what the political force of the notion of abjection actually is.[6]

Kristeva's newly formulated positions seem to have arisen from her visit to China in the early seventies and the disillusionment which her attachment to Maoism suffered on that trip. She has said that this was the end of her involvement with both socialism and feminism, and this break is marked by her privileging of individuality above collective political engagement (1983b). In the following exchange from a recent seminar Kristeva attempts to gloss this tendency:

Jacqueline Rose: . . . . your account of the political . . . is a relegation of the political to a marginal and inadequate arena of work. And in a sense your personal history . . . has a classical ring about it. It's the story of somebody who became disillusioned with politics and those very big desires for change . . . [this] leads to a move into a more personal, more individualised sphere.
Kristeva: . . . . it seems to me that if the artist or the psychoanalyst acts politically they act politically through an intervention on the individual level. And it can be a main political concern to give value to the individual. My reproach to some political discourses with which I

am disillusioned is that they don't consider the individual as a value.
(1983a, p. 27)

The question of the "value" of the "individual" is one which is not negligible
of course; indeed, it is part of the aim of this book to mark out a theoretical space
where such a question can be approached once more. But it is one thing to suggest, as Kristeva does here, that "intervention on the individual level" is a political
practice (there is no real doubt about that); and it's altogether another thing to
privilege that intervention above and beyond "political discourses" of the sort that
Kristeva now wishes to reproach. The stress on individuality cannot, in other
words, be understood as an end in itself, nor can it be taken to be logically and
historically *opposed* to political discourse, nor romanticized as suffering or mar-
tyred dissidence. Any discussion or even enactment of dissident individuality is
condemned to social marginality unless it can embrace or be embraced by more
widely insistent claims. This is what Kristeva's earlier work, which I'm subsum-
ing under the heading of "sémanalyse," itself claimed to do, but what her later
work seems to wish to avoid.

Kristeva's retrenchment into these positions is perhaps nowhere more obvious
than in her relation to feminism. It's true that Kristeva's notion of the "subject"
has been elaborated more within the horizon of Freud's bisexuality thesis than
with the aim of producing a specifically female "subject." Nonetheless the very
nature of her discussions of the "subject" in relation to language and history has
been enormously useful to feminism in its attempt to demystify and counteract
the structures and effects of masculinist power. Her linking of the semiotic to the
cultural construction and repression of "the feminine" by dint of its relation to the
maternal body has enabled some feminist thinking to critique the historical logic
of masculine privilege without conflating "the feminine" with female "subjects."
In all that, Kristeva's contribution to feminist thinking cannot be underestimated.
It is thus all the more disappointing to find her remark with some scorn that feminism is just "the latest power-seeking ideology" (1980a, p. 246) — and this in the
same book where she seems to turn a blind eye to Céline's anti-Semitism.

It seems to me, then, that Kristeva's current ideas are retrogressive in the sense
that they return to a very familiar kind of ideology of subjectivity. Even if she
has not totally abandoned a view of the "subject" as a mobile entity constructed
as it were between the semiotic and the symbolic, she has altered the significance
of such a view by relocating it within a kind of liberal humanism which defends
art and dissidence over other social practice and contestation. In other words, she
can be understood to have stated her unwillingness to engage any longer in the
kinds of social and collective struggles to which her work has nonetheless been
useful. Despite this unwillingness, Kristeva's notion of the semiotic's dialectic interaction with the symbolic and their mutually constraining roles in relation to the
"repressed" and the "innovative" in the "subject" remains by far the most sophisti-

cated attempt in the current discourses of the human sciences to account for and encourage active human agency. Equally, that attempt is explicitly bound up with the kinds of feminist critiques of the masculinist structures of power and domination which will be the topic of the next chapter. Perhaps it can be said, to finish, that Kristeva's work has been and might still be more useful for helping to demystify and counter the logic of capitalist patriarchy than her characterization of feminism as "the latest power-seeking ideology" would suggest.

Chapter 9
Feminism

Kristeva's turn away from the general political direction of her earlier work and her consequent impatience with the *"garde-fous"* of politics have been especially problematic for feminist theory, within which her work has been—and remains—especially important. There has been no shortage of attacks on her new positions and it would be merely repetitious to go through them here.[1] But at the same time some feminists have tried to salvage something, as I have just tried to do to some extent, from Kristeva's work. I want to begin this chapter by looking at one of these attempts.

Toril Moi ends her recent *Sexual/Textual Politics* (1985) with a chapter devoted to Kristeva. The overall tone and intent of Moi's book are guided by her belief that feminism currently suffers from the "absence of a genuinely critical debate about the political implications of its methodological and theoretical choices" (p. xiii). As I hope I might have established by the end of this chapter, that seems to me a quite astonishing point of view; nonetheless it is the warrant for Moi's arguments and critiques around a whole set of Anglo-American and French feminist thinkers. Moi sees herself as installing the terms of the supposedly missing debate, and she sets about her task by criticizing most of the feminists she deals with for their variously demonstrated inabilities to resist the temptation to define a specifically feminine language and a specifically feminine "subject." Moi's claim, in its strongest version, is that on the contrary there can be no politically useful notion of feminine specificity, especially not one arrived at by positing a special relation to language for women, since "there is no space uncontaminated by patriarchy from which women can speak. . . . there is simply nowhere else to go" (p. 81). Instead of the kinds of feminist thinking that she sees in operation, Moi would like to have a kind of "ideological criticism" which would address the material conditions of women's oppression under capitalist formations:

> If, as I have previously argued, all efforts towards a definition of 'woman' are destined to be essentialist, it looks as if feminist theory might thrive better if it abandoned the minefield of femininity and femaleness for a while and approached the questions of oppression and emancipation from a different direction (p. 148).

Julia Kristeva is the thinker whom Moi chooses to privilege as an example of how this "different direction" might look. But it should be noted that Kristeva emerges mostly unscathed from Moi's critical survey largely because she cannot "strictly speaking be considered a purely *feminist* theorist" (p. 149); rather, she is concerned with more general questions (or, as Moi and the left in general tend to say, "larger" questions) of marginality, subversion, and opposition. Moi's account proceeds on the assumption that this is more useful for feminism than, say, the work of Luce Irigaray or Hélène Cixous which would claim a specifically female "subject" of political practice.

Kristeva's skepticism toward the taking of political positions, her dismissal of collective feminist organization, her privileging of dissident individualism, her flirtations with anti-Semitic writing, her revindication of America, and so on—all these recent positions are rather blithely passed over in Moi's argument. Indeed, Moi's attitude toward these aspects of Kristeva's recent political choices is somewhat nonchalant. She remarks, cooly and with the illusory wisdom of much hindsight, that Kristeva's "development away from Marxism and feminism is not as surprising as it may seem at first glance" (p. 168). Apparently this is because Kristeva's thought was always tinged with "anarchist tendencies" and anarchist tendencies are just libertarianism and libertarianism is nothing but a symptom of bourgeois individualism. Despite all this, Moi is very forgiving. Her own political project needs to be able to claim some positive things from Kristeva's work (the investigations of social marginality, for instance), and this is possible, it seems, even though some of Kristeva's "most valuable insights draw at times on highly contentious forms of subjectivist politics" (p. 169).

Moi's excusing Kristeva's "subjectivism" is fairly difficult to accept, especially in a context where she also claims to be advancing the terms of a "genuine" and "materialist" political debate for feminism. However, the conclusion of her chapter on Kristeva (and thus of her entire book) takes her where such a strategy was inevitably going to lead. She ends with a long quotation from Derrida, with the arch-poststructuralist dreaming of a future where he could

> believe in the multiplicity of sexually marked voices. I would like to believe in the masses, this indeterminable number of blended voices,

this mobile of non-identified sexual marks whose choreography can
carry, divide, multiply the body of each 'individual,' whether he be
classified as 'man' or 'woman' according to the criteria of usage.
(quoted, p. 173)

Moi talks of this passage as "utopian," but in a way she is wrong to do so. It has
a place: in the narcissistic imaginary productions of poststructuralism. Thus Moi,
pretending her work to be guided primarily by the need for a materialist feminism, ends her book with the rhetoric of an entirely typical poststructuralist
public-policy statement. Her "utopia" is immaterial, turning out to be the rather
common vision of a dance of voices, the choreography of indeterminacy.[2]

I take Moi's conclusion here to be indicative of a certain difficulty in contemporary theory, feminist or otherwise: namely, its inability to think a materialist
politics without the rather hackneyed—and, not to put too fine a point on it,
naive—notion of the liberatory "free play of the signifier" (p. 172) and the always
consequent claim that "the revolution at the level of the signifier" is on hand (see
Chapter 2). More important, I think it is signal that in order to advance her arguments for Kristeva and for this extreme poststructuralist vision of indeterminate
difference beyond difference, Moi has to make a relentless critique—even a
rejection—of feminist theory in most of its recent forms. Even if the rejection of
each feminist thinker with whom Moi deals is quickly followed by an apologetic
concession to feminist solidarity, this should not be allowed to hide the fact that
Moi is ultimately attacking feminism, and doing so by confronting it with a
strange combination of the blandest clichés of poststructuralist utopianism and
rhetorical reminders of "the political." The overall effect of her work is to consistently undermine the *specificity* of feminist thought.

In what follows here, I want to make almost the opposite kind of emphasis.
I want to suggest that in its very constitution—as varied and variegated as that
might be—feminism can actually represent a fundamental challenge to the kinds
of claims which writers such as Moi make, as well as to the more general political
effects of the traditional patterns of cerning of which I have been treating so far.
My argument will be that feminism has indeed produced the hope of a political
logic and praxis which might go a long way in responding to some of the problems
that I have been worrying in this book around the question of the "subject" and
political agency.

The question of the "subject" has been a major topic for feminist theory of all
stripes over the last couple of decades. However, I think it's true to say that until
quite recently feminist investigation into and assumptions about subjectivity
revolved around two distinct, and partially contradictory, conceptual poles which
are only now being brought closer together in order to act in concert. These two
poles have often been seen as corresponding to a kind of representative division
between, on the one hand, Anglo-American feminism (with its stress on women's

experience and women's identity) and, on the other hand, French feminism (with its more psychoanalytically informed notions of female subjectivity). Indeed, this is a distinction that Moi's survey makes, just as it is a division which a book like Alice Jardine's *Gynesis* (1985) tries to mend. In its crudest forms it is stated as a division between (French) theory and (Anglo-American) practice.[3] What I will try to do here is to suggest that the division is becoming less and less clear and that, indeed, feminism's current strength resides in its coming to terms with the tensions and contradictions produced by having within itself both these manners of thinking. I will be stressing the possibly productive contradictions in this opposition out of which, it seems to me, there comes a kind of double feminist strategy perhaps capable of providing some important cues for the question of how an active political agent can be dis-cerned from the sub-jected "subject."

To approach this conflict and its effects it might first be useful to look at the way in which the notion of women's identity and experience is promoted as a fundamental feminist weapon in the field of literary studies. For over twenty years feminists, especially in America, have been attacking the masculinist literary canon for its refusal and its inability to represent women's experience. Concomitantly, women's writing itself has been championed as an at least potentially privileged locus for expressing, or place for exploring, women's experience and identity. The question of what identity women are allowed to hold in patriarchal society, and the question of what identity they might now claim have become major ones for feminists in this respect.

The claiming or reclaiming of women's identity has usually been seen as a way of fending off the exploitation, objectification, and oppression of women. In literary studies and other male-dominated institutions, this urge has given life to a two-fold enterprise, to be seen most clearly perhaps in America: first, filling in the gaps of a patriarchal tradition and history by reclaiming a women's tradition; and second, encouraging women's *active* use of the present social structures to ensure that the newly recovered women's tradition will both continue and have a continuing effect on patriarchal institutions. Thus, early in the history of the current wave of feminist literary studies, Elaine Showalter (1969) encouraged both tactics as ways of rectifying women's relation to dominant modes of literary studies and textual production, on the grounds that

> Few women can sustain the sense of a positive feminine identity in the face of [male domination of the curricula]. Women are estranged from their own experience and unable to perceive its shape and authenticity, in part because they do not see it mirrored and given resonance in literature.

Such statements have had enormous influence and effect. Promoting the positive valorization of women's *experience*, they encourage an emphasis on the installation of a new and fairer balance: the point is to reweight the literary curricula so that women can see themselves represented there. The underlying assumptions about the nature of the human "subject" here are at first sight depressingly familiar ones, relying upon a set of demonstrably humanist values and ideologies. Indeed, when taken to extremes, this kind of "humanist feminism" replicates some of the most standard mythological tenets of traditional literary criticism: some feminists can still bring themselves to speak of literature

> imitating nature by revealing its essence in imaginative language, [about] the awesome beauty of literature . . . [and of how] a modern view of the possible nobility of all human beings require that I include in my syllabus [works by women]. (Swift, 1981)

In a less Arnoldian tone, Judith Kegan Gardiner, writing specifically about women's identity, claims that

> . . . women writers *express* the experience of their own *iden-*
> *tity* . . . often with a sense of urgency and excitement in the *communi-*
> *cation* of *truths* just understood. . . . they communicate a *conscious-*
> *ness* of their identity. (1981; my emphases)

This ideology of the communication of truth, coming to consciousness, the expression of self, and so on is summed up later in Gardiner's article as the need for women's writing and criticism to ensure that "female experience is transformed into female consciousness."

One problem which immediately seems to beset feminist criticism of this sort is that the claim to identity often devolves in some fashion upon a faith in women's essential character or identity which has been chronically oppressed and suppressed by male domination. Such an identity is sometimes assumed to be the ground on which to establish the category "woman"; alternatively, indeed, "woman" is already assumed (conceptualized) by the thought which wishes to establish such a category. The latter case affirms that a "truthful" conceptualization of "woman" can be realized; and the affirmation is supposed to persuade the affirmer that the realization has already occurred. In the former case, real, "authentic" women are seen as having been put down by patriarchy in such a way that the problem of their oppression is actually one of their enforced "false consciousness" in a male world. In both cases a kind of authentic being is being imagined.

In short the goal of much of this early kind of ("American") feminist writing on literature seems sometimes to be the discovery of "woman" as some sort of "changeless essence [shining] through all the erasures of external change."[4] Much of this kind of work has been undertaken beneath the aegis — sometimes explicitly, sometimes not — of those forms of psychologism which have as their general goal the adjustment of a coherent, whole, and self-valuing ego into a society which, while seemingly structured so as to be inimical to such an ego, nonetheless relies upon its cohesion for its own proper functioning.

The assumptions here, of course, are that there *is* an identity to express, that there *are* truths to communicate, and that there can be a development of "consciousness." Insofar as such an ideology entails the establishment of the familiar cerned "subject" of humanism, it might not appear to point necessarily toward fundamental changes in the structures that we inhabit. Furthermore, if the ways of humanist thought are thought of as chronically masculinist—as indeed they are—then this form of the feminist project might seem to be inevitably compromised and to invite being caught back up into the humanistic economy, the economy of the same.

One quite frequent rejoinder to this kind of argument is that such a validation of women's experience and identity is a tactical necessity within the struggle against patriarchal power and institutions. And indeed it seems right to suggest that the valorizing of women is a necessity—perhaps the first and fundamental one—in the passes of feminist activity. But perhaps a stronger case can be made—one which does not limit the role of such valorization to a tactical and provisional exigency. The first step in such an argument would be to respond to the kinds of criticism which suggest, as Moi for example has suggested, that women's experiences and identities are limited by dint of being forged in and by patriarchy: there can be no uncontaminated place from which a female "subject" could speak or act her identity—"there is simply nowhere else to go." Moi continues to say that women's "truths" and identities can currently be represented only within a symbolic field organized on a principle of difference which works to exclude and defend against them. Thus, the possibility of women as an identifiable set of "subjects" mounting any kind of resistance to patriarchy is foreclosed upon immediately. According to such a perspective there can be no specifically female identity and therefore no specifically female agent except one committed to struggles which are in fact (as with Kristeva's current work) not specifically feminist struggles.

But in order to make such an argument, Moi and others have to forget or ignore certain fundamental—indeed, deceptively simple—truths about not only this all-embracing patriarchy, but also about feminism itself. That is, patriarchy has defined and placed women as the other with the result that, if women begin to speak and act from the same ground of cerned subjectivity and identity as men have traditionally enjoyed, a resistance is automatically effected in a sense. Women's history has not included their being regarded within patriarchy as properly full "subjects." Indeed, patriarchy has marginalized femininity as the other by means of which its own identity can be formulated and guaranteed. Thus, in the promotion of claims to women's identity there is already not only a contestation or a seeking of power, but also a contradiction at work; that is, at one important level this kind of feminism has indeed produced a form of contestatory "subject" whose demands threaten the logic of domination by a contradiction. In that light, the rejection of those theories and practices which have arisen around the demand for as it were an "equal" identity must take account of the fact that, because of the history and effective continuation of patriarchy, such demands for equality are not simply that—they also necessarily comport a threat and a resistance to dominatory structures.

This is, of course, a very basic point, even if its limitations are clear enough, both theoretically and historically. In terms of theory, there still has to be an effort to engage and critique this feminist logic of the cerned "subject" even at the point where it has the contradictory and contestatory effect that I'm claiming for it. And in historical terms, it is not altogether clear that the increasingly successful validation of women's identities has necessarily led to a sustained contestation and resistance. That is, there is room, even within feminist discourse itself, for many doubts about the actual effects of this stratagem. The institutionalization of women's studies programs in the academy, for instance, has led in some instances to a dulling of the radical edge that first produced them. Perhaps it would be true to say that this negation of contestatory energy is the result of a too sustained insistence on this rhetoric of equality, and of an ensuing assumption of the kinds of corollary values and epistemologies which patriarchal institutions promulgate. But, of course, the satisfying of the quite powerful and effective feminist demands for equality is not nothing. Thus, although the feminist appeal to the idealist notion of a cerned identity may be problematic in certain ways, it must be recognized that it has nonetheless produced significant political effects.

In terms, again, of the "subject" or the status of the human agent, many significant and significantly different theorizations of women's specific identity have been made, arising out of and elaborating upon this pragmatic strain. Feminism is constituted as a highly complex and widely diversified discourse, and one of its strengths is that it holds in tension and contradiction many different theoretical and practical propositions. Feminism is, in other words, an internally heterogeneous discourse, many aspects of which are concerned with questions of identity, subjectivity and agency. That aspect which stresses the empowered realization of a cerned identity for women has been made to work alongside other and perhaps contradictory aspects.

This question of identity particularly has undergone many elaborations by feminists. For instance, the term "identity" need not even be understood as conforming exactly to the traditional notion of the coherent and cohesive identity which historically has cerned the "subject." Rather the search for identity can equally be understood in the way that, for example, Annette Kolodny (1980) describes it: that is, as "female self-consciousness turning in upon itself attempting to grasp the deepest conditions of its own unique and multiplicitous realities." Already here the concept of identity is quite different from the idea of a "changeless essence." This definition proposes the necessity of specifying the particular *conditions* which produce a sense of identity, as well as of the fundamental multiplicity of positions into which any "subject" is called: the definition clearly no longer subvents any simple essentialism, and indeed begins to contradict notions of the "subject's" simple sub-jection.

The recognition that any theory of identity needs to be submitted to an investigation of the grounds on which it might be constructed has taken firm root by now in most feminist thinking. This is at least in part due to the influence of what is reductively known as "French feminism." The feminism which had relied upon relatively familiar, humanist theories of the "subject" has by now been supplemented by a feminism which owes much to that more radical view of the "subject" which can be read in poststructuralism and which is, more specifically, informed by the theories of Freud and Lacan. Onto the terrain occupied by the proponents of feminine identity there has come the influence of poststructuralism and its decentering of the "subject."

It is probably true to say that what is now something like a collaboration between those two aspects of feminism was a problematic tension not so long ago. The tension arose, of course, from a general suspicion on the part of feminists in regard to psychoanalysis. Many feminists saw that the definition of the female "subject" in psychoanalysis can be read as being predicated on the irremovable fixity of the phallus; that, in other words, women are situated by psychoanalytical theory just as they are by all other phallocentric institutions—in the position of other in relation to a normative and male "subject." The stick most often used by feminists to beat psychoanalysis, and Freud in particular, is this reliance upon a theory of gender difference which would establish the male as plenitude and the female as deficient in relation to that. Thus psychoanalysis is understood to posit an intrinsic, somatic and, thus, psychical inferiority in women. Throughout the 1960s—and to some extent still—that view of Freud's theories of sexuality carried a lot of weight and, as a result, psychoanalysis was often dismissed out of hand, as in the work of Kate Millett and other influential American feminists. It seems to me, however, that much of the feminist work which has made most of an impact recently has been marked (both negatively and positively) by a working through, rather than a rejection of psychoanalysis.

It is not difficult to see from where the entirely negative view of psychoanalysis has arisen. Freud's texts do exhibit exactly the normative phallocentrism of which they are often accused. On occasion, this phallocentric component is clearly a product of Freud's having to speak from within a social context that itself dictates the form of theoretical address. Even in his 1932 *New Introductory Lectures* this is the case; there, having claimed that "throughout history people have knocked their heads against the riddle of the nature of femininity," he suggests that "to those of you who are women this will not apply—you are yourselves the problem" (1964a). The historical tradition itself privileges the male as "investigator" of the feminine. (No doubt the marks of that tradition will be found in this essay too where I presume to discourse as a man on "femininity." However, I hope it will become clear that whatever criticisms of particular kinds of feminism I might allow myself to make are rooted in a desire to understand feminism and to be able to understand its role in formulating a critique of the social formations of capitalist patriarchy.)

Freud's attachment to at least the ethos of patriarchy is, as I suggested, perhaps best thought of as a historical question. His assigning to women their obligation to "react to the fact of not having received [a penis]" (1964a), or his unequivocal reference to "the fact of [women's] being castrated" (1961) cannot be thought of outside their historical context. Nonetheless these kinds of gesture remain operative in psychoanalytical theory of all stripes and even constitute a major part of its urge to establish a view of the subjective genesis in both sexes as a function of the evidential absence or presence of a penis. There is, however, room for at least a re-reading of Freud, if not a defense.

Part of that re-reading, or re-situating has been undertaken from a feminist perspective by Juliet Mitchell. Mitchell's principal argument (1975) is that, rather than prescribing a phallocentric order detrimental to women, Freud's work emerges from and more exactly describes such an order. The upshot of her argument is that in attacking Freud's supposed prescriptions feminists are led to what she sees as the politically damaging gesture of foreclosing on the concept of the unconscious and thence encouraging biologistic or psychologistic renditions of feminine identity. Mitchell's aim is to defend the radical epistemological yield of Freud's theories against the long line of his followers who, in order to overcome the difficulties set by his treatment of feminine sexuality, presuppose a natural or biological sexual division that takes precedence and pre-eminence over any unconscious process of subjective construction. The fault that Mitchell finds with such theories is that, although they are proposed as if on behalf of femininity and in order to countermand Freud's formulations of a deficiency in the female "subject," they paradoxically return to a notion of a pregiven sexuality which in no way helps explain women's oppression — much less offers practical political ways of ending it. Indeed, it might be said that such theories of the feminine stand uncomfortably close to Freud's own infamous statement that "Anatomy is Destiny." Mitchell's point is that in the debate with Freud over the derogatory implications of his theories of penis-envy and the castration complex, analysts such as Karen Horney and Ernest Jones have run the risk of distorting the project of psychoanalysis by changing it to a tendentious one: "the issue subtly shifts from what distinguishes the sexes to what has each sex got of value that belongs to it alone" (Mitchell and Rose, 1982, p. 20).

That subtle shift is what lies beneath the claims of various of Freud's commentators that sexual identity is not purely a product of the subject's passage through the oedipal stage but rather takes shape before that. By positing pre-oedipal specificity for the female "subject" and by claiming that in psychoanalysis's phallocentrism "the importance of the female organs [is] correspondingly underestimated" (Jones, 1927, p. 438), the early opponents of Freud's views began to construct an ethical path that many later analysts unhesitatingly followed, notably in the parade of American ego psychology. Jones's desire to have psychoanalysis establish a "sense of proportion" (ibid.) or fairness in dealing with female sexuality is emblematic of the liberal post-Freudian approach to concepts like penis-envy, castration, and the oedipus complex (Gallop, 1982, pp.16ff.). The ethical spirit that pervades this desire to demote the phallus from its privileged and dominant role in Freud's work is the immediate source of the feminist rejection of Freud in the 1960s; and it exhibits the same moral outrage.

Freud's own contention, on the other hand, is that the work of psychoanalysis becomes distorted through such propositions. He maintains that Jones's work, for instance, fails to "distinguish . . . clearly and cleanly between what is psychic and what is biological, [and tries] to establish a neat parallelism between the two" (quoted in Mitchell and Rose, 1982, p. 1). The result of such a parallelism would be the explanation of sexual division on purely biological grounds. The crucial psychical consequences of the imposition on the "subject" of the paternal law would then be disregarded on behalf of a liberalist claim—an ethical claim—for a kind of somatic equality or, even, equivalence.

Josette Féral, among many others, has pointed out that the feminist demand for equality, even when it is met, "implies an insufficient recognition of [women's] specificity" even though "this type of equality is no doubt a *necessary* precondition for a profound transformation of structures" (1980, p. 91). Féral is referring to socioeconomic structures, but the point can be made in relation to conceptual ones too. In terms of psychoanalysis's dealings with and definitions of femininity, the phallocentric structure has been countered by the proposition of a concentric one for women, even if it can be said that the effects of this are limited in the way I've suggested. Nonetheless, the radical conceptual changes, which come with the French feminists theorizing of women's specificity, rest upon the predicate of the concentric, as I will try to show.

Freud himself, predictably enough, suggests that in the realm of psychoanalytical inquiry "the feminist demand for equal rights for the sexes does not take us very far" (1961). The reversal or rebalancing of the phallocentric economy on the grounds of equality would ignore the way in which both male and female "subjects" are constructed within that order and on behalf of its consistency. A demand of this sort concentrates more on a conception of the static nature or status of subjectivity than on attempting to understand its social construction. Freud points out that psychoanalysis properly "does not try to describe what a woman is—that would be a task it could scarcely perform—but sets about enquiring how she came into being" (1964a). His emphasis there on the construction of the sexed "subject" allows a glimpse of the productive aspect of his thought which Mitchell, for example, wants to preserve. The genesis of subjectivity is the proper object of psychoanalytical theory, and Freud is clear that this does not permit pregiven and biological factors to be decisive. Any view suggesting otherwise will perhaps have as its corollary a certain moralism which ultimately finds its roots and guarantees in traditional humanist notions about the species, where cultural exigencies are seen as merely impositions on the natural character of the human. Against such a traditional paradigm, where the moral value of the "subject" (either male or female) is linked to the "natural" qualities of the species, and against the notions of truth and falsity implied by such thinking, Freud inaugurates an investigation of the dynamic construction of the "fiction" of sexual identity, and a deprivileging of the static economy of the "natural."[5]

This tactic of Freud's has been severely criticized by feminists such as Sarah Kofman (1980) and Luce Irigaray (1974) who are guided by the observation that the inquiry into "how she came into being" is undertaken in a historical context which still sees woman as other, as a deviation from what has been established as the normal "subject." Irigaray points out that the methodology for such an investigation would always in fact see women as the *object* of inquiry. She recognizes, too, that this object has a profoundly unsettling effect on the mode of inquiry: she claims that "especially when woman is in question, Freud's reasoning, his logic goes astray" (p. 14). He tends, for example, to talk of the "mystery" of women's sexuality, throwing the whole load of his difficulty in understanding sexuality onto the figure of femininity. At the same time he describes feminine sexuality in the pre-phallic stage as if it were the same as the masculine; in other words, the primary bisexuality that he insists on for both genders is in fact conceived of as fundamentally masculine — there is but one libido and it is male. Irigaray's point is well taken, that it is here that Freud's androcentric bias is most marked, rather than in his more controversial theories such as that of penis-envy, which at least posits a specifically feminine dimension to sexual development.

From this insight Irigaray goes on to argue against the implicitly underlying assumption in Freud's work that female pre-oedipal sexuality is finally undifferentiable, entirely subsumed under the norm of the masculine. In other words, Freud's theory of subjectivity is underwritten by a view of undifferentiated male drives so fundamental that femininity can be discerned only at the oedipal stage: before the oedipal moment every "subject" is masculine.

During the course of her arguments with Freud's texts in *Speculum de l'autre femme* (1974) Irigaray asks the same question of Freud as do Jones and psychologistic feminism: what do women have that is specific to them? When she asks rhetorically why Freud did not consider womb-envy or breast-envy, she operates with the same reversal in mind that prompts Jones's call for "fairness" and his introduction into the debate with Freud of the notion of a specifically feminine libido. The term *concentric*, coined by Béla Grunberger (1964), marks such a trend, opposed as it is to the phallocentric in a simple reversal. The concentric is that which is regarded as specifically feminine in the unconscious and is used in reference to female pre-oedipal sexuality and its organization.

Ultimately, in Jones, this specificity is founded upon somatic detail: there is a biological determination of sexuality through the sexed organs. Irigaray, however, even while adopting much the same kind of tactic as Jones, is perhaps less concerned than he to ask the "ethical" question of what women have of value that is specific to them. Rather, she can be understood as addressing a more general question to Freud's methodology and its logic. That is, she is asking why Freud's thought has finally to return to a primarily masculine definition of the species and to not exactly a marginalization of femininity but rather an elision of it altogether. With this emphasis it is possible to read Irigaray's effort as being concerned more with promoting a different kind of logic for thinking gender—a logic which would take its cue from the establishment of something like a concentric organization, but whose aim would be the dismantling of the logic of opposites altogether.

This would help explain the fact that her references to the specificity of the female body are cast differently from those of the post-Freudians. Whereas Jones will build his ideas of the concentric by reference to the visible genital differences between males and females, Irigaray talks of somatic differences in a very different way. In particular, she includes the whole female body in her attempt to draw up what she calls "a somatic scenography" (1974, pp. 155–56) of femininity. Thus, femininity is not confined and delimited in its somatic referent in the same way as it is in the liberal "ethical" argument. Irigaray instead operates a philosophical and oppositional attempt to think of the female body beyond the terms of the inequality of same and other, *as well as* beyond the terms of the equality of phallocentric and concentric. The necessity, in other words, is not just to reinstall the female body into the male economy as a kind of provocative rhetoric, but equally to re-view it in such a way that it cannot be reduced or appropriated by the phallicism of the language in which it has traditionally been thought. She is, in other words, attempting to conceptualize difference outside the terms of the phallus.

Even where Irigaray's reference is to female sexual organs, the same kind of effort is apparent. Her somewhat infamous descriptions of women's sexuality are a good example:

> Woman is in touch with herself, touches herself all the time without anyone being able to forbid it, because her sex is made of two lips continually kissing. So, within herself she is already two—but not divisible into one—and they stimulate each other. (1977, p. 25)

These "two lips continually kissing" represent, as Jane Gallop has argued, not even a description of the female body in masculinist, "phallological" terms:

> In phallo-logic the female genital is either a clitoris, phallic-same, or a vagina, phallic-opposite. . . . This either-or, same or opposite, always

seen according to phallic parameters, has constituted the alternatives for
the representation of female genital anatomy. . . . Irigaray seems to be
advocating a female sexuality that replaces the anxious either-or. . . .
ultimately choosing *not both but neither*. (1983, p. 81)

That is to say that, if it is the symbolic trap which persuades us that there is no
identity but by way of the phallus, we might be able to alter the dictates of the
symbolic by refusing to be reduced in our bodies, male or female, to the description it proffers. Irigaray's aim is thus not quite to claim a privileged essence for
women's "two lips" but to propose a radically different construct (or a radical construct of difference). She puts forward not a dualism, nor actually a reference to
any empirical body, but an attempt to displace altogether the terms of phallological discourse which has proscribed the female body because of its threatening and
irreducible otherness.[6]

Irigaray's view of the female "subject," then, is that there is not and has not
been such a thing permitted in the purview of masculinist discourse: that discourse, because of its own constitution, is unable to *specify* femininity. A woman
can thus only speak there either *as if* a man (miming the discourses of patriarchy),
or as a "subject" without specificity, without her own language. Thus women's
efforts to speak and to change patriarchy must first be subvented by a sense of
their own specific identity, and Irigaray suggests that this identity can itself be
funded by reference to a somatic specificity. These propositions have caused
Irigaray to be rejected for her supposed essentialism, as well as for her apparent
vindication of separatism. However, the charge of essentialism—common as it
is—does not necessarily or always amount to the damning criticism it is supposed
to be. Within the logic of feminism's still evolving constitution essentialist claims
are perhaps becoming more and more important. Just as the vindication of female
identity in the forms of feminism discussed above can constitute an automatic resistance on the part of the female "subject," so too does essentialism mark a moment of contestation.

Doubtless both political and conceptual risks attend this moment of resistance,
and the discussion of those risks and of how to mollify them is currently one of
the most urgent items on feminism's agenda. The desire, for example, to posit
a sexual identity for women which is not constituted in relation to the phallus but
which exists rather in or as a result of the pre-oedipal, while it is still to be considered something like the "necessary precondition" (Féral) to larger theoretical forays against patriarchy, is still open to the various charges: of essentialism, of
returning women to an extra-symbolic role, of equating women with only their
bodies, of constructing a dualism between a "natural" femininity and a "civilized"
masculinity, and so on.

Indeed, these charges have been made, and often bitterly, by various
feminists. As Monique Plaza points out in a thorough critique of Irigaray (1978),

western phallocracy has shown itself almost infallibly capable of depreciating any form of activity, process, or being that it can equate with the "natural." Or, to put it another way, the physical being of those who are physically appropriated is always given by the oppressors as the absolute *cause* of the oppression. And when those physical characteristics are extended to become psychical characteristics and then become the emblems of the great unfathomable mysteries of human existence, the same is even more the case. The essentialist "subject" is a priori susceptible to the male tendency to regard as infantile and worthless that which it has already designated as uncontrollable and unknowable. The same kind of warning as Plaza offers is repeated by the editorial collective of the journal, *Questions Féministes*:

> It is worthwhile to expose the oppression, the mutilation, the functionalization and the objectification of women's bodies . . . it is also dangerous to put the body at the center of a search for female identity. Furthermore, the notions of Body and Otherness merge easily since the most evident difference between men and women is indeed the difference in their bodies. That difference has been used to justify total domination of one sex over the other. (1981, p. 218)

These kinds of criticisms from within feminism are not inconsiderable, but they might well be seen as tactical reminders of the fact that the conservativism of which their targets have made use can return to haunt them. Even though, as I have suggested, such criticisms tend to underplay the first and oppositional moment in which the claim to identity consists, and even though something like Irigaray's reference to the female body is finally not to be understood as essentialist in any familiar way, both of the remarks quoted point to some basic problems in the project of discerning a specifically female "subject." Such a "subject" is, if not necessarily, then at least potentially available to reappropriation by the masculinist economy. Women winning equality are certainly empowered, but still within the masculine economy which underwrites that power; equally, women identified with their bodies are already the other for patriarchal logic. Clearly there is a need for continued theoretical work and vigilance in order to counter the appropriative capacities of the dominatory structures.

At any rate, it becomes important that not all of feminism's strategies rest entirely on these kinds of claim. If the "subject" of "equality" and the radically decentered but somatically located "subject" already act together as a mixed and partially contradictory element in feminist strategizing and theorizing, other efforts will be added to what can still be considered these "necessary preconditions" for radical change. For instance, whereas Irigaray's view of the female "subject" is often somewhat depressive, stressing more often than not its impossibilities, a writer like Hélène Cixous offers a much more celebratory view of femininity — almost a utopian view indeed.

Cixous's best known text in the Anglophone countries is probably "The Laugh of the Medusa" (1981). There Cixous appears ostensibly to take it for granted—by Lacan, primarily—that the symbolic world is a phallocentric organization constructed in the tight knot of "a libidinal and cultural—hence political and typically masculine—economy" (p. 249). Her argument with Lacan, however, and the source of her utopian project, is involved with the question of women's relation to language. She rejects the Freudian/Lacanian proposal that women are *necessarily* in a negative relation to the symbolic. She wants that phallological economy to be, as she puts it, *dépensé*, dépensé as in un-thought, de-thought; and also dépensé in the sense of spent, and spent by the production of a new feminine discourse. Spending refers at the same time here to the orgasmic energy of women's bodies—spending without end, spending without reserve (as Derrida might say)—so that libidinal as well as economic structures are to be undone at one fell swoop of the female body.

Cixous wants, then, to expose the male economy to a run, an uncontrollable effusion that will cause the collapse of all the stocks and entail the devaluation of the phallic stakes toward the structuring of a new economy. As Jane Gallop says, for Cixous "the heroine is she who breaks something . . . compromise attaches to the one who is shut up" (1982, p. 136). That is, the woman shut up in her room, or enclosed and silenced in a putative identity, is imprisoned by the male economy. For Cixous, if the "subject" is formed in language and is never definitively fixed, always a constant flux beyond cohesive identity, then the destructuring of the language will forge new "subjects"—in this case women, continually opening up the symbolic and expressing themselves away from the base of identity.

It is perhaps not very surprising that "The Laugh of the Medusa," when printed in the anthology *New French Feminisms*, was placed in the section on "Utopias," and her whole project has been described by Elaine Showalter as "a significant theoretical formulation" of the question of women's relation to language, but one which is addressed to "a Utopian possibility rather than an actual literary practice" (1979, p. 185). Cixous's celebratory, sometimes almost mystical writing predicates future possibilities on the disruption of all notions of psychic identity and, in that it refuses to fall back onto the idea of a primary or core identity, provides a powerful accompaniment to humanist feminist notions of cerned subjectivity. She claims that there is no firm and capacitating self for the "subject" to express, but only relations to an overbearing symbolic world and thus relations to a language that needs to be broken and destructured, or "dépensé," exhausted.

Utopian projects, as I have suggested before in this book, are more than a little problematic. Especially, I have discussed the problems that attend the notion that new forms of subjectivity will come into being through changes in discursive practices (see Chapter 2). But with Cixous there is another difficulty: in her urgency and through the undoubted necessity of establishing for women a better access to cultural modes, she is led to presuppose a category "woman" as the end of her practices. Not only is the teleological impulse somewhat idealist here, but also Cixous might be said to fall into a trap of another kind of fixed identity from the one she is ostensibly countermanding. Although she does not rely upon a fixed female psychical identity, she fixes "woman" as a function of the female body in a way perhaps more extremely than Irigaray. She almost mystically conceives of women's bodies as an infinitely capacious medium of endless orgasmic pleasure: "woman's body . . . a thousand thresholds of ardor" (1981, p. 256). And the "value" of this special kind of body resides in its unique relation to language: "More so than men who are coaxed toward social success, toward sublimation, women are body. More body, hence more writing" (p. 257). She would unproblematically attach "woman's body" to what Lacan says corresponds to desire itself, namely, the metonymic axis of language where there is a free run of signifiers never impeded by the imposition of the signified.

When Lacan establishes the assignation of the two poles of language described by Jakobson, metonymy and metaphor, to desire and the law, respectively, his claim is that no meaning can exist for the "subject" outside of the imposition of the metaphoric axis upon the metonymic. That is to say, desire in language can never be totally uninhibited: the signifier must at some point be halted and anchored, albeit temporarily and arbitrarily. Language's functioning between the metonymic and metaphoric axes entails that neither male nor female "subject" is free of language's laws in the production of meaning. However, in presupposing the utopian category "woman" Cixous simply affirms the existence of a new entity whose specification is the very function of that affirmation and of a set of unactualized practices in language. Here her statement or slogan "Her flesh speaks true" (p. 251) might be nothing more than an imposition of utopian will, colluding with the multiple uses of future and conditional tenses in Cixous's work.

Although I'm stressing Cixous's relation to psychoanalysis, it can be seen, as Alice Jardine points out, that

> Cixous's 'primary text' is Derrida . . . her primary theoretical weapon
> is 'deconstruction.' But Cixous has gone a step further than Derrida
> could or would have wanted to go: she has incarnated Derrida's 'femi-
> nine operation' by and in women. She has named Derrida's 'writing-as-
> feminine-locus': 'feminine writing.' (1985, p. 262)

Derrida's using the feminine as a privileged cipher, or his allegorizing the figure of femininity in the working through of "différance" has always seemed to me much less interesting and acceptable than it does to many of his followers, but the adoption of deconstructive methods is not uncommon in feminism.[7] Cixous's use of deconstruction sets different problems and questions than do most. Certainly she cannot be said to fail in the way that Derrida does (as I suggested in Chapter 3, by refusing to entertain the notion of agency and by denying responsi-

bility for his theories): Cixous's work is not only explicit in its uses of psychoanalytical theory but is, more important, highly politically motivated.

Yet, criticisms of Cixous might be made around the fact that, in a way quite
unlike deconstruction, her stated determination to go beyond modes of thought
constructed in "a two-term system, related to 'the' couple man/woman" (1981, p.
91 & n.) does finally posit some kind of unity—the unified space of women's privileged relation to the imaginary: it is a coherence of the imaginary that holds in
place all the deconstructive forays against the male symbolic. The female "subject" she construes is centered at the level of the imaginary, but dispersed in its
relations to language and the structures of male domination. In this regard Cixous
might well be the model of feminism's contradictory doubled strategy. However,
the female "subject" in this schema is constructed by way of a certain stratifica-
tion: dispersal and disruption at the level of the "subject's" operations in the symbolic, subvented however by a coherence at the unconscious level (in the imaginary). In other words, although Cixous's "primary text" might well be
deconstruction, the effects of that primary text are offset by the influence of psychoanalysis. But it is a use of psychoanalysis that understands an internal coherence of the "subject" which is timeless and essential. Thus, even though its essentialism is of an unfamiliar kind—a sort of essentialism of the imaginary—Cixous's
writing does indeed bring up again that old specter.

But as I have been suggesting, neither the conceptualization nor the project of
essentialism in feminism is ever unmixed or carried out in isolation. In this regard
Gayatri Spivak has recently supplied feminism with a kind of rallying call by suggesting that women "take the risk of essence" in order to increase the substantive
efficacy of feminist resistance.[8] Spivak's quoting, in support of some similar positions in her article "French Feminism in an International Frame" (1981), a number of statements by the French socio-biologist Evelyne Sullerot, underscores this
exhortation, but also shows *how* such a "risk" must be run. Sullerot suggests that
feminist interpretative systems have to be built from "observations based on
reality"—specifically on the fundamental recognition that "one is in fact born a
woman" (Sullerot 1981, pp.157–588). This rather basic reminder—that in more
general terms "the human species . . . is cultural by its very nature" (p. 158;
sic.)—constitutes a call toward a crucial component in the task of thinking the human "subject" in any context: that is, historicization. The notion of women's
specificity—even when understood to be rooted in the female body—is always to
be submitted to the demands of historical analysis, the materialist counterweight
to essentializing claims. Thus, the "risk of essence" becomes already a more complex proposition.

I suggested before that feminism was currently attending in a close manner to
precisely the multiplication of its positions (of its feminism*s*). Thus some of the
most self-conscious of current feminist thinking is concerned with actually theorizing this double strategy. In fact the strategy is something more like a quadru-

pled one; there is simultaneously an attack on traditional and masculinist notions of the cerned subject, along with the revindication of female specificity; and there is the embracing of fairly familiar poststructuralist notions of the decentered subject, as well as an increasingly frequent attempt to halt the tropological turns of that radical decentering.[9] There is in all this a recognition that neither the moment of forging a fixed "subject" nor the moment of that "subject's" dispersal is sufficient, and that both have to work at once in the service of feminism's political aims. This, I think, is something like what Jane Gallop is getting at when she says that

> Both psychoanalysis and feminism can be seen as efforts to call into question a rigid identity that cramps and binds. But both also tend to want to produce a "new identity," one that will now be adequate and authentic. I hold the Lacanian view that any identity will necessarily be alien and constraining. But I do not seek some liberation from identity. That would lead to another form of paralysis—the oceanic passivity of undifferentiation. Identity must be continually assumed and immediately called into question. (1982, p.xii)

Such multiplied versions of the "subject" help form the heterogeneity of feminism's internal constitution in aid of concerted political action.

Currently, then, it seems as if feminism's most successful strategy against patriarchy comes in the form of a simultaneous registering of these differing strands and their concomitant claims in regard to the female "subject." This "doubling" within feminist discourse and practice precludes the possibility that either the cerning or the decentering view of the "subject" should stand pre-eminent. The doubled constitution of feminism involves not only a valorizing of women—and avoiding or being very circumspect about the way in which such valorization can be recuperated—but also a continued working on the production of alternative notions of the female "subject." This further but simultaneous analysis not only remarks and exploits the contradictions inherent to dominant social structures, but also treats of its own contradictions and exploits them too.

Another description of this kind of doubled strategy has been put forward by Gayatri Spivak who suggests that feminism can best advance by seeing itself as a practice that will be both against sexism and for feminism:

> *against* sexism, where women unite as a biologically oppressed caste; and *for* feminism, where human beings train to prepare for a transformation of consciousness. (1981, p. 170)

Spivak's proposal is an important exemplum of what I am describing— the tactic of doing two or more things at once, or of putting ostensibly contradictory but overlapping items on the agenda. Spivak does not elaborate upon how these two efforts might be articulated together. It can be suggested, however, that their articulation is being made both at the level of the women's movement itself and at the level of theorizing the feminist "subject" in such a way that the kinds of subjective organization I have been proposing in this book came to be reflected in the movement itself.

That is, I have suggested that the "subject" is continually called upon to take on the marks of multifarious subject-positions but that it is nonetheless incapable of colligating these positions without contradiction (even by means of accepting the interpellation into the position of whole and coherent "self," the ideology of unity). This contradiction, or whole set of contradictions, and the negativity which underpin them and produce them are what releases the "subject" from perfect self-identity, homogeneity, and fixity. And yet the "subject" cannot subsist in radical heterogeneity. As Laclau and Mouffe point out:

> the analysis [of the subject] cannot simply remain at the level of dispersion, given that 'human identity' involves not merely an ensemble of dispersed positions but also the forms of overdetermination existing among them. (1985, p. 117)

Whereas Laclau and Mouffe talk about overdetermination as a principle of colligation among subject-positions, I would say rather more simply that what binds subject-positions together is precisely their difference. That is, the contradictions between them are a product of the negativity which enjoins the "subject" to construct, recognize, and exploit difference. It is negativity which also and simultaneously produces the human agent.

Thus, in relation to the constitution of feminism as a concerted social movement, it is perhaps possible to see writ in large there the kind of "internal" subjective constitution that I have been describing. Moreover, it seems to me that the actual "subject" that feminism is in a position now to discern is very much akin to what I have been calling the agent. At the junctures of feminism's variously posed and differently constructed propositions, a properly feminist agent can be discerned. At the interstices between a humanistically identified "subject" and some more radical or utopian and dispersed "subject," both notions operate in a mutually enabling dialectic, bound together by their very contradictions or by the negativity that underpins their heterogeneity. Understood in this context, contemporary feminist theory could perhaps be regarded as a project which recognizes that its aims would scarcely be met by either the positing of a fixed identity or the conjuring of some new and dispersed "subject." And in this respect it is almost unique—and thus salutary—among the various discourses of resistance.

If two of the more distinct (by virtue of being larger) targets of this book have been (a) the notions of fixed and cerned subjectivity inherited from traditional humanist thought in a most unexpected way by many of our currently available oppositional discourses, and (b) the poststructuralist fantasy of the dispersed or decentered subject, it might appear perverse of me to be advocating feminism's deployment of both. However, it must be remembered that I'm describing the deployment of both *simultaneously*. The effect of feminism's double-play is demonstrably to have broken down the old habit of *presuming* the "subject" as the fixed guarantor of a given epistemological formation, as well as to have cast doubt on the adequacy of the poststructuralist shibboleth of the decentered "subject." My claim, then, is that the human agent can be dis-cerned from the "subject" (indeed, perhaps the notion of the "subject" can altogether be abandoned) at the point where the contradictions between different ideas and positions of the "subject" are recognized and privileged; that is, at the point where the negativity contained in and by social discourses and systems is once again allowed the right to work.

Chapter 10
Responsibilities

(0) Both within the academy and without, feminism's critique of patriarchal culture has been perhaps the most effective and sustained contestatory discourse of the last twenty years or so. Thus its "double strategy" of which I spoke in the last chapter must be instructive. Feminism, so it seems to me, has been able to recognize the operations of subjectivity and ideology in a way at once more sophisticated and more appropriate to contemporary conditions than most of the other discourses or oppositional movements which have arisen in those years. The "subject," in the widest catchment of feminist discourse, has been formulated both in terms of its experience as dominated "subject" and also as an active and contestatory social agent.

By dint of this acceptance of the doubled nature of the "subject's" existence, feminism provides a view which counters the long and continuing history of (phallocratic) cerning of the "subject." What's important here is that this paired subject-and-agent in feminism derives from the "subject's" obeying the logic of its own oppression. That is, the interpellation of the "subject" into oppressed positions is not complete and monolithic; rather, interpellation also produces contradiction and negativity. The necessary existence of various and different subject-positions in the interpellated "subject" produces resistance to the logic of domination while still being in a sense part of, or a by-product of, that logic.

Feminism seems to have been successful in mobilizing such resistance in part because feminist discourses and politics have been consistently wary of constituting women as a homogeneous group or class and thence of assigning that grouping a pre-signified historical role. In relation to the discourses and practices which it supersedes and counters, then, feminism can be seen as precisely a difference. Feminism speaks not only for women as a *heterogeneous* grouping, but also against the homogenizing logic of masculinist domination. In addition it recognises that such a logic is not necessarily enacted by male "subjects" only (that is, female "subjects" can be its bearers too). The "enemy" for feminism, therefore, is more the institutions, logics, and discourses of the patriarchy than the real people who inhabit it. Thus feminism's allies are not perforce women only—nor to be sure, *all* women. But another component and instructive feature of feminism's difference, and a consequence of its heterogeneity and fluid constitution, is that at its best moments it need not be *exclusive*. That is to say, since there is no necessary a priori grouping, there need be none of the dramas of expectation and disappointment, or charges of betrayal which so often seem to attend the spectacle of pre-constituted classes or groups failing (inevitably perhaps) to live up to their pre-signified historical tasks or roles. There is thus a possible and productive disparity between the "subject" and object of feminism, between its self-constitution and its other.

It could well be argued that what I have just described is merely an idealizing interpretation of feminism's character; and that the history of the movement over the last twenty years would in fact produce many counter-instances and illustrations. This may indeed be true. But my point is that the *effect* of feminism *might* be as I have described; or, at least, I understand feminism to be capable of this effect. Most relevant here perhaps is the way in which feminism seems to have been articulated across the terms of what *pragmatically* has nearly always seemed to be an impossibility: heterogeneity and singularity in internal constitution still managing to produce concerted opposition to material and definable oppressions.

The "subject" of feminism's self-constitution, the agent of feminism's contestation is thus exemplary exactly because of its paradoxical articulation.

(1) The tendency and possible force of such a contradiction or paradox is what I have tried to adumbrate in all the chapters of this book.

After reading a draft of the early parts of the book, a colleague wanted to know: "So where *is* the subject?" For the most part I've wanted to not answer this question; rather I've intended to displace it. My complaint against many of the discourses of the human sciences is that the term "subject" is used there with an unwarranted confidence (even abandon), and that a certain complacency (sometimes even a marked complicity with the traditional structures of domination) is evident in that use. It has been my claim that all the discourses I have focused on presume and construct their appropriate "subject" in a way which ultimately leaves little room for consideration of resistance. If this claim is plausible, then there is nothing very encouraging about these contemporary discourses; indeed, very little can be learned from them, unless it be that a certain conservativism resides at their epistemological base, even in despite of their sometimes radical claims. In many of its current uses and roles, then, the term "subject" is a mere abstraction destined to designate nothing other than a purely dominated entity. And this is due, as I've suggested many times, to an inability to think of subjectivity beyond the parameters of the traditional mechanisms of what I've called cerning—a mechanism which has served the logic of domination and which has upheld phallocratic power for centuries.

Such a logic is predicated upon theories wherein the "subject" is a cerned entity or concept. Furthermore, as Luce Irigaray has claimed, "we can assume that all theories of the subject have been appropriated by the masculine. When she submits to (such a) theory, woman fails to realise that she renounces the specificity of her relationship to the imaginary. She subjects herself to objectification in discourse—by being "female" . . . [But] once it is imagined that woman imagines, then this object loses its fixed and obsessive character . . . [and then] what support remains for the existence of the subject?" (1974 p. 165)

Irigaray's formulation here could stand in effect as the admonitory epigraph for much of this book, objecting to the abundant totalizing and cerning theories of the "subject" in contemporary discourses and also positing feminist thinking (or imagination, more exactly) as an explicit resistance to all that. However, it seems to me not necessary, nor quite advantageous, to propose feminism (the attempt to rid women of their objecthood) as the only—or even the sufficient—contestatory discourse and practice. Part of my project has been to suggest merely that some feminist thinking and feminist practice has found ways toward solving problems which seem to me urgent ones. Feminism's instruction, its example, might be carried, not to what the left tends often to think of as "larger issues," but into the context of other kinds of theory and other kinds of struggle. My suggestion is that for progress to be made in that context all notions of the "subject" as essentially subjected and dominated need to be questioned, rejected for their incompleteness, and exploited as a basis for complaint and resistance.

So I don't mean to hypostasize feminism, nor yet to idealize it; and I certainly don't want my comments to be thought of as yet one more attempt to appropriate it. I hope, by the same token, to avoid the rather common (masculine) tendency of seeing feminism as altogether humanizing or salvational. Any of these routes would inevitably lead to the assimilation of feminism's specific energy into yet another totalizing discourse. But at the same time it would appear pointless to ignore the success that feminism has achieved in balancing the theoretical demand for the simultaneous privileging of both its "subject" and its active agent. That is to say, the force of one of feminism's older slogans—that the personal is the political—is crucial, even if it sometimes gets understood rather too simplistically. But as a lesson, such a slogan can be taken into other discourses, other contexts.

The formulation and formation of other oppositional practices and discourses within this kind of ethic are, of course, underway. One thinks immediately of the various ecological, anti-nuclear, and peace movements in both Europe and North America. Equally one thinks of the political groups which have recently been seceding from and doing battle with their old hosts in traditional party political organizations: the Rainbow Coalition in the United States or the left-wing of the British Labour Party are, it is to be hoped, just the avatars of this kind of movement. Such tendencies are being proposed and analyzed also at the level of theory. For instance, some of what I have been suggesting might find a certain resonance in Ernesto Laclau's and Chantal Mouffe's (1985) recent attempts to theorize the articulation of radical democratic demands. Their work, particularly in its ability to mark its distance from the older leftist idea of "alliance politics," redefines some of the theoretical problems traditionally associated with the articulation of heterogeneous political groupings and their demands.

One of those problems has been the demand that any given group should both maintain and profess an internal consistency, and the ensuing claim that this consistency should be reverenced even in interaction with other, perhaps contradictory, consistencies. As one possible response to such a problem feminism, maintaining a certain internal heterogeneity and contradiction while still producing solidarity and concerted action, can be considered exemplary.

Thus, perhaps feminism's hard-won successes can be seen — without idealizing or homogenizing "feminism" itself — as an avatar of multiple and even contradictory, but always positive, contestations construed in a kind of emulsion of differences.

(2) In my introduction I warned that the argument of this book would not necessarily be constructed in a conventionally linear and logical manner, leading up to a punctual conclusion. Indeed, in a way the argument can best be described as having been carried on as a series of raids from a mobile base. The targets have been multifarious, but the aim has been consistently that of countering the unificatory discourses on the "subject" that surround and inform many of the current practices in the human sciences. The principle, or ethic, has been one of non-unity, and of non-narrative, even of contradiction in internal constitution. But the book has been guided also by a recognition that it is necessary to address a concerted critique to the logic of domination which can be understood as the powerful and empowered effort to suppress such heterogeneity by establishing categories such as the "subject."

Indeed, as I suggested in my discussion of Julia Kristeva's work, it is the principle of negativity, the form of heterogeneity, that enables the maintenance of contradiction and difference at the same time as it prevents or inhibits submission to the categorical demands of the social symbolic order.

(3) The positive thesis that I want to draw from the largely critical readings I've conducted is perhaps nothing especially original but rather something more in the

order of a reminder. The simple and material existence of contradiction in the subject/individual renders both components of that unwieldy term somewhat problematical. The difficulty I have experienced in finding any more distinctive, less problematical or more graceful vocabulary to dscribe the disposition of the terms "subject," "individual," and agent is indeed a symptom of the questions I've been taking up. There is always contradiction in the "subject"; there is no warrant to accept the cerning inherent to the notion of the "individual"; and the agent is never *only* an active force, but also an actor for the ideological script.

I have therefore had recourse to the idea of subject-positions as a reminder of the subjective effect of the symbolic order in the construction (limiting and enabling) of human activity. But such a notion is quite incomplete. It needs to be supplemented at least by a proper recognition of the negativity which both binds and unbinds those subject-positions. So the "subject" is constituted heterogeneously and is continually changing. But it is those changes themselves and that heterogeneity which are the problem for most theories of subjectivity (either implicitly or not) and which are repressed there more often than not.

The "subject" subsists, as it were, amid all this flux, movement, and change through the *process* of negativity itself. Thus the colligation of subject-positions, far from entailing a fixed or cerned "subject," is effected precisely by the principle which stands against unification—negativity, the forgotten fourth term of Hegel's dialectics.

(4) The current strength and radically conservative character of contemporary social structures and their discourses in the west (and especially in the United States) derive at least in part from their consistent and continuing ability to address their claims to "subjects"; and from the fact that they can still promulgate ideologies of the "subject" in a relatively uniform—that is, overarching—manner.

However, the exploitation of negativity and contradiction in social practice is in fact now one of the most important tactics of the dominant apparatuses. In an age when actual political and administrative practice is perhaps more than usually disjunct from people's lives, dominant discourses about the social and analyses of the social no longer assume the need for logical coherence, internal consistency (or even the humanist corollary of those things—relative honesty and relevance). It would seem that the new right has understood how crucial a component of political and ideological force contradiction really is.

At the same time, the power and efficacy of contradiction are seemingly unlimited when played out against the backdrop of a morally informed conception of the "subject"—where, that is, a traditionally cerned "subject" stands in as the cover for contradiction. In other words, in the era ushered in by the likes of Reagan and Thatcher, the public sphere has made a virtue of its own internal contradictions, but equally has tried to counter (or cover) such contradiction by projecting homogeneity onto its "subjects"—and, increasingly it seems, literally legislating for that homogeneity and by many routes trying to tighten up on the traditional formations of the citizen-subject. Thus an overarching or resolutory discourse of the cerned "subject"—the dominated "subject" of all kinds of other discourses of domination—comes to stand guard over and neutralize both the heterogeneity of real "subjects" and also the epistemological contradictions from which these ideological efforts arise. Notions such as those drawn from familiar conservative moralities—the championing of self-interest, enterprise, and ambition, the revindication of the family, anti-homosexuality, religious fundamentalism, state control of marginal social activity, and so on—are perhaps the most commonplace marks of such a neutralizing discourse by which the idea of the traditional cerned "subject" is encouraged and enforced once more.

This would all seem to suggest that what I wanted to identify as the positive thesis to be drawn from my readings in this book is already at work: its features have been installed—albeit in negative ways—into the practices of the new right's contemporary form of warfare against difference, against people. But here, as always, it is the major task for oppositional discourse to keep the book open: that is, to refuse more than ever the lure of this new cerned "subject" by laying claim once again to the very principle of heterogeneity that has been appropriated by the new right.

(5) To exploit the negativity which, as I've claimed, constitutes the links of the "subject's" colligations is not to privilege the action of resistant or rebellious will. It is, rather, to try to locate within the "subject" a *process*, or a tension which is the product of its having been called upon to adopt multifarious subject-positions. This is the process whereby the "subject's" contradictory constitution is given over to the articulation of needs and self-interest.

For anyone, the question of self-interest is to a certain and necessary extent one of conscious calculation. But this is a calculation that cannot be considered as wholly an activity of consciousness; it cannot consist, for example, only in what Giddens has called "reflexive monitoring of action" (1982, p. 31), which *is* necessarily a conscious process. Rather, it must be regarded as being continually crossed by unconscious components—desire, memory, repressions, anxieties, and so on. Equally, and according to the logic of the unconscious, its articulation will bear the traces and the marks of such components of thought and language.

This is not to imply the hopelessness of achieving and articulating the calculation of self-interest; it is just to suggest that, like any other production of meaning or any other form of articulation, it is best considered as an ultimately unfixable process whose meaning is not unproblematically available. However, the actions that arise from such a process are themselves significant in the simple sense that they must enter into the world of signification; they achieve and exhibit their meaning primarily there. This is clearly the case whatever their intent or purpose might be, and whatever "reflexive monitoring" might be applied to them.

Any "subject's" motives and intentions are bound up with—indeed, in part built up by—a singular history. That is they are to be seen as firmly implicated into a particular "internal" constitution which is subvented by what is sometimes called the "subject's self-narrative." The "subject's" actions, on the other hand, are also and equally engagements or interventions in everyone else's history and have real effects there. These two histories cannot be construed as separate, of course. They are mediated in a dialectical process as the "subject" negotiates its self-interest in relation not only to itself, but to the world.

But the notion of self-interest is not being proposed here as in any sense the origin of, or final explanation for, the actions of a living person as they intersect with the actions, discourses, and representations of others. Rather, the "subject's" self-interest is in part what has to be articulated in an inevitably complex way in order for someone to be able to act at all. In this sense the active "subject" is always caught in the process of engaging the world and itself *simultaneously*.

Self-interest, since it is formed through negativity, since it has to run the gauntlet of the contradictions among subject-positions, and since it must be articulated through discourse and interaction, is unavoidably a negotiation: there is no pure self-interest, but only the quite ragged process of articulation and negotiation of histories. Such a negotiation is a *social* one; it can never be thought of as given over entirely to the demands of what I'm calling the "subject's" self-narrative. At the same time, neither is it useful to think of that self-narrative as mere noise in the processes of social negotiation: the "subject's" history informs, dialectically, the social process and is therefore a crucial pressure upon it. This is the case even at the moment where it is part of the "subject's" self-interest to see itself as and act as a properly cerned "subject."

Self-interest is, in other words, the product of the "subject's" heterogeneous constitution and the "subject's" experience, even where it most demands compliance with interpellating notions of wholeness, coherence, and consistency. It is, evidently, the process of simultaneous and momentaneous, dialectical negotiations between heterogeneous self-narrative and heterogeneous social processes. The negativity at the base of the "subject's" constitution enables contradiction and enforces a demand for the recognition of the "subject's" specificity—its history. At the same time, the social character of human existence enables articulation and forces negotiation with other "subjects."

The claim here, then, is that a recognition of both the specificity of any "subject's" history and also of the necessary negotiation with other "subjects" constitutes one of the prime conditions of oppositional practice in our day.

(6) In contemporary conditions in the west it has become more necessary than ever to adopt this kind of dialectical view of the "subject" and its relation to the social, since it is only in this way that the success of a movement like feminism

can be grasped and that even more demands and resistances against the hegemony of the new right can be articulated.

In the course of complaining about the views of subjectivity forged in prevalent discourses of the human sciences, I have often pointed out the foreclosing there of the possibilities of political resistance. I've claimed that this is the result of a number of different operations, sometimes discrete, sometimes overlapping, conducted around the category of the "subject." Such tendencies are not, I think, merely the symptom of an inherent conservativism in the theory of the human sciences, since they appear to be the end-point of even intentionally oppositional thinking such as that of Adorno or, in a different mode, Barthes or Kristeva. They have even become, as I've suggested before, a familiar narrative in which contestation cedes to a sometimes cynical, sometimes depressive view of the possibility of radical change. The most common sign of such tendencies, and the one on which I've concentrated, is the cerning of the "subject," whereby the "subject" is cut off from the real of its own constitution and history, or is abstracted from the sphere of historical action, or both.

Without commenting at any more length on the symptoms and effects of such treatments of the "subject," I think it worth reiterating here that the era of what is commonly called poststructuralism has perhaps brought with it a tendency to problematize so much the "subject's" relation to experience that it has become difficult to keep sight of the political necessity of being able to not only theorize but also *refer* to that experience. Any claim to the specificity of experience is foreclosed upon—or at least severely debilitated—by the theories of language, representation, and subjectivity which poststructuralism has conventionalized. In other words, poststructuralism's skepticism, its radical doubt, about the availability of the referent has been canonized, even exaggerated, to the point that the real often disappears from consideration.

This is not quite to say that contemporary theory is never politically motivated or politically useful. Rather, I want merely to suggest that it often shows itself unable to approach the political dilemmas left open by its own consistent and elaborate privileging of a view of difference which can best be described as *indifference*. My sense is that this theory is especially handicapped by its own theses about the nature of language and the relation to the real. However, I think that it's still not too late to claim that an articulation of the political based on the principles of heterogeneity *is* possible to theorize; but only if it is accepted that

(a) the "subject's" relation to its own history must be involved in the necessary articulation of self-interest;
(b) such an articulation demands a recognition of the "subject's" experience in all its specificity;
(c) this recognition can take place only if the "subject's" ability to refer to real conditions is unblocked by theory.

It was in order to adumbrate this last condition that I argued in Chapter 8 for the particular point in Julia Kristeva's work where she elaborates in a dialectical manner the relations between language, the "subject," and material process. The link of negativity which she establishes to carry, as it were, heterogeneity and to negotiate the finally "indissoluble relation" between self and other, identity and difference, guarantees a simultaneous movement or negotiation between them. Thus it basically vindicates the possibility of referring to each. Kristeva's work at that moment is able, I think, to counter the effects of much contemporary theory in which oppositional practice is deprived of one of its most indispensible weapons: namely, the ability to point to and analyze the material conditions, the actuality, or, in short, the reality of oppressions.

I take it that it is the responsibility of theory today to enable rather than to fore-close upon that fundamental *right*.

(7) The phrase "the responsibility of theory" might sound fairly alien in the context of the human sciences today, but in a sense it has constituted the watchword of this book. I have tried to suggest that such a responsibility exists and that it exists in relation to the lived life of what I hope will no longer be so readily dubbed the "subject." The various categorical uses of the term "subject" around which I have conducted my arguments and critiques do not seem to me to indicate any overwhelming desire to fulfill or even admit such a responsibility.

Thus I have tried to suggest ways in which theories of the "subject" might be reconsidered and the "subject" itself dis-cerned. In doing so, I have been continually haunted by a little passage in Adorno's *Negative Dialectics*. It is a saying with which I'm not sure that this book has necessarily come entirely to grips, but I think that the *sentiment* of Adorno's words is entirely in keeping with what I've been suggesting. It is a reminder of what is at stake in theory's abstraction of the "subject," and of what is at stake in discerning the "subject." Thus, I want to end with it:

Suffering is objectivity that weighs upon the subject; its most subjective experience, its expression, is to be objectively conveyed. (1973, p. 18)

Notes

Notes

Preface

1. Even deconstruction cannot altogether do away with this dialectical inconvenience, and Derrida is often at pains to point out that the concepts which underpin Western thought are as yet inescapable: "they are necessary and, at least at present, nothing is conceivable without them" (1976, p. 13). Adorno, of course, had said something like the same thing in *Negative Dialectics* (1973). See my Chapters 3 and 4.

2. This double-focus on the relations between language and representation and the construction of the "subject" has, by now, a lengthy history which need not be wholly recounted in this book. Apart from the fact that the problematic of the "subject" and language has been more or less the privileged one in contemporary critical debate, there are many fertile accounts and interpretations available which may be consulted. An especially good – if difficult to read – introduction to that history is Coward and Ellis's *Language and Materialism* (1977). This book has the advantage of covering quite thoroughly many of the theoretical matrices upon which structuralism and semiotics have been erected. A sociological perspective on much of the same theory is provided by Janet Wolff's excellent study *The Social Production of Art* (1981). Kaja Silverman's *The Subject of Semiotics* (1983) explores the terrain with a more specifically feminist intent than do either of the two books mentioned.

3. There have been many attempts to forge links of various sorts between Marxist and psychoanalytical theories. The project does, of course, seem attractive since the one claims to theorize the social and the other the "individual." However, the history of the attempts is not altogether encouraging. Work done in that regard by members of the Frankfurt School (such as Fromm and Marcuse) and the maverick Reich, for example, runs into many difficulties, some of which are discussed in Chapter 4. Those difficulties are part and parcel of more recent attempts at the same theme and often involve the weakening or even the eradication of the central notion of psychoanalysis, namely, the unconscious. This is evident, for example, in Richard Lichtman's *The Production of Desire* (1982). It is also true of Habermas, a writer who has often raised hopes that he might solve some

of the problems. The tendency of Habermas's work has, it seems to me, been toward an ever more idealist notion of the "subject," and many of the fundaments of his thought also legislate against thinking the unconscious. His work might legitimately have been expected to have been part of the discussions in this book, but my sense is (a) that his work has rightly made little impression on the human sciences and (b) that many of the arguments I make in Chapter 4 in regard to the Frankfurt School and to educational theory might be suggestive in relation to Habermas as well.

4. While I might appear to refer relatively comfortably to the notion of "fields," "areas," "disciplines," and so on, that's somewhat deceptive. In fact, one of the remarkable features of contemporary theory in the human sciences (leaving aside the question of how best to define *those* terms) is the wide miscegenation of "fields," etc. While on the one hand such a situation encourages intellectuals' interests to be less narrow than has traditionally been the case, on the other hand something of the historical and conceptual specificity of particular discourses gets lost within this expanded context. Clearly one of the reasons for concentrating on the term the "subject" is its apparently well understood and shared uses within a variety of different discourses. At the same time, my argument wants to specify those uses and to try to show how and why they commonly fail. Thus, the notion of "fields" is a difficult one since I want to show both their specificity and their commonality, and so I want here to stress a certain distance from my own use of these words.

5. That chapter has a motley history which I would like to make note of here. Its first version was presented at Wesleyan University's Center for the Humanities and was commented upon by Christina Crosby, by my students in a class on feminist theory and practice in the arts, and later by Jane Gallop. This first version was even more marked by problems of enunciation (a man talking about feminism) than the present version, but most of all it was marked by a tendency to try to legislate among feminist writers (a tendency not unconnected to problems of enunciation, of course). Another version, which has already been published (Smith 1984a), was commented upon after publication by Peggy Kamuf and then jointly by Alice Jardine and Rosi Braidotti. I requested their comments in the hope that they could be published in this book. This was a prospect which did not finally appeal to Jardine and Braidotti—and, I think, rightly so. Such an arrangement would have placed them in the position of respondents only; equally their work would have been subsumed under mine. Their comments, however, encouraged me to make some considerable changes—indeed some complete reversals—for the version which appears in this book. There is a certain irony in the fact that, while I think this is probably the worst chapter in the book, it is also the one whose construction taught me the most.

Some further elaborations on some of the same topics can be found in the various essays and dialogues in Jardine and Smith, eds., 1987.

Note on Terminology

1. Raymond Williams's entry on the word "individual" in his *Keywords* (1976, pp. 133–36) traces the history of its use and stresses its rise with the tradition of the liberal political and economic thought of the Enlightenment. But the word's rather complex history seems not to have quite shaken off the etymological meaning which Williams notes for it: "not cuttable, not divisible."

2. The term "subject" is dealt with in Williams's *Keywords* (1976, pp. 259–64) under the entry for "subjective." Williams notes the "ironic contrast" between the "subject" of political domination and the "subject" of German classical philosophy which was required to be "the active mind or thinking agent." It wouldn't be too cynical to suggest that the irony still exists and in fact becomes unfunny by the late 1980s.

Chapter 1

1. One of the obstacles to Marxism's dealing since Freud with the question of subjectivity has been what might be called an essentialism of class whereby the "subject's" constitution in and by a

class and thus by economics is always paramount to any other factor. Within the Marxist tradition there have, of course, been multifarious statements of this relation and of the subjective problematic, some of which are looked at in various moments of this book. Indeed, the problem has been a crucial one in a significant and lengthy Marxist debate between what Stanley Aronowitz calls "automatic Marxism" (1981, p. xix), favored by Rosa Luxemburg for example (where the proletariat's class position is an unchangeable constituent of the historical inevitability of capitalism's demise), and a Marxism which takes into account the cultural and ideological determinants of the "subject" under capitalism. My feeling is that Marxism in the West to a great extent owes its survival into the late twentieth century to this second party which has always tried, at least, to recognize the ideological as a determinant. The Frankfurt School clearly arises from this strand of Marxist thinking and authorizes itself to take the question of the constitution of the "subject" as a proper one: thus the first serious Marxist attempt to take account of Freud's work appears in its work. Wilhelm Reich was a contemporary of the major Frankfurt School thinkers and carried their interest in psychoanalysis to an extreme where the constitution of the social is seen as a macrocosmic version of the oedipal construction of the "subject." Reich's work is problematic exactly for its extremity, and his place in the history of Marxism is by now quite marginal (partly because of the extraordinarily naive "sex-therapy" solutions he proposed to capitalist domination). That marginality is the main reason why I have not dealt with his particular conflation of Marxism and Freudianism in this book, even though some of his work—especially some parts of *The Mass Psychology of Fascism* (1970)—is undeniably of interest.

2. See the Note on Terminology for my rationale in introducing this word. The Oxford English Dictionary defines "to cern" as a legal word meaning "to enter upon an inheritance." "To cerne" means "to surround."

3. The many different attempts on the left to question and redefine traditional Marxist categories would itself be the topic of a whole book. In America in particular, the failure of the working class to fit the shoes that Marxism has made for it has led to much radical scrutiny of the Marxist tradition. Some of this impulse can, of course, be found in Adorno and Marcuse and in the extensive consequences of their work on Marxist thinking in America; what is often called Adorno's and Marcuse's pessimism (inspiringly displayed, I think, in their essay "The Culture Industry" in *The Dialectic of Enlightenment* [1972]) can perhaps be seen as a symptom of the disappointment caused by the obvious inapplicability of classical Marxist analyses to mid-century Western capitalism. Equally, this impulse can be found in work that might once have been considered quite eccentric to the Marxist tradition, like Murrary Bookchin's in the '60s. These are just two, almost random examples. There are many others (especially from Europe—one thinks of Baudrillard's attempt to discredit the Marxist narrative of the modes of production [see 1975]); but in writing this book I've had especial dealings with two books (which have, admittedly, very dissimilar assessments and theories about the significance and future directions of all this lengthy revision): Stanley Aronowitz's *The Crisis in Historical Materialism* (1981) and Ernesto Laclau and Chantal Mouffe's *Hegemony and Socialist Strategy* (1985).

4. See Marx's "Critique of Hegel's Philosophy of Right" (Marx 1967c, pp. 164ff.) where Marx uses Feuerbach's arguments against specular synthesis to attack Hegel's view of the state as a unification of the "singular" and the "universal." Marx also points out here the paradox in Hegel's sense of democracy: "Hegel proceeds from the State and makes man into the subjectified State; democracy starts with man and makes the State objectified man." The critique of specular illusions is clearly important here and is not inapposite to contemporary—and especially American—views of democracy and "man."

5. "Epistemological break" is a term imported into Marxist thought, through Bachelard, by Althusser to indicate a disjuncture between the young Marx (say of *The German Ideology*) and the "mature" Marx of *Capital*. Althusser regards the latter text as an instance of Marx's elaborating a full and properly constituted Marxist science.

6. For a concise and informed discussion of this problematic of the "double reality" in Marxism see Sharp (1980).

7. These two questions are clearly not the same one, but it's perfectly feasible to consider the ideology/science distinction in Althusser, for example, as an attempt to insist absolutely on the priority of theory—even if he himself wants to talk of theory *as* praxis.

8. There is, of course, a lot of difference between Althusser and his followers, some of whom indeed have come to disagree with him very strongly on a number of issues. What remains constant in writers as various as Poulantzas, Macherey, and Hirst, for example, is the recognition of the permanence of ideology. I take it that this is a direct benefit of the determined anti-humanism which Althusser's own thinking exemplifies so well.

9. Particularly horrified is Jorge Larrain whose *Marxism and Ideology* (1983) is devoted to defending what he sees as an originary Marxist conception of ideology as a negative phenomenon. Althusser is apparently a proponent of a less critically enabling notion of ideology which, Larrain tries to explain, destroys the possibility of accurate class analysis and which cannot recognize contradiction in capitalist society.

10. The langue/parole doublet derives from so-called structural linguistics where "the former is a system, an institution, a set of impersonal rules and norms, while the latter comprises the actual manifestations of the system in speech and writing" (Culler, 1975, p. 8).

11. Apart from the texts from which I quote in the rest of the paragraph, many others have objected to Althusser's supposed functionalism. This may be due to a distressing inability, especially common in American social sciences, to distinguish either intellectually or historically between functionalism and structuralism. But there are intelligent critiques of Althusser: see Hirst (1979), Best and Connolly (1979), and Callinicos (1976) for example.

12. This point is elaborated in Stephen Heath's interesting but difficult article "The Turn of the Subject" (1979). The article was one of the original provocations for this book.

Chapter 2

1. For discussion see especially Belsey (1980), Eagleton (1975 & 1978), and Kavanagh (1980 & 1982).

2. The new *Screen* is considerably less theoretically orientated and also appears open to a wider range of cultural texts. For an account of some of the arguments around the old *Screen's* manners, see MacCabe (1985).

3. Pêcheux's debt to Althusser is fairly clear in this formulation, and his work does attempt to solve some of the difficulties that Althusser runs into around the question of the "subject." But it would be fair to say that Pêcheux is by and large an apologist for Althusser. His notion of the "subject form" still does not manage to explain convincingly how the "subject's" identifications can be made as concrete as he wants them to be. The concretization of the "subject's" relation to language gets its closest explanation in Julia Kristeva's work; see Chapter 8.

4. Of this move Paul Willemen's "Notes on Subjectivity" (1978) is exemplary. It should perhaps be made clear that the kind of theorizations involved here are quite distinct from those of the so-called reader response critics. The work of these latter is always haunted, to paraphrase Macherey, by the problem of replacing the old humanist myth of the creator with a mythology of the public.

5. Perhaps the best known examination of classical Hollywood's masculinist structures is by Laura Mulvey (1975).

6. I quote Rainer from a seminar discussion at Wesleyan University's Center for the Humanities, fall 1982.

Chapter 3

1. See Derrida's important essay "Différance" (1982, pp. 1–29) for his funding arguments for the tropes alluded to here. For examples of these tropes in action, see Derrida (1974, 1977, and 1978).

2. Derrida's disagreement with Lacan is perhaps more deeply embedded in his texts than that with Freud, but it emerges especially clearly in his article attacking Lacan's reading of Poe's "The Purloined Letter." For details, and for a deconstructive reading of the texts involved, see Johnson (1977).

3. Ryan's work has by and large been conveniently forgotten by many others who have attempted to talk about the political implications of deconstruction. A particularly egregious example of this can be seen in an issue of *Diacrticis*, vol. 15, no. 4, entitled "Marx After Derrida." Most of the contributors to that issue of course differ from Ryan in that they seem to want—quite desperately—to redeem Derrida from charges of being politically suspect. Ryan, at least, looks at Derrida with a critical eye.

4. Ryan seems in fact quite often unconvinced of Derrida's political health and his book is less an attempt to "cure" Derrida than to try to turn deconstructive logic into a kind of super-dialectics appropriate to late capitalist conditions. Deconstructive logic can indeed be—and often has been—seen as remarkably apt to such conditions; I'd suggest, however, that it may not be apt in the sense of being a necessarily oppositional weapon. It seems to me that it's no accident that deconstruction arises or takes root in academic discourses most firmly after the social disturbances of the late '60s have died down, and thus at the same time as the rise of neo-conservative hegemony; nor accidental that most of its enthusiastic proponents are in the American academy. It's not my aim here to prove the obviously contentious suspicion that deconstructionist thought is in fact an ally of the new right, but I'd want to say that any claim to the contrary would need to contextualize (historicize) the advent and rise of deconstruction in a way that, so far as I'm aware, hasn't been undertaken yet.

5. For example, in a lecture given around the United States in 1983, "Mnemosyne," Derrida suggested that deconstruction's hostile treatment at the hands of conservative academics in America was ironically misplaced: deconstruction had in fact come to do a job not unlike that of New Criticism. Perhaps more tellingly, Derrida's recent dealings with the topic of apartheid have been less than encouraging. For instance, in his 1986 lectures in the United States he expresses an admiration for Nelson Mandela but refrains from expressing any solidarity. This is perhaps not surprising since in an earlier article in *Critical Inquiry* he delivered himself of the view that acting against apartheid would be "too dialectical" for his taste.

6. Since the writing of this chapter, Derrida has published what must surely be one of his most bizarre—and certainly most angry—texts to date: "But beyond . . . (Open letter to Anne McClintock and Rob Nixon)" (1986). Here Derrida responds viciously to a criticism of his article "Racism's Last Word" (1985). McClintock and Nixon, graduate students at Columbia University, while giving Derrida's article credit for having spoken out against apartheid (an act of some generosity on their part, in my view), quite sympathetically remind the master that his dealings with the discourse of the Pretoria regime need to be historicized if they are to become of more than limited strategic and political value. This simple enough point becomes the occasion for Derrida to lash out not only against his immediate interlocutors (an unequal enough exchange, that) but also against all critics of deconstruction's political efficacy.

What Derrida actually says is perhaps much less interesting that the ruthless, almost hysterical way in which he defends himself (and it is without question *himself* whom he defends). But it strikes me as signal that (even while he seems obsessed with the kindness of the editors of *Critical Inquiry* in letting him take up 16 pages of their space) Derrida chooses to demolish the two students rather than say anything—howsoever vaguely—which could lead one to believe that deconstructive thought in any way entails, causes, or is even related to his own personal opposition to apartheid.

Alex Argyros, in an unpublished article which I am grateful to have read, "The Vulgar Difference: Deconstruction and History," argues to a similar conclusion about "Racism's Last Word"; he successfully questions "whether the deconstructive posture that underlies Derrida's arguments could ever in fact be the theoretical reason for his opposition to apartheid." Given the continued absence of any clear relation between deconstruction and Derrida's personal "beliefs," there seems little point in amending anything in the present chapter which is, after all, directed against deconstruction more than against Derrida the man.

Chapter 4

1. Ryan (1982) is of course the first major attempt to examine the connections. See also Stanley Aronowitz's remarks (1981 passim) and Rainer Nägele's essay on Adorno and poststructuralism (1982). Also, see my remarks in note 4 to Chapter 3.

2. As Aronowitz points out (1981, p. 71), Marcuse's use of the notion of the pleasure principle did undergo changes: in *Eros and Civilization* (1955) the pleasure principle was seen as a force subversive of the repressive mechanism of capitalism; but during the '60s Marcuse came to recognize the use of the pleasure principle in reproducing a consumer society (a recognition that led to his sharing somewhat the pessimism of his Frankfurt School colleagues).

3. Martin Jay claims that Marcuse's thought was never so unquestioningly directed toward the utopia of a communist society of non-antagonism as I think it was. Jay quotes Marcuse's admonition to Norman Brown that "Tension can be made nonantagonistic, nondestructive, but it can never be eliminated, because (Freud knew it well) its elimination would be death—not in any symbolic but in a very real sense" (Marcuse quoted in Jay, 1984, p. 239). I'd say that this quotation is a little atypical.

4. Sharp (1980) is substantially more respectful toward Marxism than is *Theory and Resistance*, but the two books complement each other insofar as Sharp's orthodoxy around the same issues as Giroux deals with can put both Giroux's strengths and his weaknesses into perspective.

Chapter 5

1. Foucault's work on the fields of discourse, on institutions, etc., and on their multifold interrelations with the construction and exercise of forms of social power is, of course, important. Still, his is work which provides no explanation, so far as I can tell, of the way in which discourses actually intersect with and in the "subject." Furthermore, the heterogeneity which Foucault (quite properly) ascribes to historical conditions, and which it is his aim to uncover, is finally a heterogeneity perceptible only from the ground of an epistemology of the cerned "subject": Foucault himself (as observer); the "subjects" in his histories (who seem to me to be studied not so much as the *bearers* of heterogeneous social forces as simply *sufferers* from them).

It may sound surprising to say this, especially since Foucault is frequently praised for emphasizing *both* the dominatory and the enabling function of power. However, it seems that Foucault's "subject" is more incapable than not of becoming an agent of large social change and that the supposedly enabling moments of power relations are subsumed under the "subject's" subjection. Symptomatically, in the very essay in which Foucault claims that "it is not power but the subject which is the general theme of my research" (1984, p. 417), the problematic of the "subject" gives way within a few short pages to a more general discussion of power and its objectifying capabilities. I'd say that this is a typical trajectory and that the actual constitution and potentialities of the "subject" in Foucault's work are usually elided by descriptions of power relations per se.

At any rate, the emphasis that I've wanted to place in this book is much less on the "objective" character of the forces which govern subjectivity and more on the "internal" construction of subjectivity. For that reason, and even while I admire and have been helped in certain ways by Foucault's work, I have felt it as somewhat tangential to my main concerns and arguments.

2. Parson's "subject" in functionalism is clearly different from what Giddens has called Althusser's "structural dupe" of a "subject." At least in Althusser there is still room for the "subject" to engage in struggle (that, after all, is Althusser's prime concern); but in Parsons the "subject" is unequivocally a "Träger."

3. Each of these works is important in the development of what might be called the philosophy of the social sciences and heavily relies upon the human agent's "explanations of his behaviour": Winch, for example, seems to assume that "man's understanding of reality," if not exactly coherent, is really the only possible parameter in which to locate "him." Oakeshott and Louch construe varia-

tions on this assumption (which clearly derives, at least in part, from Max Weber's celebrated notion of *Verstehen*); Oakeshott is probably the more extreme in his elaboration of this kind of pragmaticist version of a "knowledgeable subject."

Chapter 6

1. The attempt to "literatize" other disciplines is often made by those thinkers in them who have been most receptive and yet most threatened by the invasion of what is often called "continental" theory and by Marxism. In many cases they retain a kind of skepticism toward the actual benefits of such importations, and their supposed even-handedness leads to a certain eclecticism. Or else there is an attempt to point out the similarities—either thematic or logical—between the new work and the works of the tradition. This is the case with Rorty (1982), for example, or even LaCapra (1983). See Smith (1985), a review article in which I approach LaCapra and Geertz with this in mind.

2. See Roland Barthes's exemplary essay, "The Discourse of History" (1981)—exemplary in the sense that it acts as something like a primer of late structuralism's view of historiography.

3. When writing this I hadn't had the pleasure of reading Clifford and Marcus, eds. (1986), an excellent collection of essays by anthropologists and ethnologists. Some of these essays make arguments similar to but much better informed than my own, and also make a stronger case for these "alternative" forms of anthropology.

4. Martin Jay's meticulous book *Marxism and Totality* (1984) does a little to rectify this situation. However, Jay's quiet investment in the old Marxist attempt to see totality makes him appear both very reluctant to embrace this critique and also unable to imagine that what he calls "the post-structuralist challenge" marks anything but the fall of the Marxist empire.

5. I'd like to claim that the discours/récit pairing, despite its provenance in structuralism and its continued use in orthodox semiotics, is not necessarily a dualism. At least, I have tried not to use it as such here.

Chapter 7

1. This chapter's ambivalent view of Barthes marks a certain change from the tone of an earlier article, "We Always Fail . . ." (Smith 1982). Barthes's fascinating power, however, remains effective for me to a large extent. Heath (1983) seems to remain fascinated too. Culler (1983) is perhaps a little more skeptical. The most convincing critiques of Barthes have been very recent ones from feminists: see Schor (1987) for instance.

2. These works are not necessarily cast as autobiographies of course; even the one that specifically is (1975) radically questions the conventions of autobiography. However, I claim that they actually constitute a personalized narrative, and that is how I deal with them in this chapter in order to make a point about Barthes's view of the "subject."

With these books, as with many other French works cited in this book, I have preferred to use the original text and make my own translations. This is especially the case with Barthes's books, since they seem to me to have suffered more often than not from less than helpful translations.

3. See Chapter 8 for further explanation and remarks in relation to Kristeva's semiotic/symbolic distinction.

4. The reconsideration of structuralism has to come soon—even if only because Eagleton (1985) has made similar kinds of noises about the oppositional moment of structuralism!

5. Heath's discussion of this book (1983) gives a good sense of the movement or oscillation between pleasure and jouissance.

6. Quoted by A. Michelson in *October*, no. 12, p. 128.

7. See Rosalind Coward's explanation (1983, pp. 253ff.) of the reasons for wanting to undermine this dyad. See too Henriques et al. (1984).

8. Klein's work is today being taken more and more seriously outside its clinical context—perhaps because it is not so radically "difficult" as work in the Lacanian idiom, nor so simplistic or complicit with the aims of capitalist ideology as the standard run of American ego psychology. *Our Adult World* (1963) is a good introduction; Rivière, ed. (1970) includes work by Klein herself, but also serves as a survey of some of the more interesting object-relations psychoanalysis in the '60s.

Chapter 8

1. My article "Julia Kristeva Et Al.: Take Three or More" gives a more thorough treatment of Kristeva's later work and is forthcoming in a Cornell University Press collection edited by R. Feldstein and J. Roof.

2. This debate is taken up again in the next chapter.

3. Kristeva quotes Hegel as saying that "the highest 'form' of nothingness is *liberty*, and this is negativity" (Kristeva, 1974, p. 102).

4. Surprisingly and disappointingly Kristeva's elaborate and still exciting readings of Hegel in (1974) aren't included in full in the English translation of that book.

5. I discover that both these passages (from Kristeva and Eco) are also commented upon by Teresa de Lauretis (1984); we draw very different ideas from them, however.

6. Kristeva's political path seems to have led her most recently toward the United States; and if the political implications of her work *aren't* clear from the quotations in the text, the following should make things clearer:

> Now that the Latin American and Arab Marxist revolutions groan at the gates of the United States, I feel myself closer to truth and liberty when I am working in the space of this embattled giant which is perhaps on the point of becoming a David confronted with the growing Goliath of the Third World. I dream that, to the camp of this David, even with all his faults and difficulties, our children will go. (1983b, 54)

Chapter 9

1. See, for example, Stone (1983), or Eagleton's very different kind of attack (1983).

2. It is under this sort of banner that the work of Bakhtin is being gradually imported into the canon of post-structuralism. Ironically enough, perhaps the best accounts and deployment of Bakhtin are still Kristeva's (1980), written during her "sémanalyse" days.

3. I am using the idea of this division here as a heuristic device, even though I'm certain it does function historically as a real division. Perhaps, when the history of our current feminist theory is written, the most difficult aspect of the device to sustain will be the conflation of Anglo and American feminism (though Elaine Showalter's quip that the Anglo "stresses oppression," the French "stresses repression," and the American "stresses expression" [1979] may not be quite the way to make the distinctions). Meanwhile, the ethnocentric nature of the device is quite rightly pointed out by Spivak (1981).

4. This quotation is taken from Friedman (1981). See my article "H. D.'s Identity" (1984b) where I talk about this kind of feminist criticism and Friedman's book in particular.

5. Freud's thought is not, of course, untroubled in this respect: the natural is frequently invoked in his writings in the shape of the inherited unconscious component of the id; and the normative demands of the cultural often act as the compelling force behind his recommendations for actual analytical practice. And yet when Freud gives way in the face of one of his most long-standing theoretical difficulties (namely, the question of phylogenetic traces in the psyche) by considering himself "obliged to see such traces as part of the *archaic heritage* which a child brings with him into the world" (see *An Outline of Psychoanalysis* [1964b]), it should be remembered that it is nonetheless Freud himself who consistently protested against the biologicistic tendencies of psychoanalytic theory. Even if

Freud speaks of the "sick ego" that needs to be returned to its "normal functions," he is also at pains to make clear that cures cannot be effected if the analyst is "tempted to become a teacher, model and ideal"; such moralistic undertakings are not, he says, "the analyst's task in the analytical relationship." Through a reading of Freud's dealings with the question of homosexuality, for instance, an especially good case can be made for his refusal to submit to biologism. Such a case is made in an unpublished paper by Henry Abelove which I am grateful to have read.

6. Irigaray's claims for the specificity of women's bodies sometimes come accompanied by not very helpful diatribes against men on account of *their* bodies. For example, men's bodies are reduced in Irigaray's terms to the form of "a violating penis" which finds the vagina to be nothing but a "substitute for the little boy's hand" (1981, p. 100).

7. An interesting and timely (even overdue) attack is made on Derrida's (and Jonathan Culler's) relation to "the feminine" in Scholes (1987).

8. I quote this from one of Gayatri Spivak's interventions at the 1982 MLA meetings in Los Angeles.

9. My argument at this point touches upon and relies upon the remarkable prevalence of the notion of "doubling" in feminist theory. Naomi Schor (1987), questioning the "discourse of indifference" that she claims is promoted by poststructuralisms, suggests that

> the most active site of the feminine resistance [to it] is a certain insistence on doubling, which may be the feminine mode of subverting the unitary subject: mimeticism (Irigaray and Kolodny), the double and even double double identification of the female film spectator (Mulvey, Doane, de Lauretis), women's writing as palimpsest (Gibert and Gubar), female fetishism (Kofman, Berg, Schor), the foregrounding of the "other woman" (Gallop), the elaboration of a "doubled strategy" of deconstruction and construction (Martin) are some of the varied forms this insistence on doubling has taken and is taking. (1987)

References

References

T. Adorno 1973 *Negative Dialectics,* Seabury Press, New York.

T. Adorno and M. Horkheimer 1972 *The Dialectic of Enlightenment,* Seabury Press, New York.

L.Althusser 1971 *Lenin and Philosophy,* Monthly Review Press, New York.

———. 1977 *For Marx,* Verso, London.

———. 1978 *Essays in Self-Criticism,* Verso, London.

———. 1979 *Reading Capital,* Verso, London.

M. Apple ed. 1982 *Cultural and Economic Reproduction in Education,* Routledge, Kegan, Paul, London.

S.Aronowitz 1981 *The Crisis in Historical Materialism,* Praeger, New York.

R.Barthes 1973 *Le Plaisir du texte,* Seuil, Paris.

———. 1975 *Roland Barthes par lui-même,* Seuil, Paris.

———. 1977a "The Death of the Author," in *Image/Music/Text,* trans. S. Heath, Fontana, London.

———. 1977b *Fragments d'un discours amoureux,* Seuil, Paris.

———. 1980a *La Chambre claire,* Gallimard/Seuil, Paris.

———. 1980b "On échoue toujours à parler de ce qu'on aime," *Tel Quel,* no.85.

———. 1981 "The Discourse of History," trans. S. Bann, *Comparative Criticism Yearbook,* no.3.

J. Baudrillard 1975 *The Mirror of Production,* Telos Press, St Louis.

C.Belsey 1980 *Critical Practice,* Methuen, London.

R. Benedict 1959 *Patterns of Culture,* New American Library, New York.

M. Best and W. Connolly 1979 "Politics and Subjects," *Socialist Review,* vol.9, no.6.

P. Bourdieu and C. Passeron 1977 *Reproduction in Education, Society and Culture,* Sage Press, California.

A. Callinicos 1976 *Althusser's Marxism,* New Left Books, London.

H. Cixous 1981a "Sorties" and "The Laugh of the Medusa," in Marks & Courtivron eds., 1981.

———. 1981b "Castration or Decapitation," *Signs,* vol.7, no.1.

J. Clifford 1983 "On Ethnographic Authority," *Representations,* vol.1, no.2.

J. Clifford & G. Marcus eds., 1986 *Writing Culture,* University of California Press, Berkeley.

R. Coward 1983 *Patriarchal Precedents*, Routledge, Kegan, Paul, London.

R. Coward and J. Ellis 1977 *Language and Materialism*, Routledge, Kegan, Paul, London.

J. Culler 1975 *Structuralist Poetics*, Routledge, Kegan, Paul, London.

——. 1983 *Roland Barthes*, Oxford University Press, New York.

T. de Lauretis 1984 *Alice Doesn't*, Indiana University Press, Bloomington.

P. de Man 1979 "Autobiography as De-Facement," *Modern Language Notes*, vol.94.

J. Derrida 1972 *Positions*, Minuit, Paris.

——. 1974 *Glas*, Galilée, Paris.

——. 1976 *Of Grammatology*, University of Chicago Press, Chicago.

——. 1977 "Ltd Inc.," supplement to *Glyph*, no. 2.

——. 1978 *Writing and Difference*, University of Chicago Press, Chicago.

——. 1980 "Interview," *Literary Review* (London), no. 14.

——. 1982 *Margins of Philosophy*, University of Chicago Press, Chicago.

——. 1983 "The Principle of Reason: The University in the Eyes of Its Pupils," *Diacritics*, vol.13, no. 3.

——. 1984 "No Apocalypse, Not Now," *Diacritics*, vol. 14, no.2.

——. 1985 "Racism's Last Word," *Critical Inquiry*, vol. 12, no. 3.

——. 1986 "But beyond . . . (Open Letter to Anne McLintock and Rob Nixon)," *Critical Inquiry*, vol. 13, no. 1.

T. Eagleton 1975 "Pierre Macherey and the Theory of Literary Production," *Minnesota Review*, no. 5.

——. 1976 *Criticism and Ideology*, New Left Books, London.

——. 1978 "Aesthetics and Politics," *New Left Review*, no. 107.

——. 1983 *Literary Theory*, University of Minnesota Press, Minneapolis.

——. 1985 "Marxism, Structuralism and Poststructuralism," *Diacritics*, vol. 15, no. 4.

U. Eco 1977 *A Theory of Semiotics*, Macmillan, London.

H. Eisenstein & A. Jardine eds. 1980 *The Future of Difference*, G. K. Hall, Boston.

J.Féral 1980 "The Powers of Difference," in Eisenstein & Jardine eds. 1980.

M. Foucault 1984 "The Subject and Power," in B. Wallis ed., *Art After Modernism*, New Museum of Contemporary Art, New York.

S. Freud 1958 "Psychoanalytical Notes on an Autobiographical Account of a Case of Paranoia," Standard Edition, vol. 12, Hogarth Press, London.

——. 1961 "Female Sexuality," Standard Edition, vol. 21.

——. 1962 "Further Remarks on the Neuropsychology of Defence," Standard Edition, vol. 3.

——. 1964a "Femininity," Standard Edition, vol. 22.

——. 1964b "Outline of Psychoanalysis," Standard Edition, vol. 23.

S. Friedman 1981 *Psyche Reborn*, Indiana University Press, Bloomington.

J. Gallop 1982 *The Daughter's Seduction*, Cornell University Press, New York.

——. 1983 "Quand nos lèvres s'écrivent: Irigaray's Body Politic," *Romanic Review*, vol. 74, no.1.

J. K. Gardiner 1981 "On Female Identity and Writing by Women," *Critical Inquiry*, vol. 8, no. 2.

C. Geertz 1973 *The Interpretation of Cultures*, Basic Books, New York.

——. 1983 *Local Knowledge*, Basic Books, New York.

A. Giddens 1979 *Central Problems in Social Theory*, University of California Press, Berkeley.

——. 1982 *Profiles and Critiques in Social Theory*, University of California Press, Berkeley.

——. 1984 "Social Sciences and Philosophy," talk given at University of Chicago, October 1983.

H. Giroux 1983 *Theory and Resistance in Education,* Bergin & Garvey, Massachusetts.

B. Grunberger 1964 "Outline for a Study of Narcissism in Female Sexuality," in *Sexualité Féminine*, ed. J. Chasseguet-Smirgel, Payot, Paris.

J. Habermas 1980 "Psychic Thermidor and the Rebirth of Rebellious Subjectivity," *Berkeley Journal of Sociology*, vol. 24, no. 5.

REFERENCES □ 177

S. Hall 1978 "Psychology, Ideology and the Human Subject," *Ideology & Consciousness*, no. 3.
——. 1980 "Recent Developments in Theories of Language and Ideology," in *Culture, Media, Language*, Centre for Contemporary Cultural Studies, Hutchinson, London.
——. 1984 "The Problem of Ideology," in *Marx 100 Years On*, ed. B. Matthews, Lawrence & Wishart, London.
S. Heath 1978 "Difference," *Screen* vol. 19, no. 3.
——. 1979 "The Turn of the Subject," *Ciné-Tracts*, no. 8.
——. 1981 *Questions of Cinema*, Indiana University Press, Bloomington.
——. 1983 "Barthes on Love," *Sub-Stance*, no. 37/8.
J.Henriques et al. 1984 *Changing the Subject*, Methuen, New York.
I. Hextall and M. Sarup 1977 "School Knowledge, Evaluation and Alienation," in Young & Whitty eds., *Society, State, and Schooling*, 1977.
P. Hirst 1979 *On Law and Ideology*, Humanities Press, New Jersey.
P. Hirst and B. Hindess 1975 *Pre-Capitalist Modes of Production*, Routledge, Kegan, Paul, London.
P. Hirst and P. Wooley 1982 *Social Relations and Human Attributes*, Tavistock, London.
L. Irigaray 1974 *Speculum de l'autre femme*, Minuit, Paris.
——. 1977 *Ce Sexe qui n'en est pas un*, Minuit,Paris.
——. 1981 "This Sex which Is Not One," and "When the Goods Get Together," in Marks & Courtivron eds., *New French Feminisms*.
F. Jameson 1971 *Marxism and Form*, Princeton University Press, Princeton.
——. 1981 *The Political Unconscious*, Cornell University Press, Ithaca, New York.
A. Jardine 1985 *Gynesis*, Cornell University Press, Ithaca, New York.
A. Jardine & P. Smith eds. 1987 *Men in Feminism*, Methuen, New York.
M. Jay 1984 *Marxism and Totality*, University of California Press, Berkeley.
B. Johnson 1977 "The Frame of Reference," *Yale French Studies*, no. 55/6.
E. Jones 1927 "The Early Development of Female Sexuality," *International Journal of Psychoanalysis*, vol. 8.
J. Kavanagh 1980 "Marks of Weakness—Ideology, Science and Textual Criticism," *Praxis*, no. 5.
——. 1982 "Marxism's Althusser," *Diacritics*, vol. 12, no.1.
M. Kelly, 1985 "Interview," *Camera Obscura*, no.13–14.
M. Klein 1963 *Our Adult World*, Hogarth Press, London.
S. Kofman 1973 *Camera obscura de l'idéologie*, Galilée, Paris.
——. 1980 *L'Enigme de la femme*, Galilée, Paris.
A. Kolodny 1980 "Dancing Through the Minefield," *Feminist Studies*, vol. 6, no. 1.
J. Kristeva 1973 "System and Speaking Subject," *Times Literary Supplement*, October 12.
——. 1974 *La Révolution du langage poétique*, Seuil, Paris.
——. 1977 *Polylogue*, Seuil, Paris.
——. 1980a *Pouvoirs de l'horreur*, Seuil, Paris.
——. 1980b *Desire in Language*, ed. L. Roudiez, Columbia University Press, New York.
——. 1983a "Interview" in *Desire*, Institute of Contemporary Arts, London.
——. 1983b "Mémoires," *L'Infini*, no. 1.
A. Kuhn 1982 *Women's Pictures*, Routledge, Kegan, Paul, London.
J. Lacan 1966 *Ecrits*, Seuil, Paris.
——. 1977a *Ecrits: A Selection*, trans. A. Sheridan, Norton, New York.
——. 1977b *The Four Fundamental Concepts of Psychoanalysis*, trans. A. Sheridan, Penguin, London.
——. 1977c "Conférence," *Scilicet*, no. 6–7.
D. LaCapra 1983 *Rethinking Intellectual History*, Cornell University Press, Ithaca, New York.
E. Laclau 1977 *Politics and Ideology in Marxist Theory*, New Left Books, London.
E. Laclau and C. Mouffe 1985 *Hegemony and Socialist Strategy*, Verso, London.

J. Larrain 1983 *Marxism and Ideology*, Humanities Press, New Jersey.

C. Lévi-Strauss 1971 *Tristes Tropiques*, Plon, Paris.

R. Lichtman 1982 *The Production of Desire*, Free Press, New York.

A. Louch 1963 *Explanation and Human Action*, Blackwell, Oxford.

G. Lukács 1971 *History and Class Consciousness*, MIT Press, Cambridge, Mass.

C. MacCabe 1974 "Realism and the Cinema," *Screen*, vol. 15, no. 2.

——. 1976 "Principles of Realism and Pleasure," *Screen*, vol. 17, no. 3.

——. 1985 *Tracking the Signifier*, University of Minnesota Press, Minneapolis.

P. Macherey 1978 *A Theory of Literary Production*, Routledge, Kegan, Paul, London.

P. Macherey and E. Balibar 1982 "Interview," *Diacritics*, vol. 12, no. 1.

H. Marcuse 1955 *Eros and Civilization*, Beacon Press, Boston.

——. 1964 *One-Dimensional Man*, Beacon Press, Boston.

——. 1970 *Five Lectures*, Beacon Press, Boston.

E. Marks and I.de Courtivron eds. 1981 *New French Feminisms*, Schocken, New York.

K. Marx 1947 *The German Ideology*, International Publishers, New York.

——. 1967a *Capital: Volume One*, International Publishers, New York.

——. 1967b *Capital: Volume Two*, International Publishers, New York.

——. 1967c *Writings of the Young Marx*, eds. L. D. Easton & K. H. Guddat, Doubleday, New York.

——. 1968 *Theories of Surplus Value*, part 2, Progress Publishers, Moscow.

——. 1973 *Grundrisse*, Pelican, London.

C.Metz 1975 "The Imaginary Signifier," *Screen*, vol. 16, no. 2.

J-A. Miller 1977 "Suture," *Screen*, vol. 18, no. 4.

J. Milner 1976 "L'amour et le langage," *Ornicar?*, no.6.

J. Mitchell 1975 *Psychoanalysis and Feminism*, Penguin, London.

J. Mitchell & J. Rose eds. 1982 *Feminine Sexuality*, Penguin, London.

T. Moi 1985 *Sexual/Textual Politics*, Methuen, London.

D. Morley 1980 "Texts, Readers, Subjects," in *Culture, Media, Language*, Centre for Contemporary Cultural Studies, Hutchinson, London.

L. Mulvey 1975 "Visual Pleasure and Narrative Cinema," *Screen*, vol. 16, no.3.

R. Nägele 1982 "The Sense of the Other," *Boundary 2*, vol.11, 1/2.

M. Oakeshott 1974 *On Human Conduct*, Routledge, Kegan, Paul, London.

M. Pêcheux 1982 *Language, Semantics and Ideology*, St Martin's Press, New York.

M. Plaza 1978 " 'Phallomorphic Power' and the Psychology of 'Woman'," *Ideology & Consciousness*, no. 4.

Questions Féministes 1981 "Variations sur des thèmes communs" (editorial), *Questions Féministes*, no. 1.

W. Reich 1970 *The Mass Psychology of Fascism*, New York.

——. 1972 *Sex-Pol Essays*, Vintage Books, New York.

J. Rivière 1970 *Developments in Psychoanalysis*, Tavistock, London.

R. Rorty 1982 *The Consequences of Pragmatism*, University of Minnesota Press, Minneapolis.

M. Ryan 1982 *Marxism and Deconstruction*, Johns Hopkins University Press, Baltimore.

J.L. Schefer 1982 "Interview," *Enclitic*, vol. 4, no. 2.

R. Scholes 1987 "Reading Like A Man," in Jardine & Smith eds., 1987.

N. Schor 1987 "Dreaming Dissymmetry: Barthes, Foucault and Sexual Difference," in Jardine & Smith eds., 1987.

D. Schreber 1955 *Memoirs of my Nervous Illness*, Dawson's, London.

J. Searle 1977 "Reiterating the Differences: A Reply to Derrida," *Glyph*, no. 1.

L. Sève 1978 *Man in Marxist Theory*, Harvester Press, Sussex.

R. Sharp 1980 *Knowledge, Ideology and the Politics of Schooling*, Routledge, Kegan, Paul, London.

E. Showalter 1969 "Women and the Literary Curriculum," address to MLA Commission on the Status of Women.

——. 1979 "Feminist Criticism in the Wilderness," *Critical Inquiry*, vol. 8, no. 2.

K. Silverman 1983 *The Subject of Semiotics*, Oxford University Press, Oxford.

P. Smith 1982 "We Always Fail: Barthes' Last Writings," *Sub-Stance*, no. 36.

——. 1984a "A Question of Feminine Identity," *Notebooks in Cultural Analysis*, vol.1.

——. 1984b "H. D.'s Identity," *Women's Studies*, vol. 10, no. 3.

——. 1985 "Lettre d'Amérique," *Café*, no. 5.

G. Spivak 1981 "French Feminism in an International Frame," *Yale French Studies*, no. 62.

J. Stone 1983 "The Horrors of Power," *Politics of Theory*. Conference Proceedings, University of Essex, Colchester.

E. Sullerot 1981 "The Feminine (Matter of) Fact," in Marks and Courtivron eds., *New French Feminisms*.

C. R. Swift 1981 "Once More into the Breach of Western Literature Courses," *Women's Studies Quarterly*, no. 62.

E. Thompson 1978 *The Poverty of Theory*, New Left Books, London.

P. Wexler 1982 "Structure, Text and Subject," in Apple ed., *Cultural and Economic Reproduction*.

——. 1983 *Critical Social Psychology*, Routledge, Kegan, Paul, London.

P. Willemen 1978 "Notes on Subjectivity," *Screen*, vol. 19, no. 1.

R. Williams 1976 *Keywords*, Fontana, London.

——. 1978 "Problems of Materialism," *New Left Review*, no. 109.

P. Willis 1977 *Learning to Labour*, Routledge, Kegan, Paul, London.

P. Winch 1965 *The Idea of a Social Science*, Routledge, Kegan, Paul, London.

J. Wolff 1981 *The Social Production of Art*, St.Martin's Press, New York.

M. Young and G. Whitty eds. 1977 *Society, State and Schooling*, Falmer Press, Lewes.

Index

Index

Theory and History of Literature

Paul Smith is associate professor of literary and cultural studies at Carnegie Mellon University. He received his Ph.D. in 1981 from the University of Kent and M.A. from the University of Cambridge. Journals to which he contributes include *SubStance, Camera Obscura, PN Review, Enclitic, Art in America*, and *The Dalhousie Review*. Smith is the author of *Pound Revised* and co-editor, with Alice Jardine, of *Men in Feminism*.

Assistant professor of humanities and English at the University of Minnesota, **John Mowitt** received his Ph.D. in comparative literature from the University of Wisconsin, Madison, in 1982. He contributes to such journals as *Social Text, boundary 2, SubStance, and Criticism*.